Variety

# Variety

## A workbook for intermediate readers

*Jan Bell, Roy Boardman and Tony Buckby*

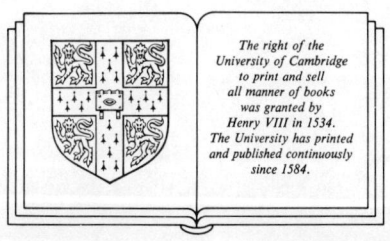

Cambridge University Press
Cambridge
London   New York   New Rochelle
Melbourne   Sydney

Published by the Press Syndicate of the University of Cambridge
The Pitt Building, Trumpington Street, Cambridge CB2 1RP
32 East 57th Street, New York, NY 10022, USA
10 Stamford Road, Oakleigh, Melbourne 3166, Australia

© Cambridge University Press 1985

First published 1985

Printed in Great Britain
at the Pitman Press, Bath

ISBN 0 521 26978 4

**Copyright**
The law allows a reader to make a single copy of part of a book
for purposes of private study. It does not allow the copying of
entire books or the making of multiple copies of extracts. Written
permission for any such copying must always be obtained from the
publisher in advance.

WD

# Contents

Thanks    vi
To the student    1

**Food and drink**    3
1  Living to eat . . .    4
2  Or eating to live    19
   Roleplay    26

**Christmas**    28
1  The spirit of Christmas    29
2  Christmas is children    36
   Roleplay    43

**Work**    44
1  In and out of work    45
2  A woman's place    52
   Discussion/Debate    62

**Education**    63
1  The happiest days of your life?    64
2  Beyond the classroom    78
   Roleplay    92

**Leisure**    94
1  The world of entertainment    95
2  The sporting life    107
   Roleplay    119

**The environment**    121
1  Preserving the countryside    122
2  Conserving energy    134
   Simulation    144

Key    146
Roles    160
To the teacher    165
Acknowledgements    169

v

# Thanks

We would like to take this opportunity to thank the many people at Cambridge University Press who have been involved in taking the book through the various stages of writing and re-writing, and in particular we would like to give our warmest and sincerest thanks to our editors, Christine and Alison. Their encouragement and help, together with their endless patience and unfailing good humour, have been much appreciated.

Thanks are also due to the staff at the various schools which tried out our pilot edition and gave us valuable feedback, and also to colleagues past and present for comments and advice.

# To the student

Every day of your life you come into contact with a wide range of written language: a letter from a friend, an advertising leaflet pushed through the door, the newspaper to be read quickly over breakfast. You may want to flick through a friend's magazine to see whether there are any articles worth reading; you may have to read instructions on how to cook something, a note from your boss, a job advert and many more items of this kind.

In *Variety*, we have taken a selection of these everyday texts which you might find in English and organised them thematically under six main headings. You don't need to work through the themes in order, of course – you can pick up the book and dip into it at whatever point you choose.

The texts may well be rather different from the kind of reading texts which you have seen before in the classroom, which may mean that they will seem more difficult at first. For one thing, they will be written in a range of different styles, from the formality of a job application to the chatty, idiomatic style of, for example, many popular newspapers. Since they are not simplified, there may be a lot of vocabulary you are not familiar with and you may be tempted to read very slowly at first, looking up every word. Because *Variety* is also a workbook, not just a collection of authentic texts, it helps you to avoid this temptation by giving you a purpose for reading, as you would have if you were reading in your own language. This purpose is given in the form of exercises, to be looked at *before* you read.

At the beginning of each unit there are exercises which encourage you to look through all the texts in that unit as quickly as possible to find specific information and ignore whatever is irrelevant to your purpose. Each text or group of texts then has further exercises which aim to develop your confidence so that you will feel able to pick up any reading text in English and cope with it.

Some of the very difficult vocabulary in the texts is glossed for you but you are encouraged to use clues from the context and the language to help you whenever possible, and there are exercises to help you to guess the meaning of unfamiliar words.

If you have to – or prefer to – work alone at home, there is a key at the back of the book which will help you to assess your progress. However, although reading skills are given emphasis, *Variety* also helps to develop your fluency in speaking, by means of roleplay and discussion activities, and obviously here you will need to work with an English-speaking friend. It is also extremely

## To the student

valuable to discuss your answers to the reading exercises with other people and this can be done very profitably in the classroom, in groups or pairs. There are also exercises which will help you to write in a variety of different styles; here, too, you will need an English-speaking person to help you.

*Variety* will help you to see how English-speaking people communicate in their language and develop strategies to help you communicate better yourself. But we also hope that you will enjoy reading it for its own sake, and that it will both interest and amuse you.

# Food and drink

Look through the texts in both sections of this unit and try to answer the following questions *as quickly as possible*. Remember that you are not looking for any other information, so it is not necessary to study the texts in detail.

1. Give page references for at least one example of each of the following types of text: a menu, a review, an article (magazine or newspaper), a chart, a coupon, a cartoon, an advertisement, a form.
2. What happens when you drink too much (according to an advertisement)?
3. How much will a meal for two, with coffee, cost at the Tudor Barn Restaurant?
4. What is the average weight of a man who is 5 ft 10 ins tall?
5. What was a man doing at a women's party?
6. Which television channel was a documentary programme about the dangers of drinking shown on?
7. What is the most popular evening meal in Britain, according to a survey?
8. Which newspaper recently published a report on why food in British restaurants is getting worse?
9. How can you lose weight and still eat your favourite food?
10. How does the Withy Trees pub describe its food?

Check your answers with a partner before looking at the key on page 146.

Now look at the exercises on pages 14–18 before reading the texts in section 1 more carefully.

*Food and drink*

# 1 Living to eat...

### The George Hotel
North Street, Bishop's Stortford. Tel: 54042
**VALENTINE'S DINNER**
**Saturday 11 February**

Homemade soup of the day.
Pieces of smoked haddock and prawn in a cheese sauce.
Spare ribs in barbecue sauce.
Button mushrooms filled with stilton, battered and deep fried.
½ Ogen melon with lemon sorbet and mandarins.
Homemade pate, hot buttered toast.
Taramasalata with pitta bread, mixed fish hors d'oeuvres

• • • • • • •

Beef Strogonoff with rice.
Breast of chicken stuffed with cheese and ham.
Pork fillet in a celery and curry sauce.
Poached lemon sole Duglere.
Veal saute in a tomato-onion wine sauce.
Roast duck in a cherry and apple sauce.
Baked cod cutlets with orange and walnuts.
Rump or sirloin steak garni.

• • • •

Vegetables

• • • •

Sweet + Coffee + Mints

**£8.95** inc VAT

PLUS A FLOWER FOR
YOUR 'LOVED ONE'

*Valentine's Day*: a special day (14 February) when lovers send each other cards/gifts
*sirloin, fillet and rump (steak)*: special cuts of beef, sold in the form of a steak

1 Living to eat . . .

### At the Sign of Ye Eight Bells, Saffron Walden.
### A Feeste for Winter
**in the Tudor Barn Restaurant**

**SAVOURY MORSELS** – fresh mushrooms filled with home-made pate covered with fine crumbs and crisply fried. Served with a spiced tomato glaze.
**HOME-MADE SOUP** – freshly made every day.
**PLUMP FRESH MUSSELS** – Salamandered with savoury butter and parsley.
**HOT GRILLED GRAPEFRUIT** – with Barbados Rum (to keep out the cold)
**DUCK LIVER PATE** – creamed with herbs and port wine.
**FRUITS OF THE EARTH** – a cornucopia of fresh young vegetables served raw to be dipped in a Herby Vinaigrette and Garlicky Mayonnaise.

**THE ROAST BEEF OF OLD ENGLAND** – carved from the silver trolley.
**FINEST LOCAL PHEASANT** – seethed in a rich cream and brandy sauce.
**LEMON SOLE** – baked with crabmeat and prawn stuffing.
**A PLUMP SIRLOIN STEAK** – grilled and served with tarragon butter.
**A GAME PIE** – baked individually to order.
**FRESH DUCKLING** – crisply roasted and accompanied with chestnut stuffing and apple sauce or with an Elizabethan Sauce of Oranges, Sherry and Walnuts.
All dishes include a choice of fresh vegetables or salads.
A selection of other dishes also available for a supplement to the inclusive price.
(A selection of home-made sweets)
All for the sum of Eight and a half pounds including our well-beloved Value Added Tax!
Coffee 40p
in the Tudor Barn Restaurant
Available until 31st March
Telephone Saffron Walden 22790 or 26237 to reserve your table

### Special Valentine's Day Menu
### Dinner for two £19.95
To include a bottle of House Wine

*feeste*: (old English) a feast; a big meal, with plenty to eat and drink

# Fish is first choice for lunch

Fish, chips and peas, followed by ice cream and coffee is the most popular lunch in Britain, while prawn cocktail, steak and gateau remain supreme in the evening, according to a Gallup survey published today.

Sirloin and fillet steaks are now more popular than rump, and meat pies have made a big comeback in the last year, displacing hamburgers and mixed grills, the *Caterer and Hotelkeeper* menu survey says. More than half of diners miss out the first course.

Scots and Welsh people favour curries, while in London chilli con carne has become fashionable and is featured on 20 per cent of menus.

Cod is still the favourite fish, followed by scampi and plaice, except in Scotland where haddock is first choice.

*Gallup survey*: an attempt to find out general public opinion about a topic, by interviewing a representative number of people

Food and drink

# When eating out leaves a bad taste in your mouth

**A meal in a restaurant can be a real test of nerves with its foreign menus, hidden costs and snooty waiters. Gaynor Morgan offers a recipe for eating out with confidence**

## TABLE FOR TWO

Booking means you promise to turn up and the restaurant promises to provide a table. If you don't show they can sue you for lost business! In practice they're usually satisfied if you tell them you're cancelling. If they forget your booking, state your case firmly and stand your ground. No restaurant *has* to serve you but they can't refuse on grounds of race, sex, or colour.

## THE HIDDEN MENU

A menu is the shop window of a restaurant and a close look will tell you more than just what's cooking and for how much. It can be quite a shock when the bill is for a lot more than the price of the food and drink. Here's how . . .

● **VAT**
Restaurants have to display a sample menu with prices at or near the entrance to the dining area and they must include VAT. But table menu prices can be exclusive of VAT, which makes them look deceptively cheap. Only a quarter of restaurants do not include VAT on *all* menus but it's best to check the small print first.

● **SERVICE CHARGE**
Many add this on for you. The going rate is 10 per cent but some places charge 12½ per cent or even 15 per cent. You have to pay it if it is prominently displayed on the menu and the service has been satisfactory.

● **TIPPING**
Ten per cent is average. But don't leave a tip if service is already added to the bill.

● **MINIMUM CHARGE**
Some places impose this especially at busy times. Watch out if you only want a snack or if one of your party isn't hungry.

● **COVER CHARGE**
This is a bit naughty. Some places impose a charge of 50p or more just for the honour of letting you sit down. It is supposed to cover the cost of laundry and they usually throw in bread and butter.
Note: restaurants are within their rights to charge for service *on top* of VAT and cover charge, adding a total of 25 per cent or more to your bill!

● **OTHER BILL BUILDERS**
"Selection of vegetables . . ." These may be charged as an extra so check what is included in the price of the main dish.
"Sweets from the trolley from 80p . . ." Beware of a sliding price scale; remember cream could be an "extra".
"Lobster s.q."—*si quaeris* (price on request)—means price varies with the market —usually expensive!

● **NO CREDIT CARDS**
The restaurant *can* insist on cash if they like.

*snooty*: snobbish
*what's cooking*: (a play on words) what's happening
*VAT*: value added tax; a government tax put on luxury items
*laundry*: washing and ironing
*trolley*: a small table on wheels (used for serving food)

1  Living to eat . . .

Fruit Juice

Compote of Fruit

Porridge

Cereals

—

*Choice of:*

Smoked Haddock

Grilled Kippers

Fried – Boiled – Poached – Scrambled Eggs

Bacon and Egg

Bacon and Sausage

Sausage and Egg

—

Toast – Rolls – Croissant

Marmalade – Honey

Tea – Coffee

"Invite everyone. We're having scrambled egg"

*Food and drink*

# IN-FACT  **CAPITAL MEALS**

Where can you eat well in London for around five pounds a head? Our selection of restaurants have been personally tested by *Company* staff and friends and they rate for ambiance and quality, as well as good value. Compiled by Bridget Freer.

**Chez Louisette**
102 Baker Street, W1 (935 2529); *tube* Baker Street; *open* 11.30-14.30, 17.30-23.00 (closed Sundays); *LVs* accepted.

There are no printed menus but one of the friendly staff will rattle off the day's dishes. Apart from a permanent selection of pâté, quiche or cheese salads (£1.50 each), the hot dishes change daily – eg. steak and salad (good value at £2.50), lamb stew (£1.45) or boeuf bourgignon (£1.95). I enjoyed the tasty and very filling saucisses d'alsace (£1.45). All dishes are accompanied by a basic but plentiful green salad in vinaigrette dressing. The cheese board is impressive and the house wine reasonable at £2.65 a bottle. Lunch times are bustling and jolly, while evenings tend to be quieter with live entertainment of the singer/songwriter genre.

**Tzabar Falafel House**
93-95 Haverstock Hill, NW3 (722 6187); *tube* Chalk Farm; *take away* yes; *licence* full; *LVs* accepted.

You could start your meal with one of three soups (borsch, bean or avgolemone), hummous or taramosalata, but when in a Falafel House why not eat falafels? These are small, flat, deep-fried rissoles flavoured with onion and spices with an optional sauce. The main courses are divided between Middle Eastern and European dishes, the former being cheaper, tastier and less familiar. There is a wide choice of salads, all worth trying. The house wine is middle eastern and definitely an acquired taste. The best pudding is their heavenly home-made cheesecake.

**Pasticceria Amalfi**
31 Old Compton Street, W1 (437 7284); *tube* Leicester Square; *open* 12.00-15.00, 18.00-23.15; *licence* full; *LVs* accepted.

You can't pass this restaraunt and fail to notice the sight of rows of homemade cakes and the smell of espresso. Inside, the decor is decidedly kitsch (pale green china sea-horses with lanterns in their mouths) but the atmosphere very Italian. The talkative waiters are not all that speedy but must rate amongst the most friendly. The menu is large with a good selection of soup and pasta for starters, and a bewildering twenty-six main courses, such as escalope milanese (around £2.50) or steak (£3.50). Choose one of the delicious cakes made on the premises for dessert.

**Porters**
17 Henrietta Street, WC2 (836 6466); *tube* Covent Garden; *open* 12.00-15.00, 18.00-23.00 (last orders); *LVs* accepted.

Named after the area's original habitués, and set in a former vegetable warehouse, Porters is very much the new Covent Garden: inside, a huge white room enhanced with a miscellany of green plants. The menu is traditional English fare and the best value is to be found in the selection of pies (from steak and kidney to game) all priced at £1.95. Side orders are extra (65p) but worth every penny. The puddings, such as treacle sponge with custard or cream, (60p) are equally delicious. House wine is £4.40 a litre; farmhouse cider 40p a half pint; but why not sample the aptly named porter (a light stout) at 55p per half pint?

**The Crown Tavern**
43 Clerkenwell Green, EC1 (250 0757); *tube* Farringdon; *open* pub hours.

Known as 'The Clocks pub' due to its phenomenal collection of timepieces – Clerkenwell was once the principal clock-making district in London. All labelled with an exotic placename, each tells a different time, apart from a quartz one labelled Clerkenwell Green to avoid confusion about closing time! Bar food is simple, homemade, cheap and good, offering such all-time favourites as cottage pies, meat pies and toad in the hole (at around £1.00).

**Geale's**
2-4 Farmer Street, W8 (727 7969); *tube* Notting Hill Gate; *open* Tuesday to Saturday 12.00-15.00; *licence* full; *LVs* accepted.

The chips are just as they should be – crisp and golden brown – and the fish exceptionally fresh. And the menu is small but select. There's homemade fish soup, smoked mackerel fillets or prawn cocktail to start with. The main course selection depends on what fish is in season but among the most commonly available are: plaice, lemon sole, haddock, cod steaks and rock salmon. One small niggle is that a portion of pickled onions costs 20p and gherkins cost 24p each. A plate of fish and chips will set you back by about £2.50 and a bottle of (decent) house wine £2.60.

"It's always been his ambition to open his own restaurant."

*LVs*: luncheon vouchers; coupons which you can exchange for a lunch in a restaurant
*kitsch*: in bad taste
*a warehouse*: a place where goods are kept before being given to the people who sell them
*fare*: food
*stout*: a kind of beer
*toad in the hole*: sausages cooked in batter
*gherkins*: small green cucumbers preserved in vinegar

1  Living to eat . . .

# Don't just swallow it
# Speak up if you find your meal out tastes awful

**Daily Mail Reporter**

The timid British diner is all that stands between the country's food industry and disaster, says the 1982 Good Food Guide, out today.

Unless he stops accepting bland restaurant meals while telling the head waiter: 'Everything is very nice', the growers, wholesalers and restaurateurs will never match their French counterparts, says Christopher Driver, the guide's editor.

Already he claims it's cheaper for people living near the Channel ports to take a day trip to Calais or Boulogne for lunch. Now he claims the quality gap is growing too.

He says: 'Food could be the next British industry to fade away. Take my particular pet hate – the overgrown, tasteless tomato, produced for profit alone without any thought of taste. It is indiscriminately marketed and pushed in front of the customer in a take-it-or-leave-it attitude.'

'That would never happen in France. There, the customers, restaurateurs and suppliers co-operate in finding the best quality ingredients. In France, the fishermen actually ask the restaurateur what he wants them to catch.'

So, if you want to get the most from a British restaurant, the guide gives this advice.

Ask questions: How dishes are cooked, which wine goes best with what and so on. If you say nothing, how is the waiter to know you care what you eat?

Don't drink too much – it numbs the palate.

When the head waiter asks 'Is everything all right?' treat it as a serious inquiry. Remember one of the great British obstacles to taking restaurant food seriously is the phrase 'please don't make a fuss.'

But never pull rank in a restaurant, like threatening to write to the Good Food Guide. And don't say you're an inspector – that counts as fraud, since real inspectors never do.

And if at the end of a meal you have enjoyed it, always say thank you with an appropriate degree of warmth. A tip isn't the same thing.

Once again the Guide highlights just how expensive eating out has become in England. Even including the £5.50 return trip from Folkestone to Boulogne, it says it's often still cheaper to eat on the other side of the Channel.

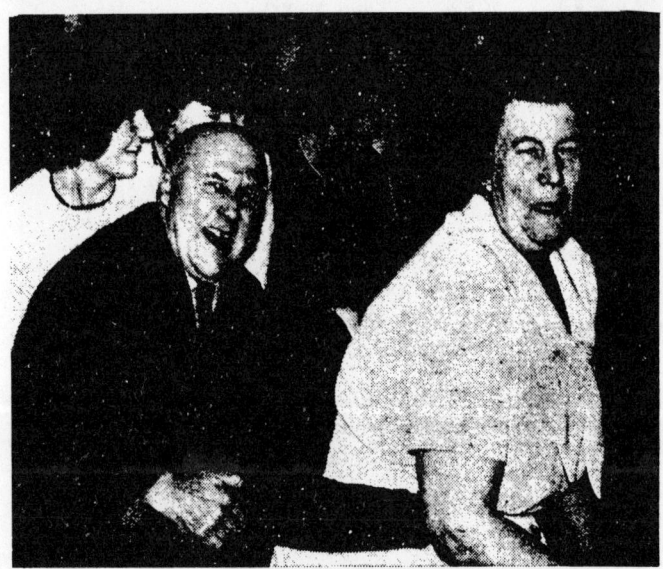

● The only man at Epping British Legion Women's Section annual party at the Methodist Hall on Monday was Mr. A. Freeman. He said he came to do the washing up.

*swallow (something)*: (play on words) to accept something (timidly)
*bland*: without much taste, uninteresting
*wholesalers*: people who sell food in large quantities to shops
*counterparts*: people who have a similar job
*numbs the palate*: prevents you from tasting something
*obstacle*: something which stops someone from doing something
*pull rank*: use your position to influence people
*fraud*: criminal deception

*Food and drink*

# 10 PUBS FOR VISITORS TO LONDON

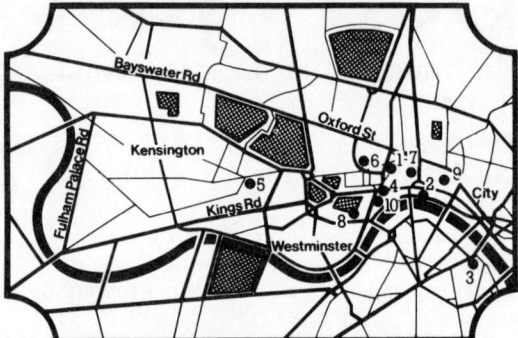

If you have only a limited period of time in London this leaflet will help you to find 10 interesting and unusual Whitbread pubs located in areas handy for sightseeing and shopping.

FOR FULLY COMPREHENSIVE FREE GUIDES TO 1000 PUBS IN LONDON & THE SOUTH EAST (24 HOURS) TELEPHONE
**01-907 4600**
OR WRITE TO:
THE WHITBREAD PUB & RESTAURANT INFORMATION BUREAU
THE TRAVELLERS REST
KENTON ROAD
KENTON, HARROW
MIDDLESEX

 **WHITBREAD**

## Key to Facilities

 Cold Buffet.

 Children's Facilities (normally in restaurant or garden).

♪ Entertainment.

 Function Room available for private hire.

 Lunchtime Restaurant (usually Monday to Friday only).

 Pool table or other pub sports facility.

 Pub Restaurant or Steakhouse open most Lunchtimes *and* evenings.

 Pub Grub and/or Bar Snacks.

 Traditional Ale.

 Wine Bar.

 Other British Pubs especially catering for tourists.

Unusual/Interesting or Historic Inns.

1  Living to eat...

**1 Blue Posts**
28 Rupert Street, London, W1. *Tel: 01 437 1415*

*Close to Piccadilly Circus, in the heart of the tourist country, this house knows well how to welcome our visitors from overseas. The lounge bar has a taste of the eighteenth century and a noteworthy collection of original oil paintings by Clifton Thompson.*

**2 Edgar Wallace**
40 Essex Street, London, WC2. *Tel: 01 353 3120*

*Houses exhibits reflecting the life and work of the famous detective author, donated by his family. The restaurant is open at lunchtime. Small function room available for private hire.*

**3 George Inn**
77 Borough High Street, London, SE1. *Tel: 01 407 2056*

*A tavern steeped in history, this, London's last remaining galleried coaching inn, has recently been carefully restored and extended. The present pub was built in 1677.
In the downstairs bar is the famous "Act of Parliament Clock", in use since the 18th Century.
Charles Dickens must have visited the "George" since he mentions it in Little Dorrit. The house now offers two bars, a wine bar and a choice of two restaurants.*

**4 Gilbert & Sullivan**
23 Wellington Street, London, WC2. Tel: 01 836 6930

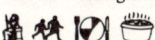

*Fascinating unique collection of old playbills, photographs, copies of the musical scores and miniature stage settings connected with the world-famous Gilbert and Sullivan operas, in a tasteful Victorian-style setting. Excellent snack bar open lunchtime and evening, except Sundays.*

**5 Grove Tavern**
43 Beauchamp Place, London, SW3. Tel: 01 589 5897

*An internationally known shopping area. Close by Knightsbridge and Harrods.*

**6 King Charles II**
18 Kingly Street, London, W1. Tel: 01 734 1170

*Close by famous Carnaby Street.*

**7 Nags Head**
10 James Street, Covent Garden, London, WC2.
*Tel: 01 836 4678*

*With the nearby Covent Garden opera house as its inspiration, this is a pub of great character used by many theatrical people. Old prints and programmes from the Royal Opera House are on view.*

**8 Old Star**
66 Broadway, Westminster, London, SW1. *Tel: 01 930 7591*

*Near the Houses of Parliament and within easy reach of the Abbey and Parliament Square, you can never be sure who you might meet in this popular pub! Serves excellent food and drink. Downstairs the Crown Vaults cellar wine bar offers a large selection of wines, pates, and continental cheeses.*

**9 Printers Devil**
98/9 Fetter Lane, London, EC4. *Tel: 01 242 2239*

*Just around the corner from the Daily Mirror building, this pub is a well-known haunt for the gentlemen and ladies of the press. The main bar features many examples of printing techniques and equipment, famous front pages, and first editions. Snacks lunchtime and evening.*

**10 Sherlock Holmes**
10 Northumberland Street, London, WC2. *Tel: 01 930 2644*

*Many foreign visitors are amazed to discover that the famous detective was in fact a fictitious character created by Sir Arthur Conan Doyle who frequented this pub when it was known as the Northumberland Arms. Mentioned in "The Hound of the Baskervilles", it has become something of a "Holmes museum" with manuscripts covering the walls of the ground floor bar. Upstairs is a restaurant in a room reconstructed to resemble Holmes' study in Baker Street.*

### The WHITBREAD PUB & RESTAURANT INFORMATION BUREAU
The Travellers Rest, Kenton Road, Kenton, Harrow, Middlesex

## 01-907 4600 (24 HOURS)

---

*steeped in history*: with a long historic tradition
*coaching inn*: an old hotel or pub where people used to stop for refreshment during a journey
*scores*: pieces of written music
*prints*: copies of pictures
*a haunt*: a place which people go to a lot
*manuscripts*: handwritten or typed pages of books (before they are printed)

*Food and drink*

The sign of good food....

## WITHY TREES

### PLEASE ORDER & PAY AT THE BAR

**HOME COOKING
GOOD AND WHOLESOME**

**Bowl of Home-made Soup** — 45p
*Made in our own kitchen. With crusty bread and butter*

**Home-made Steak, Kidney
& Mushroom Pie** — £1.45

**Chicken in the Pot** — £1.45
*Tender pieces of chicken, cooked in red wine with mushrooms and shallots*

**Home-made Turkey &
Ham Pie** — £1.45

**Traditional Cottage Pie** — £1.25
*With pickles*

**Freshly prepared Plaice
Goujons** — £1.45
*Strips of plaice, breadcrumbed and deep fried*

**Landlady's Special** — See the Blackboard
*A daily dish, made with loving care*

*All the above served with a choice of potatoes and vegetables*

### THE COLD TABLE

**Choice of Pate** — 95p
*With crusty bread*

**Ploughman's Lunch** — 95p
*Wedge of cheese, chutney, salad and crusty bread*

**Home-baked Cold Ham
Platter** — £1.45
*Served with a selection of salads*

**Cold Roast Turkey
Platter** — £1.55
*Served with a selection of salads*

*To top up*

**A selection of Sweets from
the display** — 70p

**Cheese and Biscuits** — 50p

**Cup of Fresh Filter Coffee** — 35p
*With dairy cream*

*All prices inclusive of V.A.T.*

---

*fayre*: (old English) fare; food (at table)   *wholesome*: good for you

12

1  Living to eat...

◀◀◀◀◀◀

## PLATFORM
# Let the kids in!
Peter Hain argues for changes in the pub laws

To declare an interest — I have two sons aged 4 and 2 and both my wife and I like 'real' ale. The trouble is, we can't enjoy it as much as we would like. For us, most pubs in Britain are positively anti-social — they won't admit children.

It's not that we are regular drinkers, nor that we ever have more than a couple of pints at a time. For us a visit to the pub is a chance to get away from the chores at home and from the telephone, for our family to relax together.

We enjoy sampling the different 'real' brews around the country while on holiday and in some parts we are welcomed. For example, many Cornish pubs have rooms which admit children, with Devon and Dorset not far behind.

Elsewhere you will find only the odd pub in an area that understands our problem. The Sussex Ox at Alfriston, for example, has a proper family room (with even a TV and toys) in a relaxed and homely atmosphere.

Sometimes a publican will allow us in if we eat lunch as well. Others are prepared to turn a blind eye and nod us around the corner, out of sight of the main serving area.

Although the law is pretty clear in theory — barring under-14s from rooms in which alcohol is actually being served — in practice there is room for discretion. Some publicans exercise it, others do not. For example, if a pub has an L-shaped lounge with a bar in what amounts to a distinct area, even if it is physically the same room, a publican could be broad-minded about children accompanied by adults.

But even when a separate children's room is provided, that may sidestep the real issue. Part of the attraction of a pub is its convivial, comfortable atmosphere — and if you are shuffled off with the kids into a cold side room, that may be better than nothing, but it hardly fulfils the purpose of the outing.

The real objective should surely be to bring the whole family into the pub together — not to place everyone into little compartments, separated away from each other.

Pubs would lose the image of being those places where adults let their hair down and indulge in escapism, ie, get drunk. Half of that sort of behaviour occurs out of bravado. Much youthful drunkenness occurs, I am convinced, because teenagers are anxious to show off their prowess in an adult haven. If they had been to pubs all their lives, they would not be mysterious places.

So what should we do? To begin with, we should change the law and abolish the age limit, provided of course that under-18s are accompanied by adults and are not served alcoholic drinks. On no account must we encourage the already disturbing growth in teenage drinking.

Then we should persuade publicans and breweries to turn at least one of their main bars into a family room. Ideally the whole pub should be open to families, and hopefully a new social climate could be created in which that would occur. But it should not be imposed arbitrarily on individual pubs: there should be a natural change in response to local wishes. All the law would do is enable change to occur where desired.

One factor which could foster such change would be the behaviour of children. There would be a special responsibility on adults to make sure that the children accompanying them did not run riot and spoil the atmosphere for others.

It was not long ago that women felt unwelcome in most pubs. Now attitudes have changed and so has the law. Another change has been the increasing provision of food in pubs. Now we ought to go the whole way, not just by having more children's rooms (though that would be better than nothing), but by letting the kids right in, and changing pubs from adult retreats into family places.

This would at least get parents and children to sit around a table together and talk to each other. Kids might then behave better rather than playing out their expected roles as anti-social misfits, out of sight and sound. ■

*brews*: types of different beers
*odd*: occasional
*publican*: the owner of a pub
*discretion*: individual choice
*foster*: encourage

13

*Food and drink*

## 1.1

1 Look at pages 4–5 and write down the names of:
   a) as many kinds of *fish* and
   b) as many kinds of *meat* (including birds) as possible.

2 Discuss what you have written down with a partner and, if necessary, consult your dictionary or your teacher.

3 Put a tick next to the kinds of meat and/or fish which you have in your own country. Add any others which you eat in your own country and which you know the English for. Discuss what you have written down in pairs or groups.

4 In pairs, look at the texts and find six common verbs which refer to methods of cooking meat or fish (e.g. *fry*).

## 1.2

1 Look through the whole of section 1 quickly and write down what your ideal menu would be if you were spending a day in the UK. Make notes under these headings: *Breakfast, Lunch, Dinner*.

2 Discuss your notes with a partner and try to give reasons for your choice.

3 Choose one meal (lunch or dinner) which is your favourite in your own country and write a description of it, together with explanations to help the foreign visitor. The descriptions on pages 4–5 may help, e.g.
*Savoury morsels* – fresh mushrooms filled with home-made paté covered with fine crumbs and crisply fried.

4 Work in groups. Exchange your descriptions within the group and each decide which one you like best. Ask the person who wrote it to explain how to make the meal, and take notes. Then ask that person to check whether your notes are correct.

## 1.3

1 Look at the article on page 6, 'When eating out leaves a bad taste in your mouth'. Before reading it, try to predict from the headlines what you think it will say. Then read through the article quickly and see if your predictions were correct.

# 1 Living to eat...

2 Read the article again and try to decide if the following statements are true or false according to the writer. Write T or F next to each statement.
   a) If you reserve a table, you can't change your mind about going to the restaurant.
   b) If you don't go, the restaurant will always charge you a cancellation fee.
   c) If the restaurant forgets your reservation, you should insist on having a table.
   d) A restaurant can refuse to serve women.
   e) The bill will always include food, drink and service.
   f) The service charge is usually 10% of the bill.
   g) You always have to pay 50p just to sit down.
   h) Vegetables usually cost extra.
   i) If the price of the dish isn't on the menu, it generally means it is expensive.
   j) You can always pay by cheque, provided you have a bankers card.

3 Look at the following words and expressions, as they appear in the context of the article, and discuss with your partner what they might mean. (The numbers in brackets refer to the columns in the text.) Check with a dictionary, or with your teacher.
   a) *turn up* (1)
   b) *show* (1)
   c) *sue* (1)
   d) *stand your ground* (1)
   e) *display a sample menu* (2)
   f) *check the small print* (2)
   g) *the going rate* (2)
   h) *Watch out* (3)
   i) *throw in* (3)
   j) *on top of* (3)

4 In groups, discuss the similarities and differences between eating out in Britain and in your own country. Report back to the class.

## 1.4

1 Look at the reviews on page 8. Make a note of the name of the restaurant you would go to if:
   a) you loved Italian food;
   b) you wanted to eat fish;
   c) you loved foreign food but wanted to take it back to the office;
   d) you wanted to eat something typically English;
   e) you liked a friendly, lively atmosphere.

2 Work in pairs. Ask each other which answers you chose. Then ask each other which restaurant *you* would choose to go to and why.

*Food and drink*

3 Look carefully at the reviews and try to decide what the following vocabulary might mean. Look closely at the context. Discuss your ideas in groups, giving reasons. Then check with a dictionary (or your teacher).

*Chez Louisette*
a) staff
b) to rattle off
c) plentiful
d) impressive
e) bustling

*Tzabar Falafel House*
a) an acquired taste
b) heavenly

*Pasticceria Amalfi*
on the premises

*The Crown Tavern*
timepieces

*Geales*
a) a niggle
b) to set you back

## 1.5

1 Before reading the article on page 9, look at the headlines and try to predict what you think the article will be about. Discuss your ideas with a partner.

2 Read the article quickly and decide whether the following statements are true or false, according to the writer. Write T or F next to each statement.

a) The *Good Food Guide* says that it is British people's fault if the food industry is getting worse.
b) British people have a tendency to complain in restaurants.
c) French food is worse than British food.
d) Tomatoes are always pushed in front of customers in restaurants.
e) It is French fishermen who are responsible for the good reputation of French food.
f) British waiters don't care about what the customers eat.
g) The *Guide*'s editor warns you not to cause a fuss in restaurants.
h) He says you should not pretend to be someone you are not.
i) It is always very important to say thank you after a meal in a restaurant.
j) It is cheaper to eat in France than Britain.

3 In the same article, decide what the following words refer back to, and make a note of your answers.

a) *he* (line 6)
b) *he* (line 12)
c) 'Take *it* or leave *it*' (line 22). What?
d) '*That* would never happen' (line 23). What wouldn't?
e) *There* (line 24). Where?
f) *he* (line 27)
g) *them* (line 28)
h) 'Real inspectors never *do*' (line 47). Do what?
i) 'A tip isn't *the same thing*' (lines 51–2). As what?
j) *it* (line 59)

16

## 1.6

1 Look at pages 10–11. Make a note of which of these ten well-known pubs in London you would choose to go to if:
   a) you were looking for entertainment and pub games in a fashionable area of London;
   b) you were keen on the novels and times of Charles Dickens;
   c) you liked detective writers, and had children with you;
   d) you had just been to the opera at Covent Garden;
   e) you wanted excellent food and drink near famous monuments.

2 Find words on pages 10–11 which mean the same as the following.
   a) an information guide given away free
   b) a pub (*two words*)
   c) food
   d) beer
   e) near (*five words or expressions*)

## 1.7

1 Read the article on page 13, 'Let the kids in' and choose the answer which best illustrates the meaning of the passage.

   a) Peter Hain and his wife would go out to pubs more if:
      – his wife liked beer.
      – they could drink more.
      – they could take the children with them.
      – they didn't have to stay at home and work.

   b) In Britain:
      – no pubs ever let children in.
      – the occasional pub has facilities for children.
      – you can always take children into a pub if you have a meal.
      – pubs in places like Devon and Dorset hardly ever let children in.

   c) The law says:
      – children under 14 must not go into a pub where alcohol is served.
      – children under 14 can be in a room where alcohol is served as long as it is 'L' shaped.
      – pubs must have a separate room for children.
      – children under 14 can't go into a room in a pub where alcohol is being served.

   d) Peter Hain believes that:
      – under 18s should be allowed to enter pubs and drink alcohol if they are with an adult.
      – there should be a separate room for under 18s.

*Food and drink*

- the increase in teenage drinking is a result of not allowing young people to drink alcohol in pubs.
- age limits should apply to drinking alcohol in pubs but not to entering them.

e) If pubs become family places:
- a lot of teenage drunkenness would be avoided.
- children would behave badly and disturb other people.
- children should sit quietly without talking.
- the landlord would be responsible for making sure children behaved well.

2 Find a word in the text that means more or less the same as each of the following. The number in brackets refers to the number of the column in the text.
   a) a measure of beer (1)
   b) jobs in the house (1)
   c) trying (1)
   d) allow in (1)
   e) forbidding entry (1)
   f) tolerant (2)
   g) avoid (2)
   h) sociable (2)
   i) pushed away (2)
   j) a place of safety (2)
   k) children (3)
   l) people who don't fit into society (3)

3 Now look at the passage again and decide which of the following alternatives is closest in meaning to the idiomatic expression in italics. Refer closely to the context.

   a) *to turn a blind eye* means:
      - to forbid or prevent
      - to overcharge
      - to pretend not to notice
      - to hide from the other customers

   b) *to let your hair down* means:
      - to become violent
      - to enjoy yourself without inhibition
      - to stop drinking
      - to get ready to go out

   c) *to run riot* means:
      - to drink too much
      - to race around noisily
      - to protest
      - to leave when no-one is looking

4 In Britain there are restrictions on the times that pubs can be open and the age at which a young person can enter a pub and drink alcohol. In groups, discuss your views on this, with reference to the article by Peter Hain, and to laws in your own country. Report your views back to the rest of the class.

**Before reading the the texts in section 2 more carefully, look at the exercises on pages 24–5.**

## 2  Or eating to live

# On the bier?

**Horizon**
**Monday 9.25 BBC2**

Will you be watching 'Horizon' on Monday evening, or is that when you're down at the local? HILARY MACASKILL suggests here that tuning in may be advisable

This week's Horizon: How Much Can You Drink? addresses itself to the practical issue of the dividing line between harmless normal drinking and the 'serious drinking problem' that afflicts an estimated 700,000 people in this country. Too much drinking can have dire effects on health: in the next 12 months 10,000 people may die prematurely from the effects of drink. Advertisements can no longer characterise alcohol as beneficial. Guinness is not now projected as 'good for you'. Nevertheless, social drinkers cling hopefully to that scrap of half-remembered research that suggests that a little drink *is* good for you.

Well, perhaps it is. Darts players can draw comfort from the evidence in the programme that hand tremor lessens after a few drinks. (No doubt henceforth to be cited in justification of their paunches.) Though it must be added that next day's hand tremor was greater than normal. Moderate drinking, because of the effect of alcohol on the blood, may give some protection against cardio-vascular disease.

But people's bodies vary hugely in their reactions to alcohol. The less fortunate drinkers may get cirrhosis of the liver after a far smaller alcohol intake than another drinker.

So how much *can* you drink? The answer, if you are a woman, is less than a man. The reason is not another example of blatant discrimination but that women, unfair though it may be, are more at risk from alcohol. Doc-

tors recommend a daily limit of six units for a man (a unit is ½ pt of beer, a glass of wine or a measure of spirits), four units for a woman.

That limit is the aim of those who attend Drink Watchers, formed 18 months ago, which works on similar lines to Weight Watchers. After an initial screening to ensure that they aren't physically damaged by alcohol, Drink Watchers meet weekly to analyse and discuss the daily records they keep of their drinks. 'The aim is to provide a social base as much as anything,' says National Co-ordi-

nator Geraldine Wilson. 'We replace the pub life with a different social life.'

Enjoying sensible drinking is the goal of Drink Watchers and Geraldine has some useful tips to help people stick to the limit: 'Make the first drink a soft one to quench the thirst. Alternate alcohol with mineral water. Put the glass on the table between sips. Distance the glass so you have to make a conscious effort to reach it. Make one drink last 40 minutes. Most important, plan how much to drink in an evening, count the drinks and then stop.' ●

*the local*: the pub you regularly go to
*Guinness*: a kind of beer
*cling*: hold on to tightly
*darts*: a game involving throwing small, sharp, pointed objects at a board

*tremor*: shaking
*cited*: quoted
*cardio-vascular*: heart
*cirrhosis*: a type of disease

# Food and drink

The party begins.

*I can drive when I drink.*

2 drinks later.

*I can drive when I drink*

After 4 drinks.

*I can drive when I drink.*

After 5 drinks.

*I can drive when I drink.*

7 drinks in all.

*I can drive when I drink.*

The more you drink, the more coordination you lose. That's a fact, plain and simple.

Still, people drink too much and then go out and expect to handle a car.

When you drink too much you can't handle a car. You can't even handle a pen.

Seagram/distillers since 1857.

## 2 Or eating to live

# A food-lover's way to eat and be fit

MANY popular nutritional myths are exploded in a new official blueprint for healthier eating, aimed at cutting down the high rate of heart disease, strokes and some cancer in Britain.

Such processed foods as baked beans and grilled fish fingers, for example, can be less harmful — and, indeed, less fattening — than lamb chops or steak, says the controversial report.

Red meat, in fact, is no longer considered an essential part of the daily diet. Protein in the form of fish or poultry, both lower in fat and calories than meat, is preferable.

High fibre foods such as pulses, potatoes and wholemeal bread are also held to play an important part in healthy eating. And smaller helpings are recommended as a vital contribution in the stepped-up battle against obesity.

The report, produced by the Government-appointed National Advisory Committee on Nutrition Education, recommends that we eat more fibre, fruit and vegetables, and substantially less fat, sugar and salt.

Heart disease in Britain is currently among the highest in the western world and much of it is thought to be due to too much fat in our diet.

But healthier eating does not mean that we need to become a nation of health food fanatics. Rather it is a case of modifying our existing eating habits as shown here.

Publication of the NACNE report, now presented as a discussion paper, was delayed for two years by the Department of Health and the British Nutrition Foundation, which is largely funded by the food manufacturers.

The reason given was that some of their members felt the report did not give sufficient evidence to justify the recommendations.

But the report emphasises that there is more to good health than simply altering our diet. Revised eating habits should be part of an overall change in lifestyle encompassing more exercise, less alcohol and no smoking.

**Sally Brompton**

| HEALTHY DIET | UNHEALTHY DIET |
|---|---|
| **BREAKFAST** | |
| Orange juice. High fibre cereal. Poached egg or grilled bacon. Wholemeal bread thinly spread with butter or margarine. Tea or coffee with skimmed milk and one sugar. | Fried bacon and eggs and fried bread. White bread thickly spread with butter. Tea or coffee with milk and two teaspoonfuls of sugar. |
| **ELEVENSES** | |
| Two digestive biscuits with tea or coffee. | Cheese roll with tea or coffee. |
| **LUNCH** | |
| Two rounds of chicken and lettuce brown bread sandwiches. Half pint of beer. Fruit. Yoghurt. | Pork pie. Packet of crisps. Two pints of beer. Chocolate biscuit. |
| **AFTERNOON SNACK** | |
| Two digestive biscuits. | Doughnut. |
| **DINNER** | |
| Lamb and butter bean stew. Jacket potato. Peas. Baked apple with dried fruit. | Two lamb chops. Fried potatoes. Peas. Apple pie and custard. |
| **BEDTIME DRINK** | |
| Milk drink using skimmed milk. | Chocolate or cocoa. |

**FOOD FOR THOUGHT: A typical day's meals for the carefree eater... and changes the Nutrition Education Committee suggests**

*nutritional*: related to food value
*myth*: old traditional story
*blueprint*: a plan to work from
*protein*: bodybuilding food
*calories*: energy which the body gets from food
*pulses*: kinds of seeds e.g. peas, beans (eaten as food)
*obesity*: an extreme (unhealthy) fatness
*funded by*: given money by

*Food and drink*

# IS YOUR MAN OVERWEIGHT?

Help your man look better and live longer by watching his weight – it's worthwhile!

NO ONE likes to be told they're overweight, and men are just as sensitive about it as women – although they probably won't admit it.

And, statistically, it's likely that your man could afford to shed a few pounds. Obesity has become one of our biggest health problems.

The main cause, of course, is eating too much: and over-eating is particularly harmful if he's eating the wrong foods.

Being overweight is just as ugly in men as it is in women. It also causes a general sluggishness and accelerates the onset of degenerative diseases. It has been shown that an increase of 25 pounds above the normal average weight of a man of 45 reduces his life expectation by 25 per cent.

## Lack of exercise

Another contributing factor is lack of exercise. Modern living has encouraged us to rely on the motor car, and to use labour-saving devices in the home and office more than ever before.

It is virtually impossible to devise accurate "ideal" weight charts, but we have made an *average* weight chart for men (bearing in mind that weight can vary about 10 pounds either way, depending on his overall build).

The energy value of the food we eat is counted in calories. The average man requires around 2,500 to 3,000 a day. This varies with age, build and activity. Overweight occurs when the input of calories is greater than the output. To lose weight, you must take in less than you need – when you do this, your excess body fat is used for energy.

| HEIGHT | | WEIGHT | |
|---|---|---|---|
| ft | in | lbs | stones |
| 5 | 0 | 126 | 9st 0lbs |
| 5 | 1 | 129 | 9st 3lbs |
| 5 | 2 | 132 | 9st 6lbs |
| 5 | 3 | 135 | 9st 9lbs |
| 5 | 4 | 139 | 9st 13lbs |
| 5 | 5 | 142 | 10st 2lbs |
| 5 | 6 | 146 | 10st 6lbs |
| 5 | 7 | 150 | 10st 10lbs |
| 5 | 8 | 154 | 11st 0lbs |
| 5 | 9 | 158 | 11st 4lbs |
| 5 | 10 | 162 | 11st 8lbs |
| 5 | 11 | 166 | 11st 12lbs |
| 6 | 0 | 172 | 12st 4lbs |
| 6 | 1 | 178 | 12st 10lbs |
| 6 | 2 | 184 | 13st 2lbs |
| 6 | 3 | 190 | 13st 8lbs |

It is always difficult to know what a good diet is. The best one is one that suits his condition and personal daily needs. (If he is grossly overweight, it is advisable to consult a doctor before going on a diet.)

There are hundreds of different diets around, but they all follow either the restricted carbohydrate system or the calorie controlled system. Whichever one your man decides to follow, there are a few basic rules.

He should always have at least three meals a day: breakfast, lunch and an evening meal. And each day he should have at least one portion of meat, fish, egg or cheese, as well as green vegetables and fresh fruit. Remember that if he must have milk, he should keep it to a maximum of half a pint a day. Similarly, if he insists on having bread, he should stick to wholemeal bread. A low calorie, high protein breakfast cereal is a good way to start the day and gives him a good supply of roughage as well.

## The right diet

The average low calorie diet for a man would be about 1,500 calories. With a good calorie chart, a little common sense and imagination, you can devise a diet which includes most of the foods he likes but in controlled quantities. Cut out sugar, cakes, sweets, biscuits, puddings, pastries, rice, ice cream, jams and fried foods.

Most men like a drink and would find it impossible (or at least annoying) to give up. We have therefore made a list of the calorie counts for "liquid lunches" at the pub. These calories must be included in the daily 1,500, so it might be a good idea to deduct a couple of pints' worth before you start planning each daily diet.

| | Calories |
|---|---|
| **Beer** | |
| mild (½ pt) | 120 |
| pale ale (½ pt) | 90 |
| strong ale (½ pt) | 210 |
| stout (½ pt) | 100 |
| ginger ale (½ pt) | 32 |
| ginger beer (½ pt) | 88 |
| **Spirits** | |
| brandy, gin, rum, whisky (⅙ gill = pub measure) | 65 |
| **Wines** | |
| cider (½ pt) | 110 |
| dry (1 wineglass) | 105 |
| sweet (1 wineglass) | 130 |
| port (1 wineglass) | 129 |

---

*sluggishness*: inactivity
*accelerates*: increases the speed of
*onset*: start
*degenerative*: getting worse
*carbohydrate*: foods such as sugar, flour etc.
*roughage*: rough foods such as bran

2  *Or eating to live*

# NEW Weight Watchers Food Plan
# Now you can lose weight without losing all your favourite foods

Yes, you can enjoy bread, hamburgers, potatoes, ice-cream, sausages, fish fingers, banana splits, peanut butter, even wine and beer – within limits, of course – and still lose weight! With Weight Watchers new Food Plans you can take off the pounds deliciously.

### Three ways to save money

Now you can save money while you lose weight. Start with the special offer on this page.

Then continue to save. You won't have to buy expensive foods or cook separate meals for yourself. You can enjoy the same meals as your family.

You'll save money, too, when you lose weight. Weight Watchers meetings are free when you maintain your goal weight at your monthly weigh-in.

### How Weight Watchers helps you

We show you how to use a food plan designed to suit your tastes. Our instructors were once overweight themselves – so they understand your problems. They lost weight with the same methods they'll show you.

Each week with a friendly group of weight-conscious people, you'll discover how much easier it is to lose weight when you're not doing it alone.

And any time you have a diet problem, just phone your instructor for real help.

Join a Weight Watchers class now. The most successful weight-loss Programme in the world.

**1400 weekly classes throughout the U.K. There is one near you.**

Weight Watchers (U.K.) Ltd.,
635-637 Ajax Avenue, Slough, Berkshire, SL1 4DB.

### Phone today for details

For your nearest class, call:
**Central Office Slough (0753) 70711**
Preston (0772) 23031   Cardiff (0222) 20525
Coventry (0203) 57122   Newcastle (0632) 815348
Southampton (0703) 39951
*Or look in Yellow Pages under 'Health Clubs' for phone numbers of local classes.*

### First lesson free to 'Company' readers

As a reader of 'Company' you have a unique opportunity to join Weight Watchers... *your first lesson free on registration* if you bring this reader's voucher with you. If you want to lose weight the pleasant way, this is your chance.
**Offer closes 31st April 1982.**
*This offer cannot be combined with any other offer advertised elsewhere.*

*Bring this special voucher with you*

### or post the coupon

Post to: **WEIGHT WATCHERS (U.K.) LIMITED, FREEPOST, GREATER LONDON HOUSE, LONDON NW1 1YH.**
NO STAMP REQUIRED
Please send me details of my nearest Weight Watchers classes, without obligation.
Mr/Mrs/Miss/Ms_____
(PLEASE PRINT)
Address_____
_____
_____
Postcode_____ Tel:_____

**Weight Watchers**
*'Weight Watchers and ⓡ are trademarks of Weight Watchers International Inc. and used under its control.*

*Food and drink*

## 2.1

1 The headline above the article on page 19 is a play on words – a *bier* is something you put a coffin or a dead body on; it has the same pronunciation as *beer*. Can you predict what the article is going to say? Discuss your ideas in pairs or groups.

2 Read through the article quickly and answer the following questions.

a) How many people in Britain are seriously affected by alcohol?
b) How many people are likely to die in the next year because of alcohol?
c) Can alcohol ever be good for you?
d) How much alcohol is it 'safe' to drink?
e) How can Drink Watchers help you?

3 Read the article again and try to find expressions in the article that mean roughly the same as the following.

a) switching on the television
b) very bad
c) unusually early
d) a small piece
e) big stomachs
f) very much
g) a physical examination
h) good ideas
i) non-alcoholic
j) a small mouthful (of a drink)

## 2.2

1 Turn to the article on page 21. Before you begin reading, make a note of everything you have had to eat today (or what you had yesterday). Can you predict whether the article is going to say that this is good or bad for you? If you think an item is probably *bad* for you, put a cross (X) next to it.

2 Look through the text and answer the following questions. Discuss your answers in groups or as a class.

a) Who has produced the new, official report on healthy eating?
b) What does it aim to do?
c) Why is the report controversial?
d) Why was the publication of the report delayed?
e) What is the main problem with the British diet?
f) What should we eat *more* of, according to the report?
g) What should we try to eat *less* of?
h) How can you help to prevent obesity?
i) Does the report say that it is essential to eat health foods?
j) What else, apart from diet, contributes to good health?

2 *Or eating to live*

3 Work in pairs. Ask each other about *either* what you have had to eat today *or* what you had yesterday, and make recommendations about each other's diet, e.g. 'You shouldn't eat so much...', 'Why don't you try and eat less?'. Discuss whether your predictions about your own diet were correct or not.

## 2.3

1 Look at the article on page 22. Which of the following foods is it all right to eat if you are trying to lose weight; which is it all right to eat a little of; and which should you never eat? Put a tick (✓) in the appropriate column.

|  | *always* | *a little* | *never* |
|---|---|---|---|
| meat |  |  |  |
| fish |  |  |  |
| eggs |  |  |  |
| cheese |  |  |  |
| vegetables |  |  |  |
| fruit |  |  |  |
| milk |  |  |  |
| bread |  |  |  |
| cereal |  |  |  |
| sugar |  |  |  |
| cake |  |  |  |
| sweets |  |  |  |
| rice |  |  |  |
| alcohol |  |  |  |

2 To what extent does this article on eating to lose weight agree with the one on food and fitness on page 21? Discuss your ideas in groups.

3 You know that your father is really worried about his weight, so you decide to write him a letter, giving him some advice! Don't forget to recommend that he takes more exercise, as well as telling him what food he should be eating.

*Food and drink*

# Roleplay

For groups of four to six people.

## *Roles* (pages 160–4)

Guest 1 (role 1)   Guest 4 (role 10)
Guest 2 (role 4)   Inspector from the *Good Food Guide* (role 13)
Guest 3 (role 7)   Restaurant manager (role 16)

*Note:* one or two of the 'Guest' roles can be omitted if necessary.

## *Situation*

The Cosmopolitan restaurant opened only a month ago, and serves not only English food but also food from all over the world. The restaurant would like to be mentioned in the *Good Food Guide,* so the manager has invited an inspector to go along and try the food. The restaurant claims to be able to satisfy the eating preferences of any customer, so the *Good Food Guide* inspector has invited some friends to go along with him/her; they all have very specific needs and tastes.

## *Preliminary tasks*

You will be given a certain amount of time to look through your role (at the back of the book) and prepare what you are going to say. You can consult the texts in this unit, and ask your teacher for help, but remember to read only *your* role (and no-one else's).

### *Guests*
Look through the menus etc. in this unit and make a note of what you would like to eat. Remember to study your role description carefully first.

### *Inspector*
Decide what you would like to eat and then make a note of the questions you are going to ask the manager and your friends.

### *Manager*
Make out a three-course menu which will cater for all possible tastes – choosing six items for each course.

## *Procedure*

1 The manager will tell the guests what is on the menu, referring to his/her notes.

2 The inspector will invite the guests to talk about what they had planned to order and whether the manager's menu is acceptable. He/she will also encourage the manager to justify the proposed menu.

3 If the guests are not satisfied with the menu, they should give reasons, based on their roles.

4 A limited time will be given for the inspector and guests to decide whether the restaurant lives up to its claim to be able to satisfy all tastes or not.

## Follow up

Write a series of notes stating what the restaurant had to offer, and whether it was successful in meeting the needs of these particular customers.

# Christmas

Look through the texts in both sections of this unit and try to answer the following questions *as quickly as possible*. Remember that you are not looking for any other information, so it is not necessary to study the texts in detail.

1  How long does it take to cook a 10 lb turkey?
2  What are *two* different meanings of the word *merry*?
3  What does a little boy called Nick want for Christmas?
4  Who made Christmas trees popular?
5  What kind of animal is associated with Father Christmas?
6  What is the title of the novel with a character called Scrooge in it?
7  What does eight-year-old Jo think about Christmas?
8  What is another name for Father Christmas?
9  What is the name of the silver paper that you can roast meat in?
10 What is the name of a famous cartoon by Schultz?

Check your answers with a partner before looking at the key on page 148.

Now look at the exercises on pages 33–5 before reading the texts in section 1 more carefully.

# 1 The spirit of Christmas

'A merry Christmas, uncle! God save you!' cried a cheerful voice. It was the voice of Scrooge's nephew, who came upon him so quickly that this was the first intimation he had of his approach.

'Bah!' said Scrooge, 'Humbug!'

He had so heated himself with rapid walking in the fog and frost, this nephew of Scrooge's, that he was all in a glow; his face was ruddy and handsome; his eyes sparkled and his breath smoked again.

'Christmas a humbug, uncle!' said Scrooge's nephew. 'You don't mean that, I am sure?'

'I do,' said Scrooge. 'Merry Christmas! What right have you to be merry? What reason have you to be merry? You're poor enough.'

'Come, then,' returned the nephew gaily. 'What right have you to be dismal? What reason have you to be morose? You're rich enough.'

Scrooge having no better answer ready on the spur of the moment, said, 'Bah!' again; and followed it up with 'Humbug!'

'Don't be cross, uncle!' said the nephew.

'What else can I be,' returned the uncle, 'when I live in such a world of fools as this? Merry Christmas! Out upon merry Christmas! What's Christmas time to you but a time for paying bills without money; a time for finding yourself a year older, but not an hour richer; a time for balancing your books and having every item in 'em through a round dozen of months dead against you? If I could work my will,' said Scrooge indignantly, 'every idiot who goes about with "Merry Christmas" on his lips should be boiled with his own pudding, and buried with a stake of holly through his heart. He should!'

'Uncle!' pleaded the nephew.

'Nephew!' returned the uncle, sternly, 'keep Christmas in your own way, and let me keep it in mine.'

(from *A Christmas Carol*, by Charles Dickens)

*buried*: put under the ground (when dead)
*stake*: a strong stick put into the ground (used for supporting plants etc.)
*holly*: a green plant with red berries, used for decoration at Christmas time

Glory to God in the Highest - Peace on Earth, Goodwill to all men!

# Christmas

Two 19th century figures, Charles Dickens and Prince Albert, created the Victorian Christmas – Dickens with his *Christmas Carol* and Prince Albert by popularising the Christmas tree.

A white Christmas is more often seen on Christmas cards than in reality. This is largely due to a reform in the calendar in 1752, when 11 days were 'lost' so that Christmas day fell earlier in the year. Snow is now more common in January than in December.

In Elizabethan days, Christmas dinner always began with fresh oysters served on a bed of cracked ice. Shrimps in soured cream might have been an alternative. For a main course, Victorians had turkey or roast goose, a fatty bird with succulent flesh. Like duck, it serves fewer people than its size would seem to indicate; a 10lb goose yields approximately eight servings.

Nowadays, turkey is the highlight of Christmas dinner in Britain, its popularity owing much to the classic English stuffings and the accompanying sauces. Serve the golden-brown turkey garnished with sprigs of watercress, chipolata sausages and bacon rolls. Both plain and roast potatoes are traditional, so too are Brussels sprouts, either plain or cooked with chestnuts. Bread sauce, spiced cranberries, gravy or port wine sauce are served separately.

Lastly comes the Christmas pudding . . .

## CHRISTMAS IN THE COTSWOLDS AT THE LYGON ARMS

### Seasonal Greetings

Mr. and Mrs. Douglas Barrington and I with all the Lygon team look forward to welcoming you to the Inn this Christmas.

The Lygon Arms, an Old English hostelry, in the picturesque village of Broadway, has welcomed travellers for over 400 years. This Christmas we are offering a programme that continues the tradition of welcome and hospitality.

I hope you will have a happy stay.

KIRK RITCHIE
Managing Director

*hostelry*: (old English) hotel or pub

*1 The spirit of Christmas*

## *Christmas Day*
### Sunday, 25th December

**10.30 a.m.** **Coffee** in the Drawing Room.

**11.00 a.m.** **A Tasting** of unusual and exotic teas and infusions in the Torrington Room.

**12.30 p.m.** **Christmas Luncheon**
The popular Yuletide Quiz will be handed round during lunch. You are invited to tackle this brain-teaser individually or as a family. A prize will be awarded to the winner and will be announced in the evening.

**3.00 p.m.** **The Queen's Christmas Message**
Colour television is in all bedrooms, but should you prefer company the programme will be shown in the Drawing Room.

**4.00 p.m.** **Afternoon Tea** in the Edinburgh Room.
A buffet of traditional tea dishes, including Christmas Cake and the festive Yuletide Log.

**8.00 p.m.** **Candlelit Dinner** (Black Tie)

**10.00 p.m.** **"Sound Investments"** In the Russell Room.

---

## LUNCHEON

£25.00
Inclusive of VAT

*Cream of Wild Mushroom Soup*

*Salad of Avocado and
Smoked Salmon in Caviar Dressing*

*Chilled Melon with Apricot and
White Wine Sorbet*

*Roulade of Sole and Langoustine served with a
Crayfish Sauce and Garnished with Mushrooms*

*Traditional Christmas Turkey with
Chipolatas, Bacon Rolls, Cranberry Sauce,
Bread Sauce and Chestnut Stuffing*

*Roast Angus Sirloin in Horseradish*

*Brussels Sprouts*

*Young Peas in the French Style*

*Roast Potatoes*

or

### COLD BUFFET

*Cotswold Ham in Parsley Jelly*

*Cold Dressed Salmon*

*Cold Roast Fillet of Beef*

*Game Pie*

*A Selection of Mixed Salads to include:
Lentil and Bacon*

*Coleslaw*

*Belgian Endive Walnut and Orange*

*Rice and Capsicums*

*Christmas Pudding with Brandy Butter
and Rum Sauce*

*Lygon Mince Pies and Fresh Cream*

*Peach Syllabub*

*Double Gloucester with Bath Olivers*

*Coffee and Mints*

---

*Yuletide*: (old English) Christmas
*tackle*: try
*Yuletide Log*: a traditional cake eaten at Christmas

*Christmas*

# A Merry Christmas...

## More Stuffing?

A Merry Christmas to you all . . .

"Merry", as you may know, has two meanings: a) happy, and b) drunk. If you're like a large number of British people, then your Christmas will be an alcoholic, rather than a religious, occasion.

If you walk down Piccadilly or Oxford Street just before Christmas, you will see an incredible amount of money being spent on electronic games, bottles of spirits, expensive clothes, LPs, cassettes, cameras, and a large number of luxury items. If you walk down the main street of several towns in the Third World just before Christmas, you won't see a large amount of money being spent on presents: in fact, you won't see a large amount of money being spent on anything.

80% of all disease in the world is caused by bad water supply: for millions of people, the perfect Christmas present would be a tap in the village square which would give pure, clean, water.

Do we think of these people when we sit down to our Christmas dinner? Of course not – we're too busy thinking about the turkey, the roast potatoes, and the presents sitting under the Christmas tree. The whole idea of Christmas now is completely unChristian – I'm sure that Christ would be furious if he could see what sort of celebrations are being carried out in his name.

So I'm against Christmas – I agree with Scrooge: "It's all humbug." If we're going to continue with this wasteful, thoughtless ceremony, then let's be truthful about it, and call it "Stuff-Our-Faces Week", or "Stomach Week" – but let's get rid of the hypocritical pretence that Christmas is "the season of goodwill".

*Patrick Brendan*

## Not only for Children?

Recently, a rather sophisticated woman told me shyly that she saves up all her presents until Christmas morning and then sits up in bed and opens them, just like a child. She thought I would laugh at her and say how silly she was. But in fact I was absolutely delighted to meet someone who treats Christmas as I do.

Many people today have a very different attitude to Christmas. They think it's just a time when shopkeepers make a lot of money and everyone rushes round buying presents they don't want to give and food they don't want to eat. But have they grown so far away from their own childhood that they can't remember all the good things?

First of all, Christmas takes you out of the ordinary humdrum routine of life. For children, the fun begins weeks before when the decorations are put up, and excitement gradually mounts as December the 25th approaches.

Everyone seems much friendlier to each other than usual at Christmas-time. You can lean out of a car window when you're stopped at the traffic lights and say "Merry Christmas", and people will smile and respond. You probably wouldn't think of doing that at any other time of year. Perhaps it's because most people are on holiday or because everyone knows that they are sharing a similar experience. Giving presents can be very satisfying, too, if you plan far enough in advance and really think of the right present for the right person.

Indeed, whatever shopkeepers gain out of Christmas, it is still a "holy day", the words from which "holiday" is derived, and it gives people time to pause and concentrate for a moment on non-commercial values.

*Lynne Knight*

*1 The spirit of Christmas*

## HOW TO COOK THE PERFECT TURKEY THIS CHRISTMAS

| Oven Ready Weight | Kitchen Thawing Guide (not in a fridge) | Approx Cooking Guide for Foil Roast at Gas Mark 4 350°F (180°C) |
|---|---|---|
| 5lbs | 15hrs | 2½ hrs |
| 10lbs | 18hrs | 3½ hrs |
| 15lbs | 24hrs | 4¾ hrs |
| 20lbs | 30hrs | 5¾ hrs |

**Turkey makes a really traditional Christmas**

Thaw thoroughly (see guide for thawing instructions). Remove giblets & neck. Place a peeled onion in body cavity, rub turkey with butter and sprinkle with salt: Stuff the neck end with chestnut and sausagemeat stuffing—for a 12-14lb turkey you'll need 1½ lb of sausagemeat and ¾ lb of chestnut puree. Lay bacon rashers across the breast for extra taste.

Line a roasting pan with Alcan, 12" or 20" width (300 or 500mm) bringing edges over rim. Cover turkey loosely with another sheet of Alcan, tucking edges inside rim, and cook (see table). For extra browning, remove top sheet of foil and bacon before the end of cooking time.

The turkey is cooked when the juices run clear—test with skewer in deepest part of flesh. Serve with giblet gravy, roast potatoes, sprouts, stuffings and delicious Ocean Spray Cranberry Sauce—all the Christmas trimmings your turkey deserves.

Issued by the British Turkey Federation, Ocean Spray and Alcan.

**Christmas isn't Christmas without a turkey**

*cavity*: empty space inside something
*thaw*: become un-frozen
*giblets*: the insides of a bird
*skewer*: a (metal) stick used to test if the meat is cooked
*trimmings*: the 'extras' which go with a meal, such as sauces

## 1.1

1  Look at the extract on page 29. Read it through quickly, and then try to sum up the personality of both Scrooge and his nephew in *one* word each. Compare your answers with a partner.

*Christmas*

2 Look at the extract again and try to find:
   a) *four* words which are associated with *heat*;
   b) *three* words that mean more or less the same as *happy/happily*;
   c) *three* words which mean *angry/angrily*;
   d) *two* words which mean *depressed*.

3 The following words and expressions are not used any more; look closely at the context and write down a more up-to-date version of each.

   a) *came upon him* (line 2)   d) *out upon* (line 18)
   b) *intimation* (line 3)   e) *balancing your books* (lines 20–1)
   c) *humbug* (line 4)   f) *work my will* (line 22)

## 1.2

Look at pages 30–1, and write down the answers to this Christmas Quiz. Work in groups and see which group can find the answers first.

   a) What meat do British people traditionally eat for Christmas dinner?
   b) What sometimes used to be eaten instead in Victorian times?
   c) What vegetables, traditionally, must accompany the meat dish?
   d) What is eaten for 'afters'?
   e) Why does it not often snow in Britain at Christmas?

## 1.3

1 Look at the letters on page 32. You will see various points both in favour of the Christmas celebrations, and against them. Make notes as you read, under the headings *For* and *Against*. Put a tick (✓) beside the comments you agree with. Then discuss your opinions with a partner.

2 Write a letter to the same magazine, giving *your* point of view. If you do not celebrate Christmas, then write about a similar kind of celebration in your own country instead.

## 1.4

1 Imagine that you have to write a newspaper report about the differences between a British Christmas and one in your own country (or a similar celebration there if you do not celebrate Christmas). Look through this section and make notes of any habits and customs which seem to be traditional in Britain at Christmas, under the following headings: *Food, Entertainment, Customs*.

2 Add any other details which you know of.

3 Compare your notes in groups, and see who has the most.

4 Working on your own, complete the following paragraph, which is to be the basis of your newspaper report.

Whereas in ............................... we have ............................... as traditional (Christmas) food, in Britain they eat ............................... for dinner. Other traditional food typically eaten at this time is ............................... In both ............................... and Britain, certain customs are the same, or very similar, such as ............................... Others, however, are quite different. In Britain, for example, ............................... ..............................................., while in my own country ........... ............................................................... (*Continue as you like.*)

## 1.5

Work in pairs. One of you is Student A, the other is Student B. Student B should look at the advertisement on p. 33.

*Student A*
You have just been given a 12 lb turkey, but have no idea what to do with it. Phone your friend (Student B) and find out:
a) how long it takes to defrost;
b) what you do after you've taken out the giblets;
c) if you have to cover it when it's in the oven;
d) how long you have to cook it for;
e) how you know when it's ready.
Remember to keep checking that you've got the information right.

*Student B*
A friend of yours phones you, and needs advice on how to cook a turkey. Luckily, you remember seeing an advertisement in the paper telling you how to prepare and cook one, so you can help. Remember to use the pictures as well as the text of the advertisement.

**Before reading the texts in section 2 more carefully, look at the exercises on pages 41–2.**

*Christmas*

## 2 Christmas is children

# CHRISTMAS IS...

SANTAS SLEIGH

Angels singing
Antony, 11

Christmas is snow and the trees are bare.
Richard, 8

Staying up to see if there really is a Father Christmas.
Clare, 8

playing out in the cold.
Zoe, 10

I like Christmas Because Jesus was born
Will, 8

Tinsel sparkling, turkey roasting in the oven, tree lights glittering.
Kate, 9

Christmas is kind
Michael, 7

christmas is giving and kindness
Jo, 8

opening presents at 1 oclock in the morning.
Emma, 9

## 2 Christmas is children

A Merry Christmas Mummy!
Is the turkey tender yet?
Remember Grand-Ma won't touch sprouts.
She's bet that you'll forget.

Stan thinks his present's crummy,
So he's split on Santa Claus
To Clarissa, who starts crying
While her Father Christmas snores.

Aunt Joan consults her tummy;
It could manage a mince pie!
And if it isn't too much bother
Bring it here where she can lie.

The baby's lost her dummy –
Uncle hung it on the tree.
She's lacking Christmas spirit,
She's not used to lunch at three.

A Merry Christmas Mummy!
You deserve that pair of tights.
You work so hard yet still have time
To supervise the fights.

*crummy*: (colloquial) bad, worthless
*split on*: (colloquial) told a secret about
*snores*: breathes noisily while sleeping
*tummy*: (colloquial) stomach
*mince pie*: a traditional sweet cake eaten at Christmas
*dummy*: a rubber object which a baby sucks

# Christmas

All I want for Christmas
Is my two front teeth
My two front teeth
Yes my two front teeth
All I want for Christmas
Is my two front teeth
So that I can wish you Merry Christmas.

20th December 1985

Dear Father Christmas
    Please will you bring me a soldier action man and train set or a bicycle if you could fit it down the chimney. But if you can't fit it down the chimney you can leave it outside and I will leave some mince pies and a glass of sherry on the table for you and a carrot for your reindeer. I want you to go out by the door its alright but be quiet or you will wake the dog. My room is the one next to the bathroom. When you come to fill my stocking don't get mixed up with my brothers room he doesn't believe in Santa Claus
        Love from
            Nick x

## 2 Christmas is children

26 And in the sixth month the angel Gabriel was sent from God unto a city of Galilee, named Nazareth,
27 To a virgin espoused to a man whose name was Joseph, of the house of David; and the virgin's name *was* Mary.
28 And the angel came in unto her, and said, Hail, *thou that art* highly favoured, the Lord *is* with thee: blessed *art* thou among women.
29 And when she saw *him*, she was troubled at his saying, and cast in her mind what manner of salutation this should be.
30 And the angel said unto her, Fear not, Mary: for thou hast found favour with God.
31 And, behold, thou shalt conceive in thy womb, and bring forth a son, and shalt call his name JESUS.
32 He shall be great, and shall be called the Son of the Highest: and the Lord God shall give unto him the throne of his father David:
33 And he shall reign over the house of Jacob for ever; and of his kingdom there shall be no end.

(from the *Gospel according to St Luke*, Chapter 1)

*Christmas*

## The Christmas Story

A play in two acts for children aged six to 11 years

### SCENE ONE

**A village street, with a small well downstage. Enter MARY, a young peasant girl, walking slowly, carrying a pitcher. She walks over to the well to get some water. She is humming a happy little tune for she is thinking of her coming wedding day. As she bends to fill the pitcher, GABRIEL enters quietly from the back of the stage, at first unnoticed by Mary.**

**GABRIEL**  Greetings, Mary, most blessed among women.

**MARY**  (a little frightened and shielding her eyes against the angel's brightness) Who are you? And why do you call me blessed? I am only a peasant girl.

**GABRIEL**  (gently) Don't be afraid, Mary. My name is Gabriel and I bring you good news.

**MARY**  Good news?

**GABRIEL**  Yes. You are going to have a baby and he will be the Son of God.

**MARY**  But I am going to marry Joseph, the carpenter. What would he say to that?

**GABRIEL**  Don't worry. I'll have a word with him. (Gabriel turns to leave, then, as though suddenly remembering, turns back to Mary) I nearly forgot! You must call the baby Jesus. When he grows up he will be great and loved throughout the world.

**MARY**  Will he be a king then?

**GABRIEL**  Yes, he will indeed. Well, I must fly now. (He exits. Mary clasps her hands and looks towards the audience smiling)

**MARY**  Well, fancy that! My son is going to be a king. I can't wait to tell Joseph. (She calls to someone off-stage) Joseph, come quickly. I have something to tell you. (Enter JOSEPH, carrying a block of wood and shaking one hand vigorously)

**JOSEPH**  What is it, Mary? You have just made me hit my thumb. Look, it's going black and blue already. (He holds out his thumb for inspection, but Mary is too happy to take much notice)

**MARY**  Oh dear, so it is. But never mind. I've just had a visit from an angel.

*confidingly*: as if telling a secret
*rostrum*: a platform, for public speaking
*script*: the text of a play, which the actor reads

'Get mum or dad to help you learn your lines,' suggests Ed. 'And don't forget to speak up in your best voice so that everyone can hear you.'

**JOSEPH**  Oh yes? Just dropped in to say hello, did he? (He looks disbelieving, then pointedly examines his thumb again)

**MARY**  (looking a bit disappointed that Joseph is not more impressed) Angels don't just 'drop in', Joseph. They are much too busy. He came with a message.

**JOSEPH**  Who for?

**MARY**  For me. I am going to have a baby. And he will be the Son of God.

**JOSEPH**  A likely story! (He laughs) Can I go back to work now?

**MARY**  But it's the truth. It really is. (There is a sound of voices, softly singing, offstage, and the angel Gabriel re-appears. Joseph looks startled)

**GABRIEL**  Joseph, what Mary told you is true. She is going to have God's baby and you must take great care of her.

**JOSEPH**  Well, if you say so. All right, I will. (Gabriel smiles approvingly and Mary and Joseph leave the stage. Gabriel looks confidingly at the audience)

**GABRIEL**  I don't think we will have any more trouble from him.

**END OF SCENE 1**

### SCENE TWO

**NARRATOR**  (who, ideally, should stand at the side of the stage on a small rostrum, near front. A music stand would be a useful support for the script) So it came to pass that Mary and Joseph were married. And, just as the angel Gabriel had foretold, Mary was going to have a baby. Autumn, then winter, came and Mary and Joseph set out on a journey to the city of Bethlehem to put their names down on the register, as was the custom in those long ago days. It was almost time for Mary to have her baby and the long journey on foot in the winter cold made her feel very tired. By the time they reached Bethlehem, the city was already crowded with other travellers and Joseph was quite worried that they might have great difficulty finding somewhere to stay for the night.

# 2 Christmas is children

## 2.1

1 Look at the picture on page 37. Before you read the poem, try to decide, in pairs or groups, who the people are, what they have been doing, etc. Then read the poem to see if your predictions were correct.

2 After you have read the poem, decide if the following statements are true or false, and write T or F next to each one.

   a) The family enjoyed the turkey.
   b) Grand-Ma loves sprouts.
   c) Clarissa has never believed in Father Christmas.
   d) Father is asleep.
   e) Aunt Joan is very lazy.
   f) The baby's hungry.
   g) Mother is busy.

3 In pairs, interview each other about how *you* spent last Christmas Day (or another similar festival if you do not celebrate Christmas). If you prefer, you could take one of the roles from the poem and give an imaginary account. Make notes about your partner under the following headings.
*Presents* (what your partner got, gave, liked, disliked)
*How your partner spent the day*
*Meals*
*Visitors*
*The family*

4 Write a letter to a friend or relation who was not there, describing how *you* spent the day, based on the notes made by your partner.

## 2.2

1 Look at page 39. The words underlined in the Bible extract are very different from the words we would use today. Discuss with a partner how they could be rewritten to make the language more up-to-date. Make a note of your suggestions.

2 The nativity play on page 40 was adapted from the Bible story especially for young children to act. Find words in the text that have a similar meaning to the following.
   a) a place where you can get water
   b) a container for liquids
   c) a person who lives and works in the country
   d) to protect from
   e) a man who works with wood
   f) to pay a casual visit
   g) surprised

*Christmas*

Write the word next to the corresponding letter in the left-hand column below. In the right-hand column write down any words or phrases which may have helped you to guess the meaning. The first one is done for you.

| | |
|---|---|
| a) well | to get some water |
| b) | |
| c) | |
| d) | |
| e) | |
| f) | |
| g) | |

3 Divide yourselves into groups of three and take one role each (Mary, Joseph or Gabriel). Read Scene 1 silently to yourself first of all, and decide what your tone of voice, stress and intonation patterns are going to be, depending on whether you are frightened, excited, surprised etc. Then read the scene aloud. You can then change roles and read it again if you wish.

4 At the beginning of Scene 1 there are stage directions before the scene begins. In pairs, read the summary of Scene 2 and work out what the stage directions could be for that scene. Write them out and then, in groups, decide who has the best directions.

*2 Christmas is children*

# Roleplay

For groups of five people.

## Roles (pages 160–4)

Jack Frost (father) (role 2)
Holly Frost (mother) (role 5)
Cherry Frost (16-year-old daughter) (role 8)
Nicky Frost (ten-year-old son) (role 11)
Aunt Joan (Holly's sister) (role 14)

## Situation

It is a few weeks before Christmas and the Frost family are having a discussion about how to spend the holiday. The next-door neighbours went abroad last year and have tried to convince the Frosts to go with them this year. The family have very different reactions.

## Preliminary tasks

You will be given time to read through your role (at the back of the book) and organise your arguments, adding any other points you think relevant. Consult the texts in this unit and your teacher if necessary, but read only *your own role* (and no-one else's).

## Procedure

A certain amount of time will be given for each member of the family to put forward their point of view. Attempt to persuade other members of the family to do what you want but remember that you must reach a decision within the time allotted, so you may have to compromise!

## Follow up

Write your diary for that evening, saying what happened and what decisions were reached.

# Work

Look through the texts in both sections of this unit and try to answer the following questions *as quickly as possible*. Remember that you are not looking for any other information, so it is not necessary to study the texts in detail.

1. How long has it been illegal to discriminate between the sexes when advertising jobs?
2. How many children has Diane Harpwood got?
3. How much per week does one firm of insurers value a housewife's work at?
4. According to an American magazine, what can happen to a husband if his wife is more successful at work than he is?
5. What is the name of a popular marmalade?
6. What is the weekly salary for a butcher at Safeway Stores?
7. What job is James Nolan applying for?
8. What does the 'Part-time Job Release Scheme' offer a man over 62?
9. What is the name of the industrial editor of a national daily paper?
10. Who won a prize for the star letter in a teenage magazine?

Check your answers with a partner before looking at the key on page 149.

Now look at the exercises on pages 48–51 before reading the texts in section 1 more carefully.

# 1 In and out of work

# Jobless back to 3m as school leavers sign on

**By MICHAEL EDWARDS, Industrial Editor**

THE JOBLESS figures rose above three million again this month as more than 100,000 school leavers joined the dole queues.

This means that 1 in 8 of Britain's working population—12·8 per cent.—is now without a job. And the situation will worsen next month as more school leavers sign on

The unemployment total of 3,061,229 rose from May's figures of 2,969,443 and stopped only just short of the previous peak of 3,071,000 reached in January.

Mrs Thatcher spoke in the Commons of signs of economic recovery, but this is not supported by the latest surveys carried out by the Confederation of British Industry.

TUC Secretary Len Murray said : 'Despite all the Government's optimistic and misleading talk of economic improvement, the reality is that jobs are still being lost and will continue to disappear in another summer of rising unemployment.'

*Mrs Thatcher*: British prime minister
*surveys*: asking a representative number of people their opinion about a particular topic
*TUC*: Trades Union Congress: an association of British unions

Work

# Give up half your job without giving up half your money.

Under the new Part-time Job Release Scheme you could stop working for half your normal hours.

In addition to receiving your pay for the hours you continue to work we pay you an allowance to help make up the difference.

In the example Tom Smith is 63, and apart from the war years he'd been working since he was 14.

Quite naturally he thought he deserved a break. So when he heard about the new scheme he approached his boss about it.

The company found a younger unemployed person to replace Tom for half his normal working hours, and Tom was accepted.

Now he works Tuesday and Wednesday one week; Tuesday, Wednesday and Thursday the next.

When he worked full time his take-home pay was £89.38. Now his take-home pay is £52.78 in addition to which he receives an allowance of £23.70, making a total of £76.48.

To Tom and his wife it means a difference of £12.90 a week. But they think it's more than worth it for the extra time they can now spend together.

The table shows what other married men of the same age could expect in similar circumstances, not counting the likely savings in fares and other costs of going to work every day.

Figures for half-time take-home pay include both wages and the allowance from the scheme.

| | | | |
|---|---|---|---|
| PRESENT GROSS WAGE | £90.00 | £120.00 | £140.00 |
| TYPICAL TAKE-HOME PAY | £71.08 | £89.38 | £101.58 |
| HALF-TIME TAKE-HOME PAY | £67.33 | £76.48 | £82.58 |

To qualify, men must be 62 to 64, disabled men 60 to 64, and women 59.

The main condition is that your employer takes on an unemployed person for the hours you no longer work.

If you would prefer to give up work completely and you're in the same age groups there is also the full-time Job Release Scheme.

It's worth reading through the booklets on the two schemes. Either use the coupon, or pick them up at your local Employment Office or Jobcentre.

## Part-time Job Release Scheme
Department of Employment DE

Please send me your booklets.

Name _____

Address _____

_____ Postcode _____

Post to Anne Pembroke, Job Release Scheme, P.O. BOX 702, London SW20 8SZ

*disabled*: someone who is unable to do something (usually for physical reasons)

46

*1 In and out of work*

## Plum jobs for good Oranges.

Chivers Olde English marmalade is made by the best oranges, and we pay good money for their help.

To qualify for a place with Chivers, an orange should be tasty, thick-skinned and on the larger side.

No other oranges need apply. But applications from suitable oranges are welcome at the address below.

If you're good enough, write to us. You could end up being top banana.

Write to: The Director of Oranges, Chivers, Bournville, Birmingham B30 2NA.

**CHIVERS**

Are you orange enough? Or thick enough?

*plum*: (play on words) the best; a kind of fruit
*thick-skinned*: (play on words) insensitive
*thick*: (play on words) stupid

---

Tel: 061 234 9876

102 Maynard Rd,
Manchester 13

10 June 1985

Dear Mr Logan,

I am writing with reference to your advertisement for a gardener in the 'Lancashire Evening Post' of June 9th.

I am a retired man, aged 67. For twenty-five years, before I retired, I worked for the Civil Service.

I have no direct experience of gardening, but it has always been one of my main hobbies, and at the weekend I help my son in his market garden.

I would be very interested in this job, as I like working outside and prefer flexible hours.

If you would like to contact me, my address and phone number are above.

Yours sincerely,

James Nolan

# Work

## 1.1

1 Look at the newspaper article on page 45. Work in pairs. Before reading the text, look at the headlines and try to predict what it might be about. Then read it quickly on your own and see if you were correct.

2 Read the article again, and decide if the following statements are true or false, according to the writer. Write T or F next to each statement.

   a) 3 million school leavers are out of work.
   b) A hundred thousand people just leaving school are now unemployed.
   c) Things should get better next month.
   d) These are the highest unemployment figures this year.
   e) The Trades Union Secretary disagrees with what Mrs Thatcher says.

3 Choose the best alternative to complete each of the following.

   a) You join a *dole queue* to get:
      – school examination reports
      – details of new jobs
      – food
      – an unemployment allowance

   b) *To sign on* means:
      – to leave school
      – to register as unemployed
      – to reach the age of 16
      – to receive unemployment benefit

   c) *The Commons* is:
      – a park
      – one of the Houses of Parliament
      – a London square
      – a political newspaper

## 1.2

1 Look at the article on page 46 and answer the following questions as quickly as you can. Make notes and discuss them with a partner afterwards.

   a) How many hours do you have to work under this new scheme?
   b) Who works the rest of the hours?
   c) What financial difference does this make to Tom Smith?
   d) Why does Tom Smith prefer to do this?
   e) How do you find out more information?

2 In groups, discuss your views on this scheme and put forward as many ideas as you can for solving the problem of unemployment. Report your ideas back to the rest of the class.

Work

## 1.3

1 Look at the advertisements on page 48. Make a note of the job you would apply for in each of the following cases.

   a) You are a student or old age pensioner, who would like to earn a little more money in your spare time. The time needs to be flexible and you'd like to work outdoors.
   b) You are taking your 'O' levels this month but don't know what you want to do. You like reading.
   c) You are a doctor's wife whose children are grown up. You can type quite well and are looking for an interesting, responsible job which is not too time consuming.
   d) You are a mother, looking for a part-time job while your children are at school. You can't type and must be free in the school holidays. You love small children.
   e) You are an ambitious school leaver of 18, with a lively personality. You have no experience but are willing to learn. You've just passed your driving test.

   Discuss your answers with a partner, giving reasons.

2 Now apply in writing for one of the jobs advertised (you might like to look at the letter on page 47 to give you some ideas).

3 Look at the jobs advertised on page 48 and try to classify them into jobs traditionally done by men, women, or either. If they are usually restricted to one sex only, try to decide *why*; i.e. it could be for physical reasons, or cultural, or simply because of prejudice. Complete the chart with ticks (√) in the appropriate columns and notes on the reasons and then discuss it in groups.

| Job | Men | Women | Either | Reasons (if any) |
|---|---|---|---|---|
| teacher | | | | |
| secretary | | | | |
| shop assistant | | | | |
| hairdresser | | | | |
| plumber | | | | |
| solicitor | | | | |
| traffic warden | | | | |
| accountant | | | | |
| librarian | | | | |
| gardener | | | | |
| computer operator | | | | |
| bricklayer | | | | |
| chauffeur/mechanic | | | | |
| butcher | | | | |

*1 In and out of work*

4 Which of the jobs advertised on page 48 would you *most* like and which would you *least* like to do? Choose two and try to group your reasons in the following categories.

|  | Most like | Least like |
|---|---|---|
| Name of job |  |  |
| Training required |  |  |
| Hours worked |  |  |
| Holidays |  |  |
| Salary |  |  |
| Job satisfaction |  |  |
| Career prospects |  |  |

## 1.4

Work in pairs. One of you (the applicant) is applying for the job with Kelly Girl. The other is Paul Francis. You should both read the advertisement on page 48 carefully. Look at the instructions below and prepare what you are going to say. Then begin your telephone conversation.

*Applicant*

Phone Paul Francis. Introduce yourself and say why you're phoning.

Tell him why you're interested in the job.

Admit you haven't much experience, but you're willing to learn.

Pretend you have more driving experience than you in fact have.

Agree. Ask where to go and how to get there.

Say goodbye.

*Paul Francis*

Ask why he/she's applying.

Ask about previous experience.

Tell him/her about the training course. Ask if he/she can drive.

Fix up a day and time for interview.

Explain. End conversation.

**Before reading the texts in section 2 more carefully, look at the exercises on pages 57–62.**

Work

# 2 A woman's place

**GREAT OPPORTUNITIES FOR WOMEN
VACANCIES FOR JOBS OF NATIONAL IMPORTANCE
YOUR INFLUENCE CAN SHAPE OUR COUNTRY'S FUTURE**

**WANTED:** Intelligent, cheerful, outgoing and healthy women for challenging and important work. Must be able to accept responsibility and act on own initiative but be sufficiently flexible to adapt to a secondary rôle in a small working unit on occasion. Ability to negotiate house agreements and settle disputes vital. High degree of competence in all domestic skills, including budgeting, required. Good working knowledge of nursing and psychology essential.
Understanding of, and interest in, world affairs, the environment, sport, handicrafts, music, art, literature and drama desirable. Candidates should possess all the human qualities, such as patience, discretion, kindness and humour. No A-levels, university degrees, shorthand, typing or previous experience of any kind required.
**Salary:** Non-negotiable. Nil. No promotion. Non-contributory non-pension scheme.
**Hours:** 24 daily, 7 days a week.
**Holiday entitlement:** None.
No luncheon vouchers, canteen facilities, travelling, petrol or entertainment allowances, or other fringe benefits available.

*"I'm totally against wives going out to work"*

*to act on your own initiative*: to do things independently (without needing to be told)
*on occasion*: sometimes
*negotiate*: discuss, in order to reach agreement
*settle disputes*: end arguments
*budgeting*: working out how much you can spend
*discretion*: being careful about what one says and does
*fringe benefits*: extra advantages

**SEX DISCRIMINATION ACT, 1975**

No job advertisement which indicates or can reasonably be understood as indicating an intention to discriminate on ground of sex (eg by inviting applications only from males or only from females) may be accepted, unless:

1. The job is for the purpose of a private household; or
2. It is a business employing fewer than six persons; or
3. It is otherwise excepted from the requirements of the Sex Discrimination Act.

A statement must be made at the time the advertisement is placed saying which of the exceptions in the Act is considered to apply.

In addition to employment, the principal areas covered by the section of the Act which deals with advertisements are education, the supply of goods and services and the sale or letting of property.

It is the responsibility of advertisers to ensure that advertisement content does not discriminate under the terms of the Sex Discrimination Act.

## 2  A woman's place

Diane Harpwood, an ordinary housewife, who lives at Hengoed, Mid Glamorgan, describes a day in her life. Photograph by Clay Perry

# A LIFE IN THE DAY OF DIANE HARPWOOD

"I start my day the Valium way at **7.20a.m.** when my departing husband brings me a mug of tea and a Diazepan tablet. A Valium a day keeps psychiatrists at bay.

**7.21a.m.** My two children burst into the bedroom yelling, shouting, bawling. They've been up since 6a.m., full of *joie de vivre.* Can they be mine? I go a few rounds with Ben, the youngest, who's nearly two. He wants my tea, but I must have it. I know it's unfair – he should pick on someone his own size.

When I've taken all I can, which isn't long, I drive them out screaming like a banshee and heaping curses on their beautiful, innocent little heads like a hag from *Macbeth*.

**7.25a.m.** It's washing and dressing time. My four-year-old, Miss 'Well, I'm almost five' Jodi Harpwood, presents few problems. Ben is another story. Ever seen Rod Hull wrestle with Emu? You've got the idea, except Ben is stronger and more determined.

**8.00a.m.** Breakfast time. I am exhausted, bad-tempered – drained of patience. Yes, already. Another day of soul-destroying solitude looms ahead. A de-humanising repetition of a detestable routine. I hurtle around the kitchen from frying pan to fridge and back again in response to the children's persistent demands. I worry a lot about nutrition and so they've been trained to eat a good breakfast. Anything less than porridge, bacon and egg, tea and toast and they're picketing outside the child welfare clinic.

**8.25a.m.** Jodi glowers at me from the front door. She's all ready to go and almost phobic about missing the school bus. We did once and she's neither forgotten nor forgiven me. I'm frantically wiping Ben down with the dishcloth before the congealing porridge blocks up all his cranial apertures.

**8.40a.m.** We arrive at the bus stop on time (as usual); Jodi relaxes.

→

Diane Harpwood, 33, with husband Ben, an engineering works manager, and children Jodi and Ben

53

Work

**8.55a.m.** Angela (unlikely but true name of school bus) makes an appearance. She likes to keep us waiting in the cold, especially if it's raining.

**8.56a.m.** On Fridays at this time I go to the supermarket where I don't buy cigarettes, coffee, Sunday joints, biscuits, cakes, sweets, frozen veg, washing-up liquid, tissues, kitchen paper, loo deodoriser, disinfectant, fabric conditioner, butter, or squash. All these items are either too expensive or dispensable. Not smoking makes me constipated. Can that kill you too? On other days I return home to face the overnight accumulation of dirty dishes. I could cheerfully put a sledgehammer through the lot. A friend of mine once threw out a bucket full of dirty nappies because she simply couldn't face washing another single, smelly diaper.

**10.00a.m.** The washing-up is done, dried and put away. The solidified lumps of porridge have been scraped up (wonder if it would serve to bond the leaking crack in the washing machine?). I loathe, I hate, I abhor housework, nevertheless that's what I do next. Only trendy, middle-class lady journalists like Jilly Cooper can get away with having mucky houses. Not that they want to; quite the reverse in fact. Have you noticed how it's a compulsion with them to boast about how the cat was sick in the boeuf bourgignon? Or how they failed to notice that the stripped pine dresser – picked up in a junk shop for £15 – was feet thick in dust until friends wrote rude words on it with damp index fingers? Down here in Working-class Land you'd be excommunicated for far less than that. Among us lower orders cleanliness isn't next to godliness: they are one and the same thing.

**11.00a.m.** I join Benjamin and we view *Playschool* together. He has a glass of milk, I have a cup of tea and my mid-morning fantasy about another life. Twice a week I do the washing and ironing. I've cut down to bi-weekly laundering to save on washing powder, hot water and electricity.

**1.00p.m.** Husband comes home for lunch. We share a simple meal of chips or packet soup and cups of tea.

**2.00p.m.** Husband has returned to work and theoretically I reserve the next hour for playing with Ben. In practice I usually have some housework to do, but I try to do some chasing and racing and hiding and seeking.

**3.30p.m.** It's time to meet Angela. Jodi comes home with tall tales but true about what happened in school today. She's a fair mimic and so her story telling can be quite illuminating as well as amusing. She attends a bi-lingual school (English/Welsh), so our chats are sometimes in English and less often in stumbling Welsh. I am trying to learn, too.

**5.00p.m.** The kids and I have our evening meal. My husband's meal is left to keep warm in the oven.

**5.45p.m.** is bathtime, the children adore it. I sit on the loo and watch them chuck water about.

**6.30p.m.** My better half comes home, tired out, to his two shining clean offspring, a sodden bathroom carpet and his evening meal.

**7.00p.m.** We put the children to bed. He tends to his boy. I read to my daughter until she settles down to sleep.

Every day is exactly the same except we do miss Angela at weekends and my husband doesn't go to work on Sundays so there's no tea in bed. We wouldn't know we were poor if we didn't read the adverts in *The Sunday Times* – the only newspaper we buy. They leave us gasping. Who does buy those watches at prices *from* £800? Most of our married friends are in the same financial boat. We regard our monetary malaise as a temporary condition brought on by inflation and curable in time. If we didn't we'd go insane.

We never go out, buy Chinese takeaways or fish and chips. We do take lots of walks, feed ducks, swing on swings and visit the library. I don't watch much television, but I read a lot.

Bedtime is usually around **9.30–10.00p.m.** Normally with a library book, occasionally with my husband. "

---

*Valium*: a drug, to calm the nerves
*keeps ... at bay*: keeps (the enemy) away
*go a few rounds*: play for a while
*pick on*: choose to attack
*banshee*: a female spirit that screams
*heaping curses on*: using lots of rude words
*Rod Hull*: a British comedian
*nutrition*: food value
*picketing*: (here) causing a disturbance, complaining
*phobic*: having a terrible fear of something
*congealing*: becoming solid
*cranial apertures*: (very formal) openings in the head e.g. mouth
*nappies/diapers*: a kind of towel a baby wears round its bottom
*boeuf bourgignon*: beef cooked in wine
*junk shop*: a shop which sells old objects
*tall tales*: exaggerated stories
*in the same financial boat*: in the same situation (lack of money)

*pressed*: ironed
*took for granted*: regarded as sure to happen

---

### ★ ★ IT'S A MUM'S LIFE ★ ★

Until a few weeks ago I didn't realise just how much I depended on my mother for my meals, all my lovely clean, pressed clothes, etc. I took all those for granted until she had to be taken into hospital. As my father works all day, I had to take on all Mum's jobs.

I had to take my seven-year-old brother to school, then go to school myself. On the way home I had to do the shopping for meals the following day, collect my brother, do my homework after cooking and serving tea. Before going to visit Mum I had to wash up the dinner pots, and it didn't stop there either. Before crawling into bed I had to do the ironing and get things ready for the next day.

After a couple of weeks Mum came out of hospital but the experience of having to cope with running a house made me realise just how important a mother is to a home. I know one thing for sure: I'll never take her for granted again.

L. Harper,
Harrogate,
N. Yorkshire.

(This week's winner has chosen the Boots 17 Make-Up Kit as her Star Prize.)

## 2 A woman's place

# The cost of a wife is £204 a week

**By Lorna Bourke**

The commercial rate for a housewife's work is now £204 a week, equivalent to the salary of an Army sergeant major, a bishop, or a fire chief, a recent survey conducted for the insurers, Legal & General, says.

Even costing a wife's time out at £204 a week, or £10,600 a year, her work is still valued at not much more than £2 an hour, the absolute minimum paid for domestic help. This is for a seven-day-a-week job and 12 to 14 hours a day.

Duties priced by Legal & General include cooking, child minding, waitressing, dishwashing, driving, shopping, cleaning, laundering, sewing, and other activities all based on employment agencies, average fees for different jobs.

Inflation has taken its toll. A similar survey conducted for the company in 1975 costed out a women's time at £71 a week. Although the statistics provoked considerable controversy at the time, there is little evidence to suggest that families took the lesson to heart and insured the wife's life.

A chart compiled by Gallup, which conducted the survey, shows that the housewife is fully employed for seven days a week. Her potential earnings reached a peak of £35.86 on a Thursday. They are lowest on Sunday, when she works only six and a half hours with an earnings potential of £13.

Of the married couples surveyed, a surprisingly large proportion of husbands did not see that their wives might face financial problems if anything happened to them. Half felt this would not be much of a problem or no problem at all, and 12 per cent admitted they did not know.

The survey is designed to highlight the potentially disastrous effects on the husband's finances if the wife should die, obliging the husband to hire domestic help as a replacement. Few husbands think of insuring their wife's life, and Legal & General are tackling this problem by offering an insurance scheme to employers rather than approaching the individual employees.

The scheme offers employers cover of up to £50,000 per employee for an average cost of around 0.1 per cent of total payroll.

*And that doesn't include my fee for LISTENING to your financial problems...*
— Calman

The Gallup survey commissioned by Legal & General showed that most husbands claimed to appreciate the financial value of their wives' housework, but only one husband in four had insured his wife's life.

On average, six wives in every thousand will die before their husband reaches retirement age. Legal & General's insurance cover is not designed to cover the full cost of employing a housekeeper, but to provide the financial assistance enabling the husband to carry on work while he makes alternative arrangements.

Female employees who lose a husband will be similarly entitled to benefits under the scheme, known as Coping and Caring. The company admit that the best answer would be for individuals to make their own arrangements, because cover will cease when an employee leaves his employer.

☐ Feminists were not impressed with the estimate of £10,600 a year (Lucy Hodges writes). Mrs Ann Sedley, women's rights officer of the National Council for Civil Liberties, said this was a very low price to pay for the kind of work women do at home. "I would think this is a low estimate for housewife insurance," she said.

The survey was useful to the extent that it highlighted the work done by women at home, but the concept of a housewife was rather outdated, she said.

### A WIFE'S WORTH

| Time | Activity | Cost per hr (£) |
|---|---|---|
| 7.30-8 am | Cook | 1.84 |
| | Waitress | |
| | Dishwasher | |
| 8-9 ,, | Driver | 1.23 |
| 9-10 ,, | Shopper | 1.95 |
| 10-11 ,, | Cleaner | 1.93 |
| 11-12 ,, | Laundress | 1.93 |
| 12-1 pm | Laundress | 1.93 |
| 1-2 ,, | Cost Clerk | 2.23 |
| 2-3 ,, | Cleaner | 1.93 |
| 3-4 ,, | Cleaner | 0.96 |
| | Driver | 1.23 |
| 4-5 ,, | Childminder | 1.72 |
| 5-6 ,, | Childminder | 1.72 |
| | Cook | 1.96 |
| 6-7 ,, | Childminder | 1.72 |
| | Waitress | 1.61 |
| 7-8 ,, | Childminder | 1.72 |
| | Dishwasher | 1.93 |
| 8-9 ,, | Seamstress | 1.93 |
| | **Daily Total** | **31.47** |

*taken its toll*: had its effect
*took the lesson to heart*: were influenced by this
*seamstress*: a woman who sews for her living

Work

# Man about the house, you're lazy!

MOST men are idle, useless washouts when it comes to helping with the housework.

When they do decide to do a few jobs around the home they only pick the ones they enjoy.

They refuse to do any boring jobs like cleaning the loo, changing the sheets, doing the ironing or cooking dinner.

But if they're in the mood they don't mind doing a bit of gardening or carving the roast.

And it's not too difficult coaxing them into their favourite "chore" — mixing drinks and entertaining guests.

According to a Gallup survey, the lady of the house does three-quarters of the boring household jobs ... even if she has a full-time job.

### Satisfied

But surprisingly the women don't seem to worry.

Only 20 per cent said they would like more help, 75 per cent were satisfied and the remaining five per cent said they would rather their man didn't bother.

Many women preferred to use more electrical appliances to make up for male laziness, which is good news for manufacturers such as Swan Housewares, who commissioned the survey.

# Will your success make your marriage a failure?

from **GEORGE GORDON** IN NEW YORK

A HUSBAND who earns less than his wife is doomed to an early divorce, a poor sex life and early death.

Money in marriage means power and while women have crashed through the psychological barriers to the top jobs, men have been unable to cope with the position of the lower wage earner.

The remarkable study of top earning wives and their marriages will be published next year. The magazine Psychology Today previews the research and points out that in the United States a million women now bring home more than their husbands.

*doomed to*: has something terrible waiting for him

'One of the biggest problems for both husbands and wives in marriages of unequal earnings is that there are so few model couples who have dealt successfully with the situation,' says the magazine. 'Many simply don't know how to behave in public or private.'

The hard facts are that wives who out-perform their husbands in the employment arena set a domestic scenario for disaster. Sex lives suffer and feelings of love diminish. The couples run a high risk of mutual psychological and physical abuse, which leads to a significantly higher divorce rate.

Finally for some under-achieving husbands whose wives are over-achievers, premature death from heart disease is 11 times more frequent than normal.

The exception is in cases where wives earn more but in a typically female job—secretary, nurse or researcher. Sociologist Dana Hiller who prepared the report along with William Philliber, comments: 'It's okay for your wife to have a higher-paying or higher status job, as long as she's a nurse or a teacher—because that is what women are supposed to be.'

## 2 A woman's place

# 'Every mother *is* a working mother'

HOW NICE for women's lib that people seem to think it has, on the whole, improved the lot of women: 57% tend to agree with this, while only 28% tend to disagree.

I WENT down to Plymouth and stood outside Tesco, which is in the main shopping precinct in the middle of the town, and for an hour I stopped ladies out shopping and asked them about feminism.

I stopped two much younger women about 25, young marrieds with plastic shopping bags. "I'm against these women's libbers," said one. "Yes," said the other. "They want women to work as coal miners and pick up coal. Well, let them. Not me, though."

"The man should be the man in the house. He should be the dominant one."

"But they should get the same pay if they do the same job."

"I like being whistled at. I like all that. It means they fancy you. If you don't fancy them, you just tell them to get lost. There's no problem. I'm quite happy with the way things are."

Near the front entrance sitting on a bench under a tree, was a well dressed lady of 65 with a dog on her lap, a doctor's wife with three children.

"It never occurred to me as a young woman to think for myself. I suppose I *could* have done things, they were possible, but I just didn't. My daughters went off abroad all on their own when they were very young. I wish I'd done that. They can take up any career they like—either academic or working with their hands. *All* young women are liberated today."

Two younger women, aged 19, walked past, both students at Plymouth Polytechnic, just round the corner from Tesco. They said they were Edweige Johnson and Jackie McGarvey and they approved of equal rights and equal pay, but they wouldn't call themselves radicals.

"I don't feel personally I've been exploited, not yet. Perhaps when I go for a job and a man gets it and not me, then I'll be upset and join a radical group. You have to be affected before you want to take action. But women do have it harder. They have two jobs to do, while men just have one."

"I'm glad I'm a woman. I wouldn't want to be a man. We've got the opportunity to do two things, be a mother or a career woman, though I know radicals would disagree with that thinking. Personally, I want lots of children," said Edweige.

"I don't want any," said Jackie.

I noticed a young woman in her mid-twenties, standing inside the doorway of Tesco, with bleached hair, a mini-skirt and a large black dog on a strong lead.

"It doesn't affect me," she said. "I am equal. They wouldn't try to boss me around. I once went for a job in a garage and the bloke said females weren't suited for the job. It was just on the petrol pumps. I told him to shove it up his arse."

Did she ever get whistled at?
"I should hope so, dear. I'm on the game. I'd be upset if they didn't turn and look at me."

BACK IN London, I went to Hammersmith to meet some well brought up young ladies at St Paul's Girls' School, an independent day school whose old Old Girls include Shirley Williams and Brigid Brophy.

There were eleven girls in my workshop, all very bright and keen looking, plus two or three teachers and other adults.

Out of the eleven, five had working mums, but none of them thought their mother was exploited or had a rotten life. They admitted their fathers did very little in the kitchen, or anything very much domestic, but accepted that as natural.

As for their own future, they all expected to go to some sort of college and get a professional training. Of the eleven, five were doing science, five arts and one was doing a mixture.

So far, it was all to be expected. St Paul's is a top school, with girls who are clever, motivated and come from homes where education for girls is valued highly.

But when it came to their personal future, I was surprised to discover that *all* of them planned to get married, have children, and *give up* their career, whatever it was, during the raising of their children.

"If you have children, it's not fair on them to carry on working.

"You *owe* it to your children to be a total mother.

"I'd hope my career was doing well enough, so that I could come back to it a few years later, when the children were growing up."

Wishful thinking, in an age of heavy unemployment, but they were all happily looking forward to being wives and mothers. After some discussion, they decided 24 would be a good age to get married.

I asked how many of them considered themselves to be feminists. Not one of them did.

The adults present seemed surprised so I asked one of the teachers afterwards if perhaps I'd had an untypical group. She thought not, but she had been amazed by what they'd said. "Nothing has changed in 25 years."

It's not too surprising that working-class mums, coming out of Tesco, feel feminism has nothing to do with them, but it must be worrying for the movement if intelligent, middle-class girls are equally happy to take up their traditional sexist roles.

---

*Tesco*: the name of a popular supermarket
*fancy*: to be attracted to
*boss around*: give somebody orders
*(tell someone to) shove (it) up his arse*: (very vulgar) (tell someone) you don't want it
*on the game*: (colloquial) a prostitute

## 2.1

1 Look at the large print at the top of page 52 and discuss with a partner what job is being advertised. Then read the advertisement and see if you still agree.

## Work

2 Group the information given in the advertisement under the following headings.

*Personal qualities and skills*: You must be: .................................................

You must be able to: .................................

*Knowledge*: You must know about: ...........................................................

You should know about: .......................................................

*Qualifications*: ..........................................................................................

Discuss your notes, first with a partner and then as a class.

3 Select one of the jobs advertised on page 48 and make a note of the personal qualities, skills and knowledge required for it. You don't need to be very serious! Now complete the following advertisement from your notes. If you need help you can refer back to the advertisement on page 52.

WANTED

.............................. man/woman/person for .............................. work.

Ability to .............................. vital. High degree of competence in

.............................. required. Good working knowledge of

.............................. essential. Understanding of, and interest in

.............................. desirable. Candidates should possess such human

qualities as .............................. .............................. experience needed.

Salary .............................. Hours ..............................

Holidays .............................. Benefits ..............................

4 Work in pairs. Look at each other's advertisements and try to work out what the jobs are.

## 2.2

1 On pages 53–4 there is an account of how a typical housewife spends her day. Read it quickly and see if you can re-order the mixed-up list of events in her day. Number the events below in the correct order. The first one is done for you. Then read the article again to check if you were right.

    a) meets Angela and Jodi     ..........
    b) does the washing and ironing     ..........
    c) baths the children     ..........
    d) does the shopping and/or washes up     ..........

e) has a cup of tea in bed ......1......
f) reads a book in bed ..........
g) washes and dresses the children ..........
h) husband has evening meal ..........
i) has lunch ..........
j) plays with son ..........
k) puts kids to bed ..........
l) takes daughter to the bus stop ..........
m) cooks breakfast ..........
n) watches television ..........
o) has evening meal ..........
p) does housework ..........

2 Look at the article again.
   a) Find three other verbs that are the same in meaning as, or similar to, *shout*.
   b) Find another two verbs that are the same in meaning as, or similar to, *hate*.
   c) *Laundering* means ...........................................................................
   d) *Offspring* means ............................................................................

3 Match the words from the text (in the left-hand column) with their equivalents (in the right-hand column).

   a) *mucky*     witch
   b) *loo*       emptied
   c) *drained*   fight
   d) *fair*      rush
   e) *trendy*    look angry
   f) *glower*    toilet
   g) *hag*       fashionable
   h) *hurtle*    dirty
   i) *wrestle*   quite good
   j) *sodden*    soaking wet

# 2.3

1 Look at the article 'The cost of a wife' on page 55, which appeared in a newspaper in 1981. Read it quickly and answer the following questions. Discuss your answers in pairs or groups, making reference to the text.
   a) Who else earns the same as a housewife?
   b) Who organised the survey?
   c) Why is a housewife's time costed at £133 per week more than in 1975?

*Work*

    d) Did the last survey have any effect upon people (did men begin to insure their wives' lives)?
    e) On what day is a housewife potentially earning the most?
    f) Who are the insurers offering the insurance scheme to, and why?
    g) What percentage of husbands insure their wife's life?
    h) Will the policy cover the cost of a housekeeper?
    i) Is there such a scheme for women?
    j) What are the problems of the scheme?

2  Imagine you are writing up the chart on page 55 in full for a newspaper, e.g.

'According to a survey conducted by Legal & General Insurers, an average housewife works between 12 and 14 hours a day. The day begins at half past seven when she cooks breakfast, serves it and washes up, after which she drives the children to school, stopping on the way back to do the shopping . . .'

Now continue, remembering to link your sentences together so that your report reads smoothly.

## 2.4

1  Before reading the article on page 56 'Man about the house you're lazy', look at the following list of household jobs and discuss with a partner:
    a) which of these would not normally be done by a man in your own country
    b) which you would not expect to be done by a man in Britain.
    Put a cross (x) in the appropriate column.

|  | *Own country* | *Britain* |
|---|---|---|
| a) clean the toilet |  |  |
| b) change the sheets |  |  |
| c) do the ironing |  |  |
| d) cook the dinner |  |  |
| e) do the gardening |  |  |
| f) help serve dinner (cut up meat etc.) |  |  |
| g) mix drinks |  |  |
| h) entertain guests |  |  |

2  Discuss, in groups, which jobs are traditionally done or not done by men in your own country, and report back to the class.

3 Now read the article and see if your predictions about Britain were correct. Decide whether the following statements are true or false according to the article; write T or F next to each statement and discuss your answers with a partner, giving evidence from the text.

   a) Most men are not much help in the house.
   b) Men only do the jobs they like.
   c) The writer of the article thinks that entertaining guests is hard work.
   d) The husband and wife usually divide the housework up equally if the wife works too.
   e) Most women are satisfied with the help they get from their husbands.

4 Read the text again and find words or expressions which mean approximately the same as the following. Discuss your answers in pairs and check with your dictionary or your teacher.

   a) lazy
   b) failures
   c) choose
   d) toilet
   e) feel like it
   f) cutting up meat
   g) persuading
   h) domestic job
   i) equipment
   j) compensate for

## 2.5

1 In a recent survey, several women were interviewed and asked their views on feminism, job equality, working mothers etc. Before reading the article on page 57, try to predict which of the groups below expressed which opinions.
   – 19-year-old students
   – teenage schoolgirls
   – a doctor's wife of 65
   – married women in their mid-twenties
   – a prostitute in her mid-twenties

   She/they say(s)/think(s):
   a) they want to have children and since it isn't fair to work if you have children, it is your duty to give up your career to bring them up;
   b) women have a harder life, having two jobs, but it is better to be a woman because there is a choice of having a career or being a mother;
   c) they don't want to do the same jobs as a man, and the man should be the boss at home;
   d) any young woman nowadays can take up any career she wants;
   e) women are equal, and they shouldn't worry about being whistled at.

*Work*

2 Discuss your predictions with a partner and then read the article to see if you were right.

3 Interview several people about their views on working mothers. Make notes, or tape your interviews if you can. Then write up the information you have collected in the form of a report.

# Discussion/Debate

## *Points for discussion*

1 Mothers with young children have a moral obligation to give up their jobs and stay at home to look after them.
2 The salary which is paid for a job should be reduced according to the amount of job satisfaction it gives.
3 Making people retire early would help to provide the unemployed with jobs and give older people the opportunity to develop different interests.

The class will divide into small groups, each group supporting one of the proposals above.

## *Preliminary tasks*

Time will be given for individuals within each group to make notes on the points they would like to put forward. It might be helpful to look through the texts in this section. The aim is to think of as many arguments *in favour of* the proposal as you can – it doesn't matter if you don't necessarily agree with the proposal in reality.

Discuss your points within the group; one member should be appointed to take notes and be the spokesperson.

## *Procedure*

A spokesperson from each group will have time to put forward the proposal, after which the rest of the class will be able to comment, agree, disagree etc. A vote will be taken, with the rest of the class voting for or against the proposal.

## *Follow up*

Write a balanced account of the arguments for and against the proposal, in the form of an article for a magazine or newspaper.

# Education

Look through the texts in both sections of this unit and try to answer the following questions *as quickly as possible*. Remember that you are not looking for any other information, so it is not necessary to study the texts in detail.

1. What is the name of a school bully?
2. How many different kinds of state school are there in the UK?
3. What does AP stand for?
4. Which town do you write to in order to get information about the Open University?
5. What are the names of three of 'the best teachers in Britain'?
6. What is the name of a university building where social activities take place?
7. What is the name of a method where you learn languages by listening to cassettes?
8. What does grade 'D' mean on a school report?
9. Approximately how many adults in Britain can't read or write?
10. What is the name of the person who interviewed three families about education at home?

Check your answers with a partner before looking at the key on page 151.

Now look at the exercises on pages 73–7 before reading the texts in section 1 more carefully.

Education

# 1 The happiest days of your life?

## 'WHY MY TEACHER IS THE BEST IN BRITAIN'

**My teacher**

I have a great teacher,
Mrs Griffiths is her name,
If she does much better shell end up in "Fame",
I think she is the funniest,
The greatest of the lot,
I don't know what kind of teacher the rest of you have got,
Mine is surely the best,
Writing with great zest,
She could climb mount Everest in two minutes flat,
I bet anyone elses teacher couldn't do that,
She can teach almost anything,
Maths, English and some gym,
She not like most teachers who make their lessons grim,
On her face she wears a smile,
It's probably wider than half a mile,
And if we won this computer her face would shine with glee.
To have a little genius in her class like 'me'.

---

**Why My Teacher Is The Best In Britain**

I am dyslexic, and I think the best teacher in Britain is the teacher, Mrs Davies, who helps me with my problems. She is the best teacher because she understands the things that I find difficult.

She never shouts at me or tells me I am lazy or careless if I can't spell a word.

Mrs Davies never laughs at me, only with me. For instance I find it difficult to tell the difference between a "b" and a "d" and Mrs Davies does not laugh at the funny mistakes I make, like writing baddy for daddy. She just tries to find specail ways of helping me remember.

Although Mrs Davies is kind and patient she never praises me when I know the work was not my best. So when Mrs Davies says "Well done!" I feel really pleased because I know that she understands how hard I've tried.

---

**Miss Miller**

My teacher is the best because of her personality and character. Some people would describe her as being unusual but she is also friendly, hard working and ready for a challenge.

She has mouse-brown hair and a pale complexion. Her eyes are hazelnut and are very gentle and soft. They are beautiful but tragically they are lost as she squints, and she rarely wears her glasses to help her poor eyesight.

Perhaps the most outstanding feature in her description is her height, unfortunately she does not use her height to her advantage, she slouches her shoulders, bends her back and this together with her squinting proves that she is sensitive about her appearance and lacks confidence as do many children.

I am sure her childlike, sympathetic personality most definitely is a wonderful quality, for she stays a loyal friend even after you have left the school.

---

*Fame*: a popular television programme
*two minutes flat*: only two minutes
*grim*: boring

*dyslexic*: having difficulty in reading (because of a kind of illness)
*squints*: almost closes her eyes (because she can't see well)

64

# 1 The happiest days of your life?

*Teacher of course knows everything, from why dinosaurs died out to how to tie shoelaces. A new authority threatens the home and BRIAN JACKSON, mere father that he is, has to come to terms with this challenge to his supremacy*

'Miss Goldengrove says there aren't any fairies.'
'Oh.'
'Miss Goldengrove says I've got to have a proper name tag on my raincoat—not messy pen.'
'Oh.'
'Miss Goldengrove says I've got to draw my shadow in the sun before Monday morning.'
'But darling, it's raining cats and dogs—there aren't any shadows.'
'Miss Goldengrove says I've got to.'
'Oh.'
I am a mere, mild and inoffensive dad. But suddenly Ellen, my six year old daughter, is demanding sponsored hopscotch; an end to the myth of Father Christmas; immediate access to my non-existent copies of the Encyclopaedia Britannica ('Why did the dinosaurs die out, Daddy?'). Why? Because Miss Goldengrove says.

A dagger to the heart. For the first time, someone has usurped the sovereign authority of mum and dad. Of course the opening action to take is to know your teacher. The earlier we sow that seed, the richer the harvest. The more parent visits classroom the more teacher enters home, the better for your son or daughter.

---

Dear Parents,

There will be a Parents' Evening on Thursday, 19th January, for parents of boys in the Fourth Forms. You are invited to visit the School to discuss any matters affecting the work and progress of your son with the Head of Middle School, his Year Master, Form Tutor and Subject teachers, who will be available from 6.30 to 8.30 p.m. in the School Hall and other rooms in the Main Block. Appointments may be booked through the usual booking system, and with me or the Deputy Headmaster through the School Secretary.

*fairies*: small imaginary beings
*name tag*: a label with a name printed on it
*sponsor*: give money in return for an activity (the money is usually given to charity)
*hopscotch*: a children's game (involving jumping on squares drawn on the ground)
*dinosaur*: a prehistoric animal
*dagger*: a sharp knife
*usurped*: taken wrongfully
*gruelling*: exhausting

**"I'll not bore you with my hard day at school, Mother — I can see you've had a bit of a gruelling one yourself"**

Education

# WERE THEY THE HAPPIEST DAYS OF YOUR LIFE?

Psychiatrists are forever on about parental influence, but so few ever mention the overwhelming effect that schooldays have. And yet, for a minimum of 11 years, you spend most of your time at school. Your mother and father can be blamed endlessly for your character or, if they are lucky, they can take a large proportion of the credit. So why is it teachers are never held responsible?

When you think about it, it's quite likely that, for some time, you saw more of your teachers than you did of your parents — and in your most impressionable years. Therefore, it's surely obvious that the adults you mixed with for six or seven hours a day must have had an enormous hand in shaping your life.

We talked to three people to find out how their schooldays affected them . . .

**Lucy Jackman (25):** "I hated school, absolutely loathed and detested it. I enjoyed two or three of my primary years, actually but that was all.

### "I left school at the earliest possible moment..."

"At seven, I went to a convent school for a couple of years and I think it was that which did me a lot of damage. I was a weekly boarder but it wasn't at all like I'd imagined, I remember begging my mother to let me go because I thought it'd be packed with midnight feasts and adventures — just like my Enid Blyton books. But how wrong I was. It was hard work and not much fun.

"One night, when we were all settled down in bed, a nun came into our dormitory and told us that we'd burn in hell if we told lies. What a thing to say to a bunch of kids. In fact, it was my convent experience that gave me problems in adolescence. I got very hung up about religion, was always asking God for forgiveness — and I also developed a guilt complex!

"I used to go down on my knees in the street to say I was sorry for something, but I'd always pretend I was doing up my shoelace. But then I even used to feel guilty about that, wondering if I was ashamed of praying. On top of all that, I had compulsions — I'd have to do everything three times just to make sure I didn't make mistakes.

"At the age of eleven, I went to an ordinary grammar school, and I loathed that, too. I just couldn't take all the discipline because it seemed so incredibly petty. How could I be expected to take them all seriously when they freaked out if your hat wasn't worn at a certain angle on your head? I just couldn't have respect for people like that.

"I was always rebelling — my name was constantly on the blackboard: 'Will Lucy Jackman please see the headmistress'. For some strange reason, though, the head seemed to be fond of me. Obviously, she had to tell me off frequently, but I always sensed that she liked me and, therefore, hated handing out the lectures.

"My English teacher had a soft spot for me too, but I tried hard for her because composition was my favourite subject. From a very young age, I'd always wanted to be a journalist — and I think she had hopes for me. However, she was also my form mistress and I know I used to drive her round the bend occasionally.

"My other love at school was music, but the mistress in charge was the Deputy Head and she couldn't stand the sight of me. I really wanted to join the school choir but, as a punishment she decided that I wouldn't be allowed to. It's quite sad, really — if she'd given me some encouragement, I would have put a lot of effort into that and perhaps gone on with it in some way. She was a dragon, that woman. For a detention, she once said, 'Right, from the moment I choose to clap my hands, you are not allowed to move a muscle'. I had to sit absolutely still for forty minutes. One day, I was given a load of lines to do but I refused. It had finally dawned on me that there was nothing she could do about it. Once you stop being frightened of teachers, there's no way they can hurt you and, of course, they realise that.

"I left school at the earliest possible moment, without any O-Levels or anything, but I certainly don't regret it. As my mother said, anything I want to learn I can find out from books. I did become a journalist, too, and I really love my work. I didn't need GCEs to do it, but I did need drive and determination. Fortunately, these were things I was born with, and not taught."

# 1  The happiest days of your life?

**Jillian Hall (23):** "I don't remember a bad moment from my schooldays — they were certainly a lot happier than my working life has been. Maybe it's just because I'm not used to it yet. School to me was my family, if you know what I mean, and I really miss the security of those familiar faces.

## "School to me was my family..."

"Because I'm quite small, I was always babied and, maybe because I didn't present any threat to anyone, I got on with almost everybody — teachers and pupils alike. But, as a result, I'm now virtually incapable of looking after myself.

"I'm absolutely hopeless at making decisions. I can't even decide what to wear in the mornings. Everything, right along the line, was decided for me, even my career. My class mistress thought I ought to go into a bank, and that's just what I've done.

"Thinking back on it, my school was pretty bad like that. They never really encouraged people to think for themselves. They worked on this great team spirit thing, which eventually suffocated the majority of individualistic instincts. One girl just wouldn't conform, though, but she was thrown out.

"I didn't work particularly hard — there didn't seem to be any real need. I always muddled through, scraped by somehow. I just didn't have any incentive to slog my guts out. Anyway, I think I was my form teacher's pet and so she never got cross with me.

"I come from a very large family and I often felt rather left out, so maybe that's why school was so important to me. When I first went there, I was always doing my best to please people, to get on the right side of them and, happily, I succeeded. But that attitude will stay with me, I think. Even if I don't like someone, I'm nice to them.

"I miss the cocoon of school, but now I do regret that they didn't teach me to stand on my own two feet. I don't like my job — money and figures have never really fascinated me — but I don't know what else I'm capable of. Anyway, I think I'd be too nervous to make the change!"

**Stephen Parker (23):** "My parents sent me to public school and, as they initially spent a lot of money that they didn't really have, they were determined I would succeed. But I'm not too sure whether I'm doing it.

"The basic problem with my school was that the teachers expected you to go into university or a profession, and that really was the be all and end all. I am studying accountancy now, but I'm not too sure whether I'm doing it because I want to.

## "My parents backed up every decision my teachers made..."

"My parents backed up every decision the teachers made. If I got punished for something, they agreed with it wholeheartedly. They didn't support me on anything. Even if I'd been suspended, they'd have been right behind it. Because of all this, there was no conflict — that's why I was pushed from both sides into doing what I'm doing now.

"It'll be good in the long run — when I'm thirty-five or forty I'll be raking the money in, but I'd really almost like to have two lives. I'd like to do something that my heart wants to do rather than my mind, something a bit more adventurous. Accountancy is what everyone thinks it is — it's all mapped out and there's no question mark about the future. If you qualify, you're guaranteed six thousand a year or so. Actually, I do enjoy it, but I think I could equally well enjoy bumming around the world. But, then again, I've been trained into thinking ahead. In six or seven years' time, I'll have something to show for all the hard work. And, as a result of various influences, that's quite important to me.

"I am easily influenced, though, in the way that I tend to change my moods and attitudes to suit. I was very naive when I came out of school, but I would have been worse if I'd been a boarder. When I entered the big, wide world, I honestly thought that everyone played the game honourably, all jolly good fellows and so on. How wrong I was. I think teachers should spend more time at school telling kids about people and life in general outside school walls."

---

*on about*: (colloquial) talking about
*Enid Blyton*: the author of very popular children's books
*convent*: a building where religious women live to serve God
*nun*: a woman belonging to a religious order
*form mistress*: the teacher in charge of the class
*initially*: at first
*accountancy*: a profession concerned with the financial affairs of a business
*jolly good fellows*: nice people

# Education

THE COUNTY HIGH SCHOOL, SAFFRON WALDEN

The School opened in January 1951, as a bilateral school to provide secondary education for Saffron Walden and the villages in the Rural District within a radius of about eight miles.

In September 1967 it was re-organised as a comprehensive school for pupils aged 11 to 18 and in 1971/72 a substantial programme of extensions and alterations enlarged the original buildings to cater for 1320 pupils i.e. an 8-form entry school plus a sixth form of 120. However, rising numbers have led to a 9-form entry organisation and the sixth form has increased to about 200. The original rural catchment area has twice, in 1975 and 1979, had to be reduced in order that the increasing population in Saffron Walden itself can be accommodated.

In recent years, public examination results have been consistently much above the national average at all levels.

Accommodation
The School, which is set in very pleasant grounds at the southern end of the town, near to Audley End Mansion, is a large, modern two-storey 'E' shaped building. There are separate blocks housing Technical Studies and Physical Education departments and there is also a large Farm Unit.

Specialist facilities available include eleven science laboratories and a large farm rural studies unit with greenhouses, an animal house with dairy facilities and an allotment area; modern languages rooms including a language laboratory; a Technology block of seven work areas; a Home Economics unit with three domestic science and two needlework rooms; four Art rooms and a photography studio; two Music rooms and two practice rooms; a Drama Studio, a Commercial Studies room; sixth form private study, common and dining rooms, sixth form seminar rooms; Mathematics, English, History, Geography, Religious Education and remedial rooms, a large Library with Librarian's Office, a Careers room, a large assembly hall with stage and green room; three dining rooms; two gymnasia with changing rooms and showers; an open-air heated swimming pool and extensive playing fields including hard play areas and tennis courts. Mobile classrooms, including two for science teaching, have been erected more recently to cater for increasing numbers on roll.

Extra-Curricular Activities
The School has established a reputation for its many clubs, societies, extra-curricular activities and educational visits. It has a very strong musical tradition and there is a Saturday Morning Music School. Individual instrumental music tuition is available. Exchange visits exist with Schools in France and Germany. Field Studies courses are regularly organised by the Geography and Biology departments for senior students. Other clubs and activities include the Farm Club, chess, art, drama, guitar, Christian Union, Science Club, the School Bookshop, and United Nations Association.

The School takes a leading part in area and county sporting activities both in Essex and Cambridgeshire, with considerable success. Rugby, soccer, hockey, netball, badminton, basketball, swimming, cross-country running, athletics, cricket, tennis, gymnastics and golf are featured. In recent years, ski-ing visits to Italy have proved very popular.

Uniform
The wearing of the School uniform is expected from pupils in Years one to five as an integral part of School discipline. It is considered that this promotes good standards, avoids feelings of inferiority or superiority from some pupils and acts as a good image in the eyes of the community. Sixth formers need not wear school uniform but they are expected to dress smartly.

Uniform is available from Gray Palmers, High Street, Saffron Walden or from Robert Sayles, St Andrew's Street, Cambridge. Parents are, of course, free to purchase suitable items elsewhere. A uniform list with the approximate cost of items is available on request at the School.

Interviews with Headmaster
An introductory meeting is held each October for parents of prospective new admissions. In early July an Open Evening is held for the parents of pupils who will be joining the School in the following September.

The Headmaster will be pleased to see any parent who would like further information about the School but it is advisable to telephone or write to make a firm appointment.

*bilateral*: having two sides
*catchment area*: an area from which children who attend the school are taken
*two-storey*: with two levels
*allotment*: an area of land to grow vegetables on
*extra-curricular*: outside the school syllabus

## 1 The happiest days of your life?

# SCHOOL UNIFORMS

I am all for uniforms. If pupils were allowed free choice in dress, richer children would tease the poorer ones about their clothing. Girls would want to show off a new 'mod' outfit, but this might get spoilt after one day at school. I should like a modern dress, with pockets, in a warm, inexpensive material for winter, and the same in cotton for summer. Skirts are so hard to keep in good shape, mothers hate ironing white shirts and girls despise wearing ties. A dress is less expensive and far more comfortable.
Sheila, 15

There would be no school uniform at all and the pupils would wear whatever they wanted. I am sure they would soon learn which clothes were suitable for school and which were not - even if it caused several members of the staff frequent nightmares wondering what Jane or Jimmy would be wearing tomorrow. Everybody has to form his own individual dress sense, and how can this be done if everybody is forced to dress exactly alike for most of the day?
Ruth, 15

A great number of people have put forward the suggestion that when everyone is dressed differently, one becomes too absorbed in clothes to work. It is much easier to work when you feel comfortably dressed, and very rarely are school uniforms comfortable.
Angela, 15

It is still seriously thought that if we all wear the same type of clothes, we'll all go round thinking our parents earn the same amount of money. Pupils should be allowed to dress in the manner in which they feel comfortable, and any good head teacher will use his own discretion in tactfully censuring the odd exhibitionist.
Roy, 15

I go to a school which has a uniform, and I am glad it does. There is no problem deciding what to wear each morning, no class distinction at school, and no one trying to look better than the person next to them, everyone is equal.
Jane, 15

*tease*: laugh at / make jokes about
*'mod'*: (colloquial) modern
*nightmares*: bad dreams
*censuring*: expressing disapproval (of)

### ALL ABOUT EDUCATION
#### MAINTAINED (STATE) SECTOR
PRIMARY SCHOOL: there are 23,200 of these in England and Wales, mostly co-educational and taking children from five to 11-years-old.
MIDDLE SCHOOL: designed to provide eight to 12-year-olds or sometimes nine to 13-year-olds with an easy transition between the informal class teaching of early years and the more structured secondary school subject teaching.
COMPREHENSIVE SCHOOL: there are 4,049 comprehensive schools in England and Wales, covering 86 per cent of the secondary school population in England. Comprehensives take pupils aged 11 to 18 or 11 to 16 in areas which are served by separate Sixth Form Colleges.
GRAMMAR SCHOOL: providing a mainly academic course for selected pupils from 11 to 18, they number 200 in England and Wales. There are 33 local education authorities still offering grammar school education.
**Choice of schools in the state sector.** The 1944 Education Act provides that 'so far as is compatible with the provision of efficient instruction and training and the avoidance of unreasonable public expenditure pupils are to be educated *in accordance with the wishes of their parents'.* You are entitled to state a preference for single sex education or a Church of England foundation, but in reality this statutory freedom of choice is circumscribed by the discretion of the local authority; if the authority say no, the parents do then have the right of appeal under the 1980 Education Act.
**Assisted places.** In September 1981 the government reintroduced a scheme to offer 5,000 to 6,000 assisted places a year at 230 independent schools. These places are provided for the most able children, whose parents must apply to the school. They are offered financial help with tuition fees on a sliding scale, according to family income.
#### INDEPENDENT (PRIVATE) SECTOR
PRE-PREPARATORY SCHOOL: prepares four to seven or eight-year-olds for Preparatory school.
PREPARATORY SCHOOL: the Incorporated Association of Preparatory Schools represents 550 of the boys' and girls' schools catering for girls usually aged five to 12, boys aged eight to 13. Boys are prepared for the Common Entrance Examination into their chosen senior school. Girls may sit a (different) Common Entrance Examination but they usually have more choice, as many senior girls' schools select from their own examination, and girls can therefore sit more than one examination.
PUBLIC SCHOOL: the term is used to denote the 210 (mainly) boys' secondary schools belonging to the Headmasters' Conference. There are 230 girls' senior schools in membership of the Girls' School Association. About 100 Headmasters' Conference schools now admit girls, either at sixth-form level or on a fully co-educational basis.
SCHOLARSHIPS: the remunerative as opposed to the honorary value of scholarships varies widely. Some scholarships are worth only £30 reduction in fees a term; only a handful each year provides total remission of fees to the parents of the most brilliantly academic children, regardless of family income. Some music and art scholarships are also available. Most schools also offer bursaries to assist children in need who might not qualify for scholarships.

*scholarship*: } a sum of money which pays
*bursary*: } for someone's education

*Education*

HUTTON GRAMMAR SCHOOL                                          CODE OF CONDUCT

Boys from Hutton have always <u>maintained</u> a high standard of <u>conduct</u> and <u>in consequence</u> the School has <u>stood high in public esteem</u>. This is a <u>state of affairs</u> which we all wish to <u>preserve</u>.

Good behaviour is not just obeying a set of rules. It is having consideration at all times for other people. If we exercised this consideration properly we could get along with very few rules. However, in a School we are dealing with people who are still learning how to behave properly. We have, therefore, to <u>lay down</u> some basic rules and, since there unfortunately will always be <u>people</u> who will not voluntarily do what is right, we have to <u>ensure</u> that the rules are <u>observed</u>.

Some of the rules or standards of conduct which we observe are <u>set out</u> below, but we must not forget that not everything which we should, or should not do, can possibly be covered by a rule.

Good behaviour of boys in a School <u>stems</u> from respect for the Masters, for each other, for themselves and <u>for</u> the buildings and <u>surrounds</u>.

Boys should be co-operative towards Masters. They should greet them on meeting. They should not approach them with hands in pockets. They should automatically stand up when a Master enters the room except that, when a lesson is in progress, they should only stand for the Headmaster, Deputy Headmasters or Visitors. They should be ready to open doors and to stand back and allow precedence to Masters in corridors or in using doors. In similar manner boys should always <u>defer</u> to Visitors and should try to be as helpful as possible. If a Visitor appears uncertain, <u>approach</u> and say 'Good Morning. Can I help you?' or something similar.

"I know you'll like the location—just a stone's throw away from the school"

*a stone's throw (away from)*: (play on words) very near

# FULWOOD COUNTY HIGH SCHOOL

HEADMASTER: T. BOAK, B.Sc.

REPORT FOR PERIOD ENDING: 9.7.76

NAME: Michael BELL   FORM: 4Q
ABSENCES: 12

| SUBJECT | SET | PROGRESS | EFFORT | REMARKS | INITIALS |
|---|---|---|---|---|---|
| ENGLISH LANGUAGE | 1/5 | B+ | C | Capable of excellent work but too readily assumes a responsibility to entertain and distract the class. Nonetheless he should do well at "O" Level. | |
| MATHEMATICS | 4/6 | C | C | Has settled down in Set 4 but still has to realise that worthwhile results come through hard work. | |
| OPTION 2 Art/Pottery | | A | A+ | Michael has ability and a lively imagination. His tenacity and application is far above average. | |
| OPTION 1 History | GCE | C | C | Would do well if he had more confidence in his own abilities | |
| OPTION 3 Geography | 1/2 | C | D | Michael needs to make a more determined effort to maintain his concentration | |
| OPTION 4 English Literature | | A | B+ | Michael has very considerable ability in this subject and invariably produces excellent work. | |
| OPTION 5 Biology | 2/3 | C | C | Has ability, but lacks drive. | AFB |
| P.E./GAMES | | C | C | Quite satisfactory | |
| RELIGIOUS STUDIES | 2 | A | B | Michael is able & aware. His written work is good but oral contributions lack confidence. | |

GRADING: A – EXCELLENT   B – GOOD   C – SATISFACTORY   D – WEAK   E – UNSATISFACTORY

FORM TEACHER: A very patchy report. I have no doubt that Michael is very able but that his determination varies according to subject. He has a very lively mind and could do well in all subjects.

YEAR HEAD: There is clearly the basis for some success next year. It is up to Michael as to how much he achieves.

*Education*

# The Bully Asleep

One afternoon, when grassy
Scents through the classroom crept,
Bill Craddock laid his head
Down on his desk, and slept.

The children came round him:
Jimmy, Roger, and Jane;
They lifted his head timidly
And let it sink again.

'Look, he's gone sound asleep, Miss,'
Said Jimmy Adair;
'He stays up all the night, you see;
His mother doesn't care.'

'Stand away from him, children.'
Miss Andrews stooped to see.
'Yes, he's asleep; go on
With your writing, and let him be.'

'Now's a good chance!' whispered Jimmy;
And he snatched Bill's pen and hid it.
'Kick him under the desk hard;
He won't know who did it.'

'Fill all his pockets with rubbish —
Paper, apple-cores, chalk.'
So they plotted, while Jane
Sat wide-eyed at their talk.

Not caring, not hearing,
Bill Craddock he slept on;
Lips parted, eyes closed —
Their cruelty gone.

'Stick him with pins!' muttered Roger.
'Ink down his neck!' said Jim.
But Jane, tearful and foolish,
Wanted to comfort him.

(from *The Roundabout by the Sea* by John Walsh)

## 1.1

1 A publishing company and a women's magazine recently organised a competition where children had to write in, saying 'Why my teacher is the best in Britain'. Make a note of what *you* think are the essential qualities of a good teacher. Compare your notes with a partner. Then look at the responses on page 64 and make a note of the children's criteria. Discuss these in groups or pairs.

2 Write *either* a poem *or* a short article describing your favourite teacher. It need not be true! Exchange your work in groups and decide which one would win the competition, and why.

## 1.2

1 Read the article by Brian Jackson on page 65 and decide if, according to him, the following statements are true or false. Write T or F next to each statement.

   a) Ellen's teacher has complained that her raincoat hasn't got her name on it.
   b) Ellen won't be able to do her homework because it's raining too hard.
   c) Ellen will be able to find out from her father's encyclopedia why dinosaurs no longer exist.
   d) Ellen's father thinks that teachers have become more important than parents.
   e) He thinks that parents should learn to work harder in the garden.

2 In Britain, schools have 'Parents' Evenings', where parents can meet their children's teachers. In groups, discuss how much contact parents have with schools in your own country. Could the situation be improved? If so, make suggestions about how this could be done. Then each of you should write a letter to your child's headmaster or headmistress, putting forward your suggestions.

## 1.3

1 Look at the article on pages 66–7 and try to predict from the quotations in dark type what the three people interviewed are going to say in answer to the question at the top of page 66.

*Education*

2  Look through the three interviews quickly and fill in the chart below.
   Discuss your answers in pairs or groups.

|  | Lucy Jackman | Jillian Hall | Stephen Parker |
|---|---|---|---|
| Age |  |  |  |
| Feelings about school |  |  |  |
| Reasons |  |  |  |
| Present job |  |  |  |
| Feelings about job |  |  |  |

3  Look at the interview with Lucy Jackman.
   a) Try to guess the meaning of the following words or phrases, looking carefully at the context to help you.
   
   *loathed* (line 2)           *a soft spot* (line 44)
   *boarder* (line 7)           *dragon* (line 59)
   *dormitory* (line 15)        *load of lines* (lines 63–4)
   *bunch of kids* (line 17)    *drive* (line 75)
   *petty* (line 32)

   b) Try to find a phrasal verb or idiomatic expression which is similar to each of the following.
   
   comfortable/peaceful            giving out
   emotionally disturbed           make (someone) exasperated
   tying                           hated
   acted very emotionally          became clear
   speak severely to someone
      about their faults
   
   Discuss your answers to (a) and (b) in pairs or groups and consult the dictionary or your teacher if necessary.

1 *The happiest days of your life?*

c) What words or ideas do the following refer to? Work on your own first, and then discuss your answers with a partner.

*that* (line 6)  *people like that* (lines 35–6)
*it* (line 8)  *therefore* (line 43)
*it* (line 10)  *that . . . it* (line 58)
*It* (line 12)  *that woman* (line 59)
*that* (line 25)  *it* (line 66)
*all that* (line 26)  *that* (line 68)
*them* (line 33)  *it* (line 71)

d) There are several verbs in this article which express degrees of liking or hate. Arrange them in order of strength along this line, and then discuss your answers with a partner.

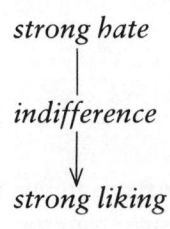

*strong hate*
|
*indifference*
↓
*strong liking*

4 Look at the interview with Jillian Hall.
a) Try and guess the meaning of the following words and phrases, looking closely at the context to help you.
*babied* (line 8)
*form teacher's pet* (line 30)
*cocoon* (line 39)

b) Try to find a phrasal verb or idiomatic expression which is similar in meaning to each of the following.

had a good relationship with   work very hard
told to leave   ignored
reached the end, despite inefficiency   to make (yourself) popular with
only just succeeded   be independent

Discuss your answers to (a) and (b) in pairs or groups and consult your teacher or the dictionary if necessary.

5 Look at the interview with Stephen Parker.
a) Try to guess the meaning of the following words and expressions, looking carefully at the context.
*the be all and end all* (lines 8–9)
*wholeheartedly* (line 13)
*suspended* (line 15)
*conflict* (line 16)
*in the long run* (line 19)
*guaranteed* (line 27)

75

*Education*

b) Try to find a phrasal verb or idiomatic expression which is similar in meaning to each of the following.
agreed with / supported
in favour of
earning lots of money
arranged/planned
not having a regular job

Discuss your answers to (a) and (b) in pairs or groups and consult your teacher or the dictionary, if necessary.

6 Work in pairs. Interview each other about your schooldays and write up your notes so that you have a similar interview for the magazine. Remember to invent a headline.

## 1.4

1 Look at page 68 and find answers to the following questions as quickly as possible. Discuss your answers with a partner, giving evidence from the text.
 a) How long has The County High School been comprehensive?
 b) Where do you have to live in order to go to the school?
 c) What kind of academic standards has the school got?
 d) What facilities are there for sport?
 e) What has the school got a reputation for?
 f) What facilities are there for sixth formers?
 g) Who has to wear uniform?
 h) What do you have to do in order to get an appointment with the headmaster?

2 Work in pairs. Interview each other about the differences between secondary schools in your own country/countries and this one in Britain. Make notes and then report back to the class on the main differences.

## 1.5

1 Think of as many advantages and disadvantages of having a school uniform as you can, and note them down (refer back to the text on page 68 for some ideas). Then read the comments about school uniform by schoolchildren on page 69.

2 After reading, make a note of any more advantages and disadvantages which are mentioned, and discuss them in groups.

*1 The happiest days of your life?*

3 Working on your own, decide on your ideal school uniform (bearing in mind comfort and cost as well as fashion) and write a letter to your present or past headmistress/headmaster, putting your suggestions forward.

## 1.6

Look at the Code of Conduct on page 70. This is written in a very formal style. Try to replace the underlined words with a more everyday equivalent and then rewrite the text in the form of a note to a friend, stating what you *should*, *have to* and *are not allowed to* do at this school.

## 1.7

Make a list of the school subjects usually studied by a 14 year old in your country. Compare them with the list on page 71 and discuss the differences in groups.

## 1.8

From the texts you have read, and the notes you have made in this section, write up a summary in the form of a newspaper article, showing the principal differences between schooling in your own country and in Britain. Remember to include factors such as:
a) types of secondary education
b) subjects studied
c) discipline
d) extra-curricular activities
e) contact with parents
f) uniform
and any others you can think of.

**Before reading the texts in section 2 more carefully, look at the exercises on pages 87–92.**

Education

## 2 Beyond the classroom

# ALTERNATIVE EDUCATION

**Thousands of parents have decided to take their children's schooling into their own hands. Carol Baker talks to three families who are making home education work**

Education is compulsory, Schooling is not. As parents, we have primary responsibility for our children's education and although we usually delegate this to schools, it is not obligatory.

The 1944 Education Act (section 36) states: 'It shall be the duty of the parent of every child of compulsory school age to cause him to receive efficient full-time education suitable to his age, ability and aptitude, either by regular attendance at school or otherwise.' (Scotland and Northern Ireland have similar clauses in their Education Acts of 1962 and 1947 respectively.)

It is the 'or otherwise' clause that has left the door open for parents to educate their children themselves.

Recently published figures suggest that there may now be as many as 70,000 children being taught at home.

But how many parents feel emotionally equipped to cope with their children seven days a week, year in and year out? How many are willing or able to write off a second wage packet or organise two jobs so that one parent is always available for child care? One positive aspect of unemployment may be that parents have more time and interest to devote to their children's education.

Families who undertake their children's education come in all shapes, sizes and income brackets – and their reasons are equally varied. Some parents who are opposed to schools in principle argue that they are educationally unproductive and socially restrictive, herding children into age and ability ghettos.

Others have taken on the responsibility, often reluctantly in the first place, when problems such as unhappiness, serious bullying or dissatisfaction with educational standards have left no alternative.

Although the Education Act establishes the general principle that children should be educated in accordance with their parents' wishes, it also requires Local Education Authorities (LEAs) to ensure that children of 'compulsory school age' are educated. So parents must satisfy the LEA that their child is receiving efficient full-time education suitable to age, ability and aptitude. 'Efficient' and 'suitable' are not defined, however, and parents and LEAs usually cooperate to reach an agreement. Occasionally, LEAs may be hostile and, in very rare instances, may bring a court action. It's important, therefore, that you check the position carefully if you're contemplating home education. Education Otherwise (address at end of this feature) gives detailed advice.

A child already attending a state school must be deregistered when he/she is withdrawn. This is done by writing to the headteacher and to the LEA. Where a child is not registered at a state school, then the procedure is more straightforward and it is not necessary to seek permission from the LEA, although they may monitor the situation in due course.

A child is not registered . . .
□ if he/she has only just reached school age and has not yet been registered at a state school;
□ if he/she is attending a private school;
□ if the family has moved into a new area;
□ if he/she is between lower and middle school or middle and upper school and has not yet accepted a place at the next school.

LEAs vary in the way that they supervise home education. Some ask for a timetable or curriculum while others will have an informal chat with the family. An adviser may visit the home each term or annually, but some parents report that they have never had a visit.

One local authority representative I spoke to visits education-at-home families twice a year. He looks at the children's work, talks with them and discusses any problems with the parents. Basic literacy and an excitement for learning are the qualities he looks for. Professionally, he thinks his job is to strengthen what the parents are doing. Personally he admits to reservations about home education. (Children may be missing out socially when they don't have to adapt to other children, and the lack of a routine can limit academic progress in those subjects that need to be approached systematically.)

## 2 Beyond the classroom

**Elaine and Roy Fullwood from Yorkshire**
**Children: Alex, Anna, Miriam, John, Luke – all taught at home.**

Elaine and Roy Fullwood had no intention of educating their children themselves until things went badly wrong at school. When a new headteacher with what Roy describes as 'trendy educational methods' took over at the local school, the work of their eldest child, Alex, plummeted and she became bored and aimless. Worried, Elaine and Roy went to discuss Alex with the headteacher, who dismissed her as a slow child.

They asked for an assessment from an educational psychologist – it showed Alex to have a well-above-average IQ. Despite a meeting with the Deputy Director of Education and other concerned parents nothing changed. At this point Elaine and Roy decided to take Alex, aged 8, and Anna, aged 6, away from school. 'It was on a trial basis originally', says Elaine. 'We just wanted to catch up on lost ground and get the basics over to them to start with.'

A year later Elaine was concerned about whether the girls were making enough progress. 'They were enjoying themselves but only working for a few hours a day and I wondered if they'd be better back at school. For advice, we took the girls' work to the heads of the schools where they would have been pupils. In both cases they were well ahead for their age. This reassured us that we were on the right track.'

Alex and Anna have now been at home for two years and are joined in their morning studies by six-year-old sister Miriam, who has never been to school. Four-year-old John occasionally joins in and 14-month-old Luke is often crawling nearby.

How does Elaine cope with five children under her feet day in and day out? 'There are times', she admits, 'when I feel I have a dirty house full of dirty children. If it gets me down then we all stop and clear up. I'm interested in working with them and they're happy – that makes it worthwhile.'

The children usually work for about 3 hours in the morning. Although they have a large say in what they do, subjects like maths and spelling, for which they have a weekly test, are structured. Afternoons are for playing, following their own interests or going out. Elaine has bought some text books and the children use the library for projects. Having no teacher-training, it was necessary to plan work very carefully in the early days but now, Elaine finds that it's become second nature.

Roy trained as a teacher but has never actually taught. Now he spends as much time with the family as his job allows.

Roy and Elaine make it quite clear that being at home is not a soft option. They put a lot of emphasis on responsibility and self-discipline. For example, Alex and Anna are in charge of the animals – hens, a horse and a goat – which they have to feed and clean out in all weathers. No one stands over them but they know that if they shirk their responsibilities then the animals will go. 'Discipline,' says Roy, 'is helping children to see what's right and to enjoy doing it'. The children themselves will decide whether they want to do 'O' and 'A' levels. Roy and Elaine certainly won't try to influence them.

The Fullwoods are clearly a close-knit family but they also have many friends. Although the children may never go to school again there is no anti-school feeling in the home. 'The door's open. If ever they want to go they can.'

**Victor and Sally Wilkins from Leicestershire**
**Children: two elder children being educated at home, two younger ones pre-school age.**

Nine months ago Victor and Sally Wilkins withdrew their two elder children from a small country school which, Sally says, 'had nice teachers and a friendly atmosphere.' It was not this particular school but a belief that all schools have a damaging effect that prompted the withdrawal of Seth, aged nine, and Esther, aged six and a half.

Sally feels that schools rob children of the personal responsibility for use of their own time. She also thinks that children are exposed to conflicting opinions and examples which confuse them. The influence of television also worries her.

But the reasons are by no means all negative. She believes passionately that children need to develop educationally and emotionally at their own pace in a caring and loving environment. Both Victor and Sally have a strong sense of the family unit and the important role of parents in guiding by example.

A typical education-at-home day begins with a few domestic chores. These done, Seth and Esther settle down at the table in their cosy, jumbled kitchen. The children usually choose what they do, though Sally encourages regular practice in the three Rs. Seth selects three or four subjects from a list which includes story-writing, English work books, reading, a topic of each child's own choice, maths games and puzzles, science, history, PE (press-ups or running several lengths of the block of cottages) and music (practising the recorder). The children keep a daily diary of their work and Sally corrects the balance if on occasions she feels something is being neglected. She also encourages them to finish whatever they begin. After a couple of hours it's time for refreshments and a story. The afternoons, when Victor is sometimes free to join them, are usually spent out of doors – gardening, or enjoying an outing or nature walk. During the evenings and at weekends the children often attend local clubs.

Victor admits that he was a bit uneasy about home education when Sally first talked about it. 'I suppose I thought that other people might think we were being irresponsible. In fact it's quite the opposite. I was also worried that it would be too much for Sally to take on. What clinched it for me was going to a conference organised by Education Otherwise and finding that even academics were disillusioned with the school system. After that we decided to give it a year's trial. Now that I see how happy the children are I wouldn't dream of sending them back to school – unless they

## Education

asked to go.'
Like the Fullwoods, these children will also make their own decision about 'O' and 'A' levels and further education.
In the early days, Sally had occasional doubts: 'There were moments,' she says, 'when I thought, "Help, what have we done?" I was sure that home education was right for the children, but there were times when I wondered if I could handle it all. I felt a bit insecure about breaking away from a familiar routine, but as we got established and the children flourished, so my confidence increased.
'Of course it's quite physically tiring – and noisy – having four children ever-present, and we can only survive by going to bed early to re-charge for the next day.
'That doesn't leave a lot of time to follow my own interests, but those can come later. If you really believe in something then you just learn to live with the difficulties. In fact, the problems are insignificant beside the excitement and satisfaction of seeing four human beings developing at their own pace and growing into independence.
'In these few months I've seen the children become happier and more creative and the whole family atmosphere has become more harmonious. Fortunately I like and enjoy my children – you can't do this job if you don't.'

### Nicholas Everdell from Cambridgeshire: studying for 'A' levels at home.

Nicholas has 7 'O' levels, all grade 'A' and a conditional place for Cambridge University. Nothing too unusual about that, except that Nicholas left school just before his 13th birthday and studied for his 'O' levels at home by correspondence course.
School life became unbearable for Nicholas when, because of his academic progress, he was put into a higher class. 'I was treated like the runt of the class,' he says: 'There was a lot of verbal abuse and I was isolated and terribly unhappy. School seemed the next thing to a prison camp – I just didn't feel it was my life.' His mother, Janet, was concerned about the effect on his health. 'He seemed very depressed, unable to sleep and his appetite disappeared.'
Janet suggested that Nicholas leave school and study at home. 'I spent a couple of weeks thinking it over,' Nicholas says. 'It seemed such a big step but I was so miserable that there didn't seem to be much choice.' Although she felt that leaving school was the only way to regain Nicholas' health and happiness, Janet admits that she had doubts. 'Would he be too lonely? Would he be able to settle down on his own? Would he later become too different? – he was already different because he wouldn't play around like the others. My husband wasn't convinced it was the right thing to do and I was really going on instinct.
'I felt a bit strange and cut off', Nicholas admits, 'but I soon found I could do so many things that I'd never had time for previously. I learned about electronics and made a radio, took up photography and learned to develop and print my own films.' Nicholas also pursued his interest in astronomy and joined the Astronomy Society in Cambridge.
Although physics, chemistry and biology were among his 'O' level subjects, he didn't particularly miss laboratory facilities. He improvised on the kitchen table. His parents were unable to help academically but listened to his problems and talked them over.
To study for his 'A' levels Nicholas registered at the local technical college, but he still does most of his work at home. 'Coming back into the system was a bit of a shock,' says Nicholas, 'but not an unpleasant one. I found it a bit hard to communicate at first, but I got over it fairly quickly and even became Chairman of the Students' Society.'
Nicholas wouldn't have missed his learning years at home. He believes that the respite from bullying has enabled him to become more confident and at ease with the world. Above all he appreciates having read and learned more than would have been possible at school, where 'so much time is lost moving from class to class and hanging around.'
How does Janet feel about things now? 'I've been amazed by the enormous potential that children have for learning on their own. If I had the benefit of hindsight,' she said emphatically, 'none of my children would have gone to school.'

*take . . . into their own hands*: do it themselves
*write off*: do without
*monitor*: check
*in due course*: at some time later
*crawling*: moving on hands and knees
*close knit*: intimate
*concerned*: worried
*got over it*: recovered

## 2 Beyond the classroom

# What degree of success can you expect from the Open University?

The short answer is "a lot." BA degrees from the Open University carry the same value as those from "Oxbridge" or any redbrick university. The main difference is that you learn at home, not at a full-time college.

Once you've earned your degree, you'll be much more valuable to an employer, either current or future. Plus, of course, you'll have the self-satisfaction of having reached a personal goal and you will probably have discovered new things about yourself.

**Q: What does studying for an OU degree mean?**

**A:** To be honest, it means a great deal of hard work. But don't be discouraged. Since it was started, some fifteen years ago, over 65,000 people have been awarded degrees. The subjects covered range through arts, social sciences, education, mathematics, science and technology.

The University genuinely is open to everyone. It doesn't matter what your background is, nor do you need 'O' or 'A' levels.

Everyone is equal at the OU and previous academic achievements are not necessary. All we ask is that you are 21 years or older and that you live in the UK.

**Q: "Distance Teaching" – how does it work?**

**A:** The majority of your course will come through the post – specially commissioned, high quality teaching material to help you study at home. There are TV and radio broadcasts and home experiment kits for some of the subjects.

At the OU, we've gained a worldwide reputation for our advanced "distance teaching" methods. It's experience which we know will be of great value to you.

**Q: Would I ever have personal tuition?**

**A:** Of course you would. There are over 5,000 part-time tutors around the country and one will be assigned to you.

The OU also has local study centres and a national network of fully staffed regional offices. Some courses even have a one-week residential summer school.

**Q: How many? How long? How much?**

**A:** In all, there are 138 courses from which you can choose, each one running from February until November. On passing you are awarded a 'credit'. To achieve your degree you must gain six credits in all.

The fees vary but all are subsidised. There are easy payment methods available and grants could be provided for those on a low income or unemployed.

**Q: How successful have others been?**

**A:** People study for different reasons. Some purely for the broadening of their knowledge or the developing of their minds; others because they wish to further their career. More than half of our graduates have reported a significant career benefit since gaining their degree.

And practically everyone acknowledges the new confidence and awareness the OU study experience has given them. You could start to share that reward this year. Places on the courses are limited and it's essentially first come, first served.

So send the coupon for the FREE Guide for Applicants to: The Open University, PO Box 48, Milton Keynes, MK7 6AB.

**Q: How do I start?**

**A:** This coupon is your first step. Complete and return it and we'll send you the FREE Open University Guide for Applicants.

Name (Mr/Mrs/Ms): _____
(PLEASE PRINT)
Address _____

_____ Postcode _____

**THE OPEN UNIVERSITY**
PO Box 48, Milton Keynes, MK7 6AB

SU13

---

*Oxbridge*: Oxford and Cambridge universities
*redbrick*: older British universities

*commissioned*: gave someone the authority to do something

*Education*

# Art of learning at leisure

PEOPLE living in East Anglia have been busy getting themselves educated — as the number of Open University graduates shows. More than 500 have stuck to the course and come through with Bachelor of Arts degrees — accounting for more than 10 per cent of those awarded nationwide. The graduates come from all walks of life, and nearly half are women. The "News" has taken a look at just a few. They are a grandmother, a vicar, and a former model.

WHITTLESFORD grandmother Mrs Loise O'Shea has been awarded an Open University degree — 50 years after she gave up school.

Mrs O'Shea, 77, put down her text books in the Roaring Twenties. She picked them up again eight years ago because she had "time on her hands."

"It was a challenge to me because I'm not academic by nature. As a schoolgirl I did the minimum amount of work and just scraped by. I left at the earliest possible opportunity — at 17," she said.

But when her husband died Mrs O'Shea, of Royston Road, decided she had to do something with her time.

Mrs O'Shea believes she may have been the oldest Open University Degree student on the Arts Course. "I was always a joke gran or great aunt," she said.

"It has been very fruitful and enjoyable. I was very tempted to drop out at times because it was quite a bind. I had to be very strict with myself — I usually worked every morning," she said.

Mrs O'Shea is now enjoying her new-found leisure time — without homework — but says she may consider going for an honours degree in a few years' time: "I'll see how I feel between my 80s and 90s."

For former model Mrs Gail Homer, working towards a bachelor of arts degree with the Open University was more than just an interest; it kept her wits together during a personal crisis.

Her son, Anton, was just a few months old, and her husband had left her. Studying for her Humanities degree was a welcome diversion.

Now seven years after she started the history of art course she has successfully completed television, radio and correspondence studies and is to be presented with her certificate at Cambridge in July.

Mrs Homer, now 35, started the course after a friend did so. She studied Greek and Roman works up to the Renaissance period.

## Brood

"I attended school in Cambridge and summer school. My husband left me, and the Open University was quite a Godsend, because it was discipline that I needed.

"I had to do something by a certain time, so I couldn't brood a lot. Looking back on it I wonder how I did it."

When she was at school Mrs Homer, of Thaxted, was not top of the class — although she said she managed to get good examination grades and she earned a diploma in modelling.

That put her into the realms of television work, and she was often seen on the screen in commercials or as an extra for Independent Television programmes.

## Research

"At school my grades were okay but I was a rebel. I went into modelling because I was fascinated with it, and my mother did the same.

"I have learnt a lot, and things have been opened up to me — this has given me more interest.

"Now I would love to go into some sort of research or I would like to write, not necessarily about art history, but fiction or something connected with history."

The vicar of Wickhambrook, near Haverhill, the Rev Bill Davis, took up studying sociology because he wanted something more demanding than just a hobby.

The 66-year-old clergyman spent four years studing for his BA, and has just received confirmation that he has been successful.

"I took it up as something to keep my mind occupied. I wanted something with more discipline than just taking up a hobby," he said.

Mr Davis, who has been vicar for 13 years, is also stand-by chaplain at the nearby Highpoint prison. He used to be the prison chaplain, but there is now a full-time chaplain, and Mr Davis acts as his deputy.

"It has been a very valuable exercise, and I enjoyed the studies tremendously," he added.

---

*scraped by*: just succeeded
*drop out*: stop
*a bind*: (colloquial) a restriction
*kept her wits together*: helped her to continue thinking normally
*brood*: think about (her) troubles
*chaplain*: a priest (usually in a chapel) attached to an institution

## 2 Beyond the classroom

# Polishing up those old school skills

IS it several years since you did any studying, or perhaps you have never studied?

The popular Return to Study course at Cambridgeshire College of Arts and Technology is designed for mature students who feel they missed out on education, or feel their study skills are rather rusty.

It is a basic course which helps you to recognise and develop those skills necessary to students who eventually would like to take A levels, or a degree, or just want to start to study again for their own interest.

The course is friendly and relaxed in atmosphere, and you will gradually be asked to produce small pieces of written work.

All the essential study skills are covered: note-taking, group discussion work, organising your time, and essay writing.

The pace of the class moves according to the needs and demands of the students and there is plenty of time and space to discuss problems and questions about how, when and why to study? and how to fit studying in around a busy life.

You will soon find that you gain confidence in your own abilities, begin to develop skills necessary for further study, and also begin to define what course will suit you.

The course caters for your individual study needs, and gives information and guidance to decide what future course best suits you.

The course runs on Tuesday afternoon 1-3 pm for ten weeks starting on September 27, enrolling either then or the first week of term — September 19th and 20th. It also runs from January to April.

The cost is £24 although, if numbers are above the minimum, people on supplementary benefit could pay a reduced fee.

Contact Gina Wisker at the Cambridgeshire College of Arts and Technology, telephone: 63271 and the secretaries will provide the necessary information.

## Qualified success

MOST people have heard of O and A Levels. Even if you left school fifty years ago, you can study for a G.C.E. O or A Level in a wide range of subjects. Community colleges and village colleges offer some O and A Levels for adults on a part-time basis, day and evening.

Adults can do O levels at the Cambridge College of Further Education and A levels at the Cambridgeshire College of Arts and Technology, full or part-time, day or evening. C.S.Es., similar to O levels (a grade one pass is equivalent to an O level) are not easy to take outside a school, though it is possible.

Instead, however, there are many other qualifications which may be more use.

The R.S.A. and the City and Guilds offer a range of clerical and technical examinations at all levels for people who want to improve their employment prospects.

The Business Education Council and the Technical Education Council (B.E.C. and T.E.C.) also offer vocational qualifications.

Some of these involve day-release studies, that is, you have to have a job before you can start your studies.

Ask at C.C.F.E., for further details.

For information about all qualifications, including H.N.D., degrees and beyond, ask at the Job Centre Education Desk, or visit the Careers Library in County Hall, Hobson Street.

*rusty*: out of practice / forgotten
*pace*: speed
'O' and 'A' levels: British public examinations (usually taken at the end of secondary school)

## The fast way to speak French

...or any of 28 languages.

With the Linguaphone Method, you can learn a second language in much the same way you learnt English.

Simply by listening, understanding and then speaking.

It's the fastest, most natural way to learn. In fact, you could be speaking your new language within three months.

So why not prove it for yourself.

Just send for our free demonstration lesson on cassette or record now. The sooner you do, the sooner you'll be speaking your second language.

### Linguaphone
The first word in languages.

FREE INTRODUCTORY RECORD OR CASSETTE
Please send me my free introductory pack on record ☐ / cassette ☐, complete with full colour brochure.
I am interested in learning French ☐, German ☐, Spanish ☐, other language (please state) _____
I WOULD LIKE INFORMATION ON THE NEW FRENCH VIDEO PROGRAMME ☐
Mr/Mrs/Miss _____
BLOCK CAPS                                     AGE IF UNDER 18
Address _____

Send to: Linguaphone Institute Ltd, Dept DA33, 209 Regent Street, London W1R 8AU.

83

*Education*

ENGINEERS / SCIENTISTS — MANAGERS / TECHNOLOGISTS

"IMPROVE YOUR MANAGEMENT POTENTIAL!"
with
**THE CERTIFIED DIPLOMA IN ACCOUNTING AND FINANCE**
For free brochure contact
THE ASSOCIATION OF CERTIFIED ACCOUNTANTS (NRY)
PO Box 244, London WC2A 3EE
Tel: 01-242 6855, Ext 251 / 2

Evening courses in preparation for this qualification are to start at the following college in September:
**Cambridge College of Arts and Technology**

---

**LEARN TO TEACH ENGLISH TO FOREIGNERS**
RSA Prep Cert TEFL Course
(PART-TIME)
no experience needed
For details contact
BELL SCHOOL OF LANGUAGES
Tel: 247242

---

**Cambridge Computer College**

Learn computing using the BBC Micro.
Intensive courses for beginners in BASIC and Word Processing

Each student will have exclusive use of a BBC Micro for the duration of the course. Only a limited number of places are therefore available.
For details write to:
Cambridge Computer College
3 Newnham Walk
Cambridge CB3 9HQ
Tel: (0223) 350819

---

St Mark's Community Centre
**NEWNHAM**
Cambridge

Offers a wide range of activities for adults, children and young people
These include:

| DAY | EVENING |
|---|---|
| Aerobics | Bird Watching |
| Dressmaking and Tailoring | Depressives Anonymous |
| Dressmaking for Teenagers | Keep Fit for Men |
| French Conversation | Ladies' Keep Fit |
| German Conversation | Painting and Drawing |
| Jazz Ballet | Speaking in Public |
| Keep Fit (Over 60s) | Tales from Six Continents |
| Painting and Drawing | The Visitor in Cambridge |
| Typewriting | Yoga (Mixed Group) |
| Writers and Writing | Youth Club |

Programmes from the Central Library, Lion Yard or the Hon Sec at 67 Grantchester Meadows (stamped env.)

---

# VOTE FOR EDUCATION

## EDUCATION FOR WHOM?

- An estimated 6 million adults in this country lack basic reading and writing skills.
- Last year over 40% of young people received no education and training after 16.
- Less than 13% entered higher education—fewer than in any other major industrialised country.
- It costs less to send a young person to college than to keep him or her on the dole.
- Many groups don't get a fair deal from the current system—working people, women, the disabled and the ethnic community.

## WHAT'S BEEN HAPPENING?

- Many large educational institutions are now faced with severe contraction, some with total closure.
- Many fully qualified potential students are being turned away from college.
- Grants for study are being reduced and have disappeared altogether for many courses. Any loans system would prevent many more from continuing education after school.
- 60,000 higher education places will be lost from our colleges, polytechnics and universities.
- As our schools are starved of resources, the government plans to end teacher education places at 10 colleges.

## STAND UP FOR EDUCATION

- As we approach the 21st century we urgently need an expansion of education as a crucial investment in the future.
- Education, research and training are not a luxury, they are essential to meet the challenge of unemployment and new technology.
- We all pay for education, and everyone should have the opportunity to benefit from it to help them participate in our highly complex society.

Published by: ASTMS, AUT, NALGO, NATFHE, NUPE, NUS in conjunction with the Education Alliance.

---

*on the dole*: receiving an unemployment allowance
*fair deal*: just treatment
*disabled*: not able to do something, physically or mentally
*ethnic*: from a different culture
*contraction*: getting smaller
*grants*: sums of money given by the government or another organisation
*resources*: materials or supplies

## 2 Beyond the classroom

## ☞ A.P.?

The aim of this Alternative Prospectus is to give you, the prospective student, some idea of what life at University is like, and in particular, what you can expect from any of the courses offered at Birmingham. It is important to use this A.P. in conjunction with the official prospectus and other departmental literature to gain more factual information about course structure etc. What we are seeking to do is partly give a students-eye view of the courses, but also to "fill in the gaps" in the official view - the realities of a course are often very different. All the submissions are written by students on the courses, but as far as possible, they have been checked by staff/student committees, so any opinions should be general rather than personal ones.

One of the greatest problems facing new students is the sheer multiplicity of choices they have to make: which course, which university, where to live, what activities to get involved in, even whether to go to university at all. These are choices you must make (not let someone else make for you), but make sure you know the reasons behind your decisions - too many students come to university with no clear ideas for their futures, and end up realising they've chosen the wrong course.

Finally, try not to hold any illusions about student life. It can be great fun and very fulfilling, but also it can be very hard, and some people find they just do not enjoy it at all. We hope you will fare better! Make the right choices and it could be an experience from which you will never really recover ...........

## THE GUILD

The focal point of the University for students is the Guild, or at least its physical manifestation, the Union Building. The many and varied facilities in it provide a centre for social and other activities of all kinds.

Many societies exist within the Guild for ethnic, political and departmental groups, as well as for such diverse activities as ballroom dancing, CND, hang-gliding, and eating jelly-babies (to name but a few). By getting involved in such societies, you get the chance to experience activities too expensive or difficult to be attempted alone!

What follows is a brief description of just some of the services provided in the Union:

## GAMES ⊕
All the latest pinball, electronic and table games are to be found in the Games Room, which is on the ground floor next to Founders.

## SNOOKER ✓✓
We have an excellent Snooker Room, down by the Cellar Bar, with eight full-sized tables. Open every day until 10.30 p.m.

## niteline ✯

Unfortunately, life at University is not always the fun-filled action-packed experience you were promised, and everyone, at times, runs into problems. Niteline is a confidential telephone service run by students, to call and talk to every night between 6 p.m. and 8 a.m. We provide a sympathetic ear for anyone wishing to talk over problems of loneliness, depression, overwork, etc. We also offer a very comprehensive information service, and have access to information on almost anything - from such mundane things as the time of the last bus home to your digs, what entertainments are available on a certain night, to whom to contact if you want to be put in touch with professional help - e.g. pregnancy advice.

General Meetings are held to discuss very important issues. Above, 850 people discuss whether or not to hold a rent strike against proposed Hall fee increases.

Education

## ⟨ TRAVEL OFFICE ⟩

This is situated near the Coffee Bar and provides a comprehensive range of travel services at competitive rates, including bus passes, rail cards, and ISIC cards. It also books flights to any destination in the world and trains to Europe.

## *Welfare*

Welfare deals with Student problems on almost every subject - everything from traintimes, supplementary benefit, to accommodation, arrest and eviction. Even if Welfare is stumped for an answer there is always someone or somewhere else you can be referred for the information. A Welfare Card is produced, which gives some very basic information and sources of help. The Welfare Office is on the ground floor of the Union.

## CATERING

The Union provides excellent cuisine (well, it's cheap!) from its 5 catering outlets - from 8.30 a.m. to 9 p.m. We aim to cater for all ranges of tastes and appetites, serving such delights as main meals, steaks, grills, pizzas, salads, fresh rolls, pasties and pies - all served with chips (if desired!).

Hopefully, by the summer our new "McDochertys" will be open (i.e. our own version of a McDonalds) - which will be Brum's answer to the American Hamburger.

## STALLS

During the year, various traders are invited to the Union to sell their goods at bargain prices e.g. there is a weekly record stall, plus others selling sports goods, watches, jeans etc.

## BATHS!

These are available free, whenever the building is open, in the Basement area. (Just leave your Guild card - whilst you borrow a plug!)

## BARS ☆

The Union has three bars. The Cellar bar, which sells real ale and hosts the infamous Cellar bar discos and Cellar bar bands.

The Mermaid bar, which adjoins the Mixed Lounge (which has a colour television) and is very popular.

Founders bar hosts the (always packed) and very popular _free_ Events discos on Fridays, whilst during the week it is available for societies to hire out for parties etc.

## SHOP

The Union Shop has recently been expanded and now offers a wide range of groceries; frozen goods, tinned food, toiletries, pharmaceuticals, cigarettes and a large variety of stationary, all at unbeatable prices. It also sells sweatshirts, T-shirts and bags sporting the University crest.

## SILKSCREENING

We have a silkscreening service, where posters, T-shirts etc. can be printed and also a Reprographics Dept. for posters, invitations, tickets, leaflets etc.

## *Accommodation*

Having made the choice to come to Birmingham, you have to decide where to live. The choice is basically between university accommodation (whether halls of residence or self-catering flats) and "living out" in houses, flats or lodgings. Birmingham guarantees all its first-time students a place in university residence, so the choice is yours! Here is some indication what to expect from each:

The advantages of hall are numerous - friendly atmospheres, many social functions such as formal (dress) meals, bars, TV's, telephones, laundries, baths, showers, hot water, warm rooms and so on. If you are prepared to put a lot into hall, then you will get a lot out. However, hall life does not please everyone. Whilst the food isn't wonderful unless you are really faddy, it is certainly tolerable. Those who don't like hall tend to be those who are most active outside it, and consequently find the meal times restrictive. Also, many people don't like being tied down to weekend lunch because they've paid for it, and those who can't get up before 9 o'clock moan about breakfast too!

Most halls of residence are on the Vale site, a landscaped setting with a lake infested with ducks and geese, all about ten minutes walk from the university. If you decide on a place in hall, bring plenty of posters and cups and enjoy yourself!

The main advantage of self-catering flats over halls is greater freedom. At the cost of having to put some effort into looking after yourself, and losing some of the ready - made social life of halls, you gain the freedom of being your own master, as well as living much more cheaply. There is the disadvantage of not having any choice of flatmates when you first arrive, but if you're a reasonably sociable person, you should have no problems making friends. A great advantage is not (usually) having to clear out your room for the two short vacations, and generally you are much less restricted by rules and regulations than in hall. If you feel that you can cope with the disadvantages, self-catering accommodation can be a lot of fun.

Living out is not advisable to first time students, unless living with parents, friends, husband/wife etc., as it can be very lonely. However, many students do choose to move out for their 2nd and/or 3rd years, once they've made friends they can get on with. Accommodation in Birmingham is not generally as difficult to get as in other cities, but nevertheless can often be sub-standard, overpriced and scarce. If intending to rent non-university accommodation, be very cautious - housing sharks do exist, so be warned! Much of the available accommodation near the university is passed on from one group of students to another, so you can get an inside view from the existing tenants! Usually, if you look hard enough (and early enough!), good, low-priced accommodation can be found, not too far away from campus.

## HALLS

### Lake/Wydd

To reach this particular haven of rest (oh ..... and study!) one must tackle traffic and geese, not to mention the hoards of students that seem to loiter around the Vale Halls of Residence.

But once one has surmounted these difficulties the Lake/Wydd 'holiday complex' is really quite nice (some would say the best!). These two halls, one for men, one for women combine the advantages of having the privacy of a single sex hall and the 'fun and games' (well .... life's what you make it) of a combined hall. We share such luxuries as a launderette, T.V. lounge and that most sociable of places.... the dining hall (more appropriately the mess room!) Oh but how could I forget the bar? People flock from miles around to go there, and then there's the J.C.R. (Junior Common Room - the place where the future drop-outs lounge) where you can find table football, pinball and electronic machines as well as a pool table and a juke box.

---

*prospectus*: information (provided in advance) about something
CND: Campaign for Nuclear Disarmament
*hang gliding*: a kind of sport
*jelly babies*: a kind of sweet

*Brum*: (colloquial) Birmingham
*faddy*: very critical about what one eats
*being your own master*: doing what you want
*housing sharks*: people who try to make a lot of money by renting houses

# 2.1

1 Look at the title of the article on page 78. Discuss in pairs what 'alternative education' might mean, and how it might work.

2 Read the first page of the article and answer the following questions.

   a) What does the law say about going to school?
   b) What are the practical problems involved in teaching children at home?
   c) What is an LEA?
   d) What, in general, is the attitude of the LEAs to educating children at home?

*Education*

    e) What are some of the ways in which an LEA may supervise education at home?
    f) What different reasons are there for wanting to educate children at home?
    g) What do you have to do when you take a child away from a state school?

3 What views do *you* have on this system of education? Before reading the interviews which follow, make a note of the potential advantages and disadvantages so that you can compare them with what the families say.

4 *Either* read all three of the interviews and fill in the chart below in note form *or* work in threes and each read just one of the interviews; then find out the rest of the information from your two partners by interviewing them.

|   |   | *The Fullwoods* | *The Wilkins* | *Nicholas Everdell* |
|---|---|---|---|---|
| a) | Reasons for removing child/children from school | | | |
| b) | How long he/they has/have been educated at home | | | |
| c) | Typical working day for the child/children | | | |
| d) | Any problems which the parents have had | | | |
| e) | Advantages of this form of education for the child/children | | | |

5 Find words or expressions in the text which are similar in meaning to the following.

*The Fullwoods*
a) modern, fashionable
b) fell suddenly
c) intelligence level
d) do what had not been done before
e) in front
f) going in the right direction
g) takes part
h) an alternative involving only a little work
i) avoid/neglect

*The Wilkins*
a) took away
b) was the reason for
c) small jobs
d) unsure/worried
e) decided
f) did well

*Nicholas Everdell*
a) inferior person
b) considering something
c) isolated
d) short break
e) using strength or power to overcome someone weaker
f) wasting time
g) looking back from the present time (into the past)

## 2.2

1 Look at page 81 and, with a partner, try to predict what the 'Open University' might be.

2 Read the advertisement to find the following information. Discuss your answers in pairs, giving evidence from the text.
   a) Does an Open University degree have the same value as any other university degree?
   b) What are the differences between studying with the Open University and an ordinary university?
   c) What qualifications do you need to join the Open University?
   d) Who is it closed to?
   e) What helps you to study?
   f) Do you always work alone?
   g) How much choice of course do you have?
   h) What do you have to do to pass your degree?
   i) Do you have to pay?
   j) How do you find out more information about the Open University?

*Education*

## 2.3

Read the article on page 82 and fill in this chart in note form. Discuss your answers with a partner.

|  | Mrs O'Shea | Mrs Homer | Rev. Davis |
|---|---|---|---|
| a) Why did he/she choose to do an OU course? | | | |
| b) Age | | | |
| c) Job | | | |
| d) Views on the course | | | |
| e) Subject(s) studied | | | |
| f) Future plans | | | |

## 2.4

1  Look at pages 83–4, and find the following information as quickly as you can. Make notes and compare them with a partner.

    a) Where can you study for 'O' levels, if you have left school?
    b) What are CSEs?
    c) What course can you take to help you to study?

2 *Beyond the classroom*

    d) Where can beginners learn about computers?
    e) What method will teach you to speak French fast?
    f) Where can you go if you want to do birdwatching or yoga?
    g) What course can you do if you want to teach English to foreigners?
    h) What exams are useful for clerical and technical work?
    i) Where can you find more information about qualifications?

2 In pairs or groups, discuss the opportunities for continuing your education once you have left school, both in Britain and in your own country. Report back to the class. Then, individually, write a short summary, in the form of a newspaper report.

## 2.5

1 On pages 85–6 you will find some information about the University of Birmingham Guild. Look through these pages quickly and make a note of where you would go or what you would do if:
    a) you wanted a rail card;
    b) you were having personal problems and wanted to talk them over;
    c) you wanted to drink real ale;
    d) you wanted to go to a free disco on a Friday night;
    e) you had problems with the police;
    f) you wanted to play table games.

2 Work in pairs. Interview each other about aspects of university life in your own country/countries, and how it differs from the UK. (You may need to make a list of questions to ask your teacher.) Focus on aspects such as:
    a) entrance requirements
    b) subjects offered, how many studied
    c) financial aspects
    d) social life
    e) facilities for books, etc.
    f) how easy/difficult it is to find a job if you have had a university education.

3 Write up your findings in the form of a brief paragraph, highlighting the differences between the different countries.

*Education*

## 2.6

1 On pages 86–7 you will find some information about accommodation for young people going to university in Britain. Read the extract quickly and make notes of the advantages and disadvantages of the various kinds of accommodation.

|    |                                          | *Advantages* | *Disadvantages* |
|----|------------------------------------------|--------------|-----------------|
| a) | Halls of residence                       |              |                 |
| b) | Self-catering flats owned by the university |              |                 |
| c) | Flats/lodgings etc.                      |              |                 |

2 In groups, discuss your experiences of living in various types of accommodation and discuss the advantages and disadvantages of the British idea of moving away from home to live in a different university town. Report your views back to the class.

# Roleplay

For groups of any number of students.

## *Roles*

Schoolchildren (aged 11 upwards)   Parents   Teachers

## *Situation*

There has been growing discontent about the quality of secondary education in state schools. Because of this, many parents have felt a need to educate their children privately, or even educate them at home.

The local education authority of a new town in the north-east of England, Compton, has decided to set up a committee composed of representatives of each of the following groups: the children who attend state secondary schools at the moment, their parents, and the teachers at these schools. The aim of the committee is to decide on the characteristics of a 'model' school. The new secondary school which is due to open in Compton next year will be run in accordance with the guidelines drawn up by the committee.

Inevitably, there will be disagreement among members of the committee and some kind of compromise will have to be reached.

## *Preliminary tasks*

The class will be divided into three groups (schoolchildren, parents and teachers). Within each group, individuals will be given time to decide what they feel would comprise an 'ideal' school, and what they definitely do *not* want to see in a school. Opinions must be backed up by reasons.

It may be helpful to look through texts in this unit, and the teacher is available for consultation, but it is important to remember what role you are playing, and consequently what reaction you might have.

It might be helpful to focus on the following areas:
a) subjects to be taught
b) aspects of teaching such as class size, length of lessons, kind of teachers, methods, exam-oriented teaching etc.
c) discipline, rules, punishment
d) school buildings, facilities etc.
e) meals, uniforms etc.
f) parental involvement
g) out of school activities, clubs, trips, sport etc.

After time for initial thought, members of each group should decide among themselves what they are going to insist on, and what they don't want. The teacher will set a time limit for this. A secretary should be appointed, to take notes on the discussion and to act as a representative who will report back to the other groups.

## *Procedure*

1 A chairperson should be elected to keep order and to make sure the representative from each group has an opportunity to express their point of view within the time given. A secretary should take notes of decisions reached.

2 The representative from each group will report back to the committee the views of the group on the topics discussed (above).

3 An open discussion will follow, and a compromise should be reached within a time limit. If this proves impossible, the groups can meet again to discuss what concessions they are prepared to make.

4 The chairperson will give a summary of decisions reached.

## *Follow up*

Make a summary of the decisions reached at the meeting to report in the local paper.

# Leisure

Look through the texts in both sections of this unit and try to answer the following questions *as quickly as possible*. Remember that you are not looking for any other information, so it is not necessary to study the texts in detail.

1. Why can't a football fan go to his girlfriend's brother's wedding?
2. Who wrote a comedy about Rita, and which company acts it?
3. What film is on at the Screen on the Hill?
4. How many main television channels are there?
5. How old do you have to be to learn to play cricket at Linton Village College, and how much does each lesson cost?
6. What is on at the London Coliseum?
7. Where did British football supporters cause so much trouble?
8. What was Toyah Wilcox interviewed about?
9. What is the name of a book investigating which sports make you physically fit?
10. How old do you have to be to see the film *Lianna*?

Check your answers with a partner before looking at the key on page 155.

Now look at the exercises on pages 103–6 before reading the texts in section 1 more carefully.

# 1 The world of entertainment

*"I only tear the tickets—so you can imagine . . ."*

**Magistrates act to keep theatres open**

**Queen sees Fonteyn take 10 curtains**

STAR'S BROKEN
LEG HITS
BOX OFFICE

Leisure

## English National Opera

### The Barber of Seville
Rossini

Sept 10/15/17/23/29 at 7.30

"effervescent comedy returns in fine fettle"
*D. Mail*

"lively... hilarious performance"
*D. Telegraph*

"huge fun... highly enjoyable evening... the audience laughed so long and so often"
*Financial Times*

**Tonight at 7.30 Some good seats available**

**London Coliseum**
St. Martins Lane
(by Trafalgar Square)

Box Office 01-836 3161
CC Bookings 01-240 5258
**GENERAL STANDBY** — £5.00 from 6.45 pm

---

## Lyric Theatre Hammersmith
King St. W6  01-741 2311

5 August – 18 September

### She Stoops to Conquer
a comedy by Oliver Goldsmith
director William Gaskill

*She Stoops to Conquer* is the best loved and most English of all Eighteenth Century comedies, one that has held the stage more persistently than almost any other since Shakespeare.

William Gaskill returns to the field of Eighteenth Century comedy, one he dominated with such productions as *The Recruiting Officer* and *The Beaux Stratagem* for the National Theatre.

**See this show for only £3.50 by booking your tickets before 10 August** (Mondays to Thursdays subject to availability).
Normal seat prices £6.00, £5.00, £4.00

---

## 'THE LAUGHTER NEVER STOPS!'
*Sunday Mirror*

### PASS THE BUTLER
**GLOBE THEATRE** 01-437 1592

---

### Magic Circle Easter Show
**APRIL 12-17**
International Acts In Great Family Show

**WESTMINSTER THEATRE**
Book Now 01-834 0283
Mat & Ev Performances

---

## WIGMORE HALL

### SIBELIUS SONGS

Four recitals to mark the 25th anniversary of Sibelius's death

**Friday, September 17, 1982**
TARU VALJAKKA
soprano
Gustav Djupsjöbacka, piano
Sibelius, Berg, Rautavaara

**Tuesday, November 23, 1982**
JORMA HYNNINEN
baritone
Ralf Gothoni, piano
Sibelius, Wolf, Vaughan Williams, O. Merikanto

**Tuesday, April 26, 1983**
HELENA DOSE
soprano
Geoffrey Parsons, piano
Sibelius, Strauss, Stenhammar

**Tuesday, May 17, 1983**
TOM KRAUSE
baritone
Irwin Gage, piano
Sibelius, Ravel, Duparc

Subscription booking opens August 2
**FOUR CONCERTS FOR THE PRICE OF THREE**
£10, £9, £7.50, £5.

Please send s.a.e. and cheque made payable to Jeremy Parsons Management: 19 Hyde Park Square, London W2 2JR.

---

25th Anniversary Season

Hetherington Seelig in association with the Greater London Council presents

### Les grands Ballets Canadiens

with the
**ROYAL PHILHARMONIC ORCHESTRA**
17-28 August

A rare visit to Britain by one of the world's great ballet companies.
"The Company to cheer about... they dance with gleaming polish and pure pleasure"
NEW YORK TIMES
"An eye-popper... beautifully danced... it's a great crowd pleaser" THE STANDARD

**Greater London Council**
**The Royal Festival Hall**
Tel. 928 3191 C.C. 928 6544/5

23, 27, 28 August
Concerto Barocco/Double Quartet/The Firebird/Tam Ti Delam

24, 25, 26 August
Polonaise/Four Temperaments Etapes/Scherzo Capriccioso

Tickets: £2.50-£7.50
Concessions and group discounts available.

---

### ANDY CAPP
A NEW MUSICAL!
STARRING TOM COURTENAY ALAN PRICE
**ALDWYCH THEATRE**

"THINK MY BILLING'S BIG ENOUGH, PET?"

# 1 The world of entertainment

Willy Russell's new comedy *Educating Rita* was specially written for the Royal Shakespeare Company. It received its first performances at The Warehouse before transferring to the Piccadilly Theatre as a co-operative project of the Royal Shakespeare Theatre and Omega Stage Ltd.

Willy Russell is also the author of the award-winning play about the Beatles. *John, Paul, George, Ringo and Bert* and *Breezeblock Park*, both of which were seen in the West End; also of the television plays *Our Day Out* and *The Daughters of Albion*.

**BOOKING INFORMATION**
Piccadilly Theatre, Denman Street, London W1
**BOX OFFICE**
Open from 10am 01-437 4506 Telex 299107
OMEGA 24-Hour Information Service
01-836 1071
**CREDIT CARD SALES**

01-379 6565 (from 9.00am) With these Credit Cards you can buy your theatre tickets over the phone and be given your ticket numbers at the same time:
**SEAT PRICES**
Stalls £4.90, £6.90, £7.90* Royal Circle £5.90, £6.90, £7.90* (*Saturday evening performance £8.50)
**SCHOOL PARTIES**
01-836 3962 Special schools' rates on application.
**GROUPS**
01-836 3962 Reductions £5.90 to £4.90, £6.90 to £5.90, £7.90 to £6.90. For groups of 12 or more for performances Monday to Friday only, subject to availability.
**HAPPY FAMILIES**
Young people up to the age of 18 can see the show for only £3.90 when each is accompanied by a regular priced ticket holder. Bookable in advance. Offer applies to performances Monday to Friday, subject to availability.
**STANDBY TICKETS**
Best available seats £3.90 from 10am on the day or £3.50 half an hour before the performance to students, members of recognised youth organisations, under 24 Rail Card holders, schoolchildren, unemployed and senior citizens. One ticket per applicant, subject to availability. Please bring appropriate identification.
**PERFORMANCE TIME**
Monday to Saturday at 7.00pm. Matinee details to be announced.
Performance lasts approx. 3½ hours.
**HAPPY HOUR**
The Circle Bar is open one hour before the performance serving champagne by the glass at £1.40. Refreshments and usual bar facilities also available.
**PARKING AND TRANSPORT**
NCP Car Park in Denman Street. Special reduced price car parking can be booked at the same time as your theatre tickets. For details and credit card booking please ring 01-379 6565 or Box Office 01-437 4506 for non-card bookings.
⊖ Piccadilly Circus. British Rail: Charing Cross. Bus numbers 3, 6, 12, 13, 15, 23, 53, 88, 159, 500.

*Leisure*

## CINEMAS

**ACADEMY 1** 437 2981. Isabelle Huppert in **AT FIRST SIGHT** (15) at 2.00 (not Sun.) 4.10, 6.25, 8.45.

**ACADEMY 2.** 437 5129 Panillov's prize-winning **VASSA** (PG). Progs 2.50 (not Sun.) 5.35, 8.20.

**ACADEMY 3** 437 8819 Kurosawa's **SEVEN SAMURAI** (PG) at 4.00, 7.30.

**BARBICAN** 628 8795. Moorgate Tube. Today 2.30 Visconti's **DEATH IN VENICE** (15). 4.45 Visconti's **LUDWIG** (15).

**CAMDEN PLAZA** 485 2443. GODARD'S prize-winning film **FIRST NAME CARMEN** (18) Progs. 1.30, 3.20, 5.15, 7.10 & 9.10.

**CHELSEA CINEMA** 351 3742 Ingmar Bergman's masterpiece **FANNY AND ALEXANDER** (16). "Without question BEST PICTURE OF '83" D. Robinson Times. Film at 3.20 & 7.15.

**CHELSEA CINEMA** 351 3742. 206 Kings Road.

**CURZON**, Curzon St. W1. 499 3737. Jeremy Irons, Ben Kingsley, Patricia Hodge "Are all superb" F.T. in Harold Pinter's **BETRAYAL** (15) "A film not to be missed" Barry Norman Film '83. Progs. at 2.00 (not Sun or Tues) 4.10, 6.20, 8.40. **LAST WEEK** From Friday Carlos Saura's **CARMEN** (15).

**GATE BLOOMSBURY, 1 & 2.** 837 8402/1177 Russell Sq. Tube
1: Bob Fosse's **STAR 80** (18) 3.00, 4.55, 6.50, 8.45.
2: **STAR STRUCK** (PG) 3.30, 5.15, 7.05, 9.00. (N.C.P.) parking 30p anytime, Sat & Sun, Mon-Fri after 6pm. Licensed Bar. Access/Visa.

**GATE MAYFAIR** 493 2031. MAYFAIR HOTEL, Stratton Street, Green Park Tube. **THE LEOPARD** (PG) 4.50, 8.00.

**GATE NOTTING HILL** 221 0220 727 5750. **DANIEL** (15). 1.55 (Sat & Sun only) 4.10, 6.30, 8.45.

**LUMIERE CINEMA** 836 0691 Coppola's **RUMBLE FISH** (18). Film at 1.05, 3.00, 5.00, 7.00, 9.05.

**ODEON HAYMARKET** (930 2738). **TO BE OR NOT TO BE** (PG). Sep. progs. today 2.00, 5.55, 8.35. ALL SEATS BOOKABLE IN ADVANCE. ACCESS AND VISA. TELEPHONE BOOKINGS WELCOME.

**ODEON LEICESTER SQUARE** (930 6111). Info. 930 5250/4259. **TWO OF A KIND** (PG). Sep. progs. Doors open Today 4.00, 8.00. ADVANCE BOOKING FOR LAST PERFORMANCE ONLY BY POST OR BOX OFFICE. ACCESS AND VISA ACCEPTED FOR ADVANCE BOOKING ONLY.

**ODEON MARBLE ARCH W2** (723 2011) Walt Disney's **THE JUNGLE BOOK** (U) & **MICKEY'S CHRISTMAS CAROL** (U). Sep. progs. Today Doors open 2.00, 5.00, 7.45. REDUCED PRICES FOR CHILDREN.

**SCREEN ON BAKER ST.** 935 2772 (96-98 Baker St. W1). (1) **LIANNA** (18) 2.20, 4.40, 7.00, 9.15. (2) **TRADING PLACES** (15) 2.00, 4.20, 6.40, 9.00. Lic. Bar. Tickets bookable.

**SCREEN ON ISLINGTON GREEN.** 226 3520. William Hurt in **THE BIG CHILL** (15). 2.55, 5.00, 7.05, 9.10. Club show. Inst. memb.

**SCREEN ON THE HILL** 435 3366 **LIANNA** (18). 2.20, 4.40, 7.00, 9.10. Lic Bar. Tickets bookable. Club show. Inst. memb.

**Rumble Fish** (Siamese fighting fish) is the story of a complex relationship between two brothers, Rusty-James (Matt Dillon), and The Motorcycle Boy (Mickey Rourke).

Set in a decaying city, now or later, the brothers are products of their environment—broken home, alcoholic father, and street gangs. The Motorcycle Boy, at the age of about twenty-one colour blind, and partially deaf from years of fighting, has seen and done it all. His kid brother looks up to him as a god. The Motorcycle Boy has left the city and lives in California, but returns like a homing pigeon to see how things are.

That is all that happens, yet Coppola, whose eleventh film this is, has created a stark, atmospheric tone poem, which, while you may not *like* it, is totally absorbing.

Filmed in black and white, with only the rumble fish of the title in colour, Coppola has created a city against racing cloudscapes, desert dust, billowing smoke and shadows. The photography pays homage to Cocteau, Bresson, Brassai, Robert Maplethorpe and Dianne Arbus.

There is a stunningly choreographed fight scene which, in spite of its Dolby stereo violence, has a background of desolation, passing trains, pigeons and breaking glass. A fight has rarely been better done in the cinema in that, rather than gratuitously playing up the violence, Coppola has photographed it in such a way that it manages not to be offensive, yet you can smell and feel the atmosphere. *That* is quite an achievement.

With the marvellous soundtrack (by Stewart Copeland of The Police) that is half percussion and half something that sounds like permanent interference, *Rumble Fish* is a sort of 'Apocalypse Then': a hymn to misplaced youth in the best traditions of James Dean, and a hymn to the great movie traditions of the past. It is also a film that manages to look backwards and forwards at the same time with style and perception.

---

□ **Daniel** hits about the same emotional nerve as did *Sophie's Choice*, only there are no laughs. The historical event that inspired the movie was the 1953 trial and execution of the Rosenbergs who were sentenced to death for conspiring to steal atomic secrets for the Russians.

In this film, names have been changed but the storyline is obvious. Timothy Hutton (who made his debut in *Ordinary People*) is brilliant as Daniel, son of the Isaacsons. And Amanda Plummer gives an excellent performance as his sister Susan. The film examines Daniel's relationship with his parents and his sister as he explores what really happened to his parents and their motives. In the process he unravels a fascinating historical record from the depression and WW2, through the McCarthy red-under-the-bed era and on to the anti-war marches of the 60s. It really is compelling stuff but perhaps just a little too graphic for the faint-hearted. □

---

*decaying*: falling into disrepair
*stark*: bare
*stunningly*: wonderfully
*The Police*: a famous pop group
*perception*: the ability to notice something

## 1 The world of entertainment

**Star 80** is the story of Vancouver-born model and actress, Dorothy Stratten, who became *Playboy's* 1980 Playmate of the Year and was tragically murdered by her estranged husband Paul Snider.

Bob Fosse's obsession with the background to the story has resulted in an interesting and workable little vehicle for twenty-one-year-old Mariel Hemingway as the fated Dorothy, and a wonderful performance by Eric Roberts as the scheming exploiter and opportunist, Paul Snider, whom Dorothy eventually marries simply because she doesn't know how to refuse him.

It was Snider who pushed Dorothy on the road to stardom by submitting photographs of her to Hugh Hefner. Then, anxious to get to the top himself, even if it was on the back of someone else, he hung on in there until he made Dorothy's life such a claustrophobic misery that she left him.

Roberts epitomises the cheap, flashy little loser. 'He had the personality of a pimp,' is Hefner's first opinion of him, and that was the way he stayed.

The movie is conveyed a little like a dramatised documentary, with a series of interviews with people who knew Dorothy and Paul: Hefner himself (a much too kindly performance from Cliff Robertson), the owner of the club where Snider worked, the doctor they shared a house with in Los Angeles, and her first photographer whom Snider ripped off. The rest of the story is told in flashback.

It is Eric Roberts' film, although clearly it isn't meant to be. Snider is such a paranoid, complex personality that he can't help but steal the show. He tries to ruin Dorothy's life, and eventually destroys her completely, as well as himself.

It is a tragic tale, and Fosse's handling of it is sympathetic and low key. Moral tales about the corruption of innocence, it seems, still carry a great deal of dramatic impetus when transferred to the screen at the hands of a master.

**The Big Chill** Large American universities in the sixties weren't so much training centres for future employment as testing grounds for political, sexual and social activism.

Opening with Marvin Gaye's *I Heard It Through The Grapevine*, seven old college friends learn that Alex, the one they all loved, the one who inspired them and had the most promise, has committed suicide. They come in from various parts of the country for the funeral and a weekend of reminiscing and soul-searching. They want to know, was all that idealism simply a passing fashion?

The weekend hosts are Harold (Kevin Kline) and Sarah (Glenn Close). He was Alex's best friend. Sarah is a doctor who had an affair with Alex. They invite Sam (Tom Berenger) and Karen (Jobeth Williams), who try to get an affair going again. Meg (Marykay Place) wants to have a baby and she's hoping that one of her old mates will be a volunteer father. She mistakenly turns to Nick (William Hurt), but Michael (Jeff Goldblum) wants to be the one for the job.

There isn't a bad performance in this rare ensemble of now and future stars. Larry Kasdan, the co-writer (with Barbara Benedek) and director, has come up with a clever script. There's so much in this film – a soundtrack which includes the Stones, Aretha Franklin and the Beach Boys – that you'll want a second viewing to take it all in.

Sun 19 - Sat 25 February
**BETRAYAL (15)**
Director. David Jones; with Ben Kingsley, Jeremy Irons, Patricia Hodge.
USA 1983. 95 mins.

David Jones' adaption of Pinter's stage play is an economical description of a cultured middle-class triangle. Pinter's theatrical device of revealing the progress of an illicit love affair in reverse, from epilogue to prelude, slyly forewarns us of every deceit and makes us privy to the secret thoughts of the deceivers that lie behind the prattle of social chitchat. It all sounds so artless and commonplace; but it is Pinter at his best with every word having its special place and significance. And the three stars slip each word into its appointed place with all the seeming nonchalance of the media people they portray, who have learned all the arts of gracious living and abandoned the old fashioned virtues of honesty and chastity. Every casual glance, every hint of a nervous twitch, every over-emphasised attempt at face saving humour comes over as a secret to be shared with the viewer who knows the score.

---

*Playboy*: a famous 'girlie' magazine
*scheming*: working out secret plans
*exploiter*: someone who takes advantage of someone
*pimp*: a man who finds clients for prostitutes
*ripped off*: took financial advantage of (by stealing etc.)
*nonchalance*: casualness

99

Leisure

# TELEVISION SPECIAL "NOT THAT I WATCH IT, OF COURSE..."

**WELL, DO THE PUNDITS REALLY KNOW WHAT THE PUBLIC LIKE? PRUE LIGHTFOOT SWITCHED ON TO A FEW FAMOUS PEOPLE'S VIEWING HABITS**

**NEIL KINNOCK
LABOUR MP
FOR BEDWELLTY**

The hours of the House and the dreadful winter weekend schedules finally persuaded my wife and me to buy a video and record programmes during the week for Saturdays and Sundays, which is the only time I can watch the box. Before the arrival of that miraculous invention most of my viewing was the odd glimpse, including 23 minutes of *Dallas*, after which I was prepared to shoot JR myself. Once I actually made a point of watching *Sale of the Century* after I'd seen some graffiti describing Nicholas Parsons as "the opiate of the masses". It was absolutely disembowelling in its awfulness! What I enjoy most of all is rugby, soccer, cricket, athletics and practically any film, though I'm besotted about Westerns. I also like David Attenborough documentaries, *The Two Ronnies*, and Tommy Cooper or any of his derivatives.

As an MP, possibly I should make a point of watching current affairs programmes but I can't see myself doing so over breakfast since this is the only regular daily contact I have with my wife and son and daughter. Anything that split up the family at this time would be bad news.

**BARBARA CARTLAND
ROMANTIC
NOVELIST**

*MASH* is my favourite because it's one of America's best and funniest series and because it has something to do with health, which appeals to me. Normally I watch television in bed from 8pm onwards, but never very late, unless it's something like Lord Mountbatten's life story. He was a personal friend of mine of course, as were Edward VII and Wallis Simpson.

The abdication series was excellent and I thought everybody looked exactly like the characters they portrayed — except, that is, for Edward Fox, good actor though he is. I told him: "Now everyone's going to think the Prince of Wales looked like you".

I enjoy watching the News — it keeps the brain active — but I'm sick to death of murder, ugliness and violence, which are bad for the brain.

I hope that Channel 4 will show us some more good news, more educational films and more historical documentaries. Visual history is far more interesting than some dreary book, and television is after all a visual medium.

Kitchen sink dramas and suspense are tiresome after a busy day; I prefer beauty, amusement and romance, but

# 1 The world of entertainment

not overt sex, of which I disapprove, and which is such a mistake for young people to see — an awful lot of them aren't like that at all, you know.

**TOYAH WILCOX**
**SINGER AND**
**ACTRESS**

I don't like religion or football or miserable films on all three channels on Sundays. Sundays should be happier with more sci-fi or horror movies and comedy, especially *Soap* or *Benson*, which I like for their black humour. Even though politics bore me, I do make a point of watching the News once a day. Breakfast telly sounds intriguing but I can't help thinking the contents will be rubbish. As someone who enjoys educational programmes I hope they start with cookery or keep fit to set me up for the day. Just so long as they don't show sport on it at the same time as the others, I'm all in favour of a fourth channel.

**MAC**
**DAILY MAIL**
**CARTOONIST**

I got rid of my television several months ago and have found not watching it has broadened my interests and made my days a lot longer as well as a great deal more fulfilling! □

*pundits*: experts
*Dallas*: The name of a famous American soap opera on television
*JR*: a character in *Dallas*
*Sale of the Century*: a famous quiz programme on television
*opiate*: a kind of drug which induces sleep
*disembowelling*: absolutely terrible
*Two Ronnies*:
*Tommy Cooper*: } British comedians seen on television

*"Send the children to bed. There's a thriller on tonight."*

Leisure

# TV PROGRAMME GUIDE

*Programme not in colour

## BBC 1

- **6.20** OPEN UNIVERSITY (ends 8.50)
- **9.0** POSTMAN PAT: A See-Saw repeat.
- **9.15** WORSHIP: Jesus and his enemies.
- **10.0** ASIAN MAGAZINE: A trick or two from young magician Guru Rangeela.
- **10.30** PLAY IT SAFE! 10.40 MATHS HELP.
- **10.55** GREEK — LANGUAGE AND PEOPLE.
- **11.20** INSIDE YTS: Assessing progress.
- **11.45** INDIAN COOKERY COURSE: Lemony chicken (rpt). **12.10** SEE HEAR!
- **12.35** MAKING THE MOST OF THE MICRO.
- **1.0** FARMING and Weather for farmers.
- **1.25** TAKING STOCK: Loss and Change.
- **1.50** NEWS.
- **1.55** FILM*: The Bells Of St Mary's (Bing Crosby is the star).
- **3.55** BONANZA: Winter Kill. Bitter cold threatens to wipe out the Ponderosa's livestock.
- **4.45** ONE NIGHT IN NOVEMBER: Terry Wogan talks about the Children in Need appeal.
- **5.15** GOODBYE MR CHIPS: Part 5 of serial.
- **5.45** NEWS; WEATHER.
- **5.55** HOLIDAY: The far pavilions of India, a ski village in southern Spain.
- **6.30** STREETWISE: How to prevent a pickpocket chancing his arm.
- **6.40** SONGS OF PRAISE: Hallelujah, it's gospel time in South London. Southwark Cathedral is the unusual venue, and among the gospel music fans is the only black mayor in Britain, Southwark's Sam King.
- **7.15** ONE BY ONE: Donald is even more convinced that his own future lies elsewhere.
- **8.5** MASTERMIND: Two women are quizzed on the history of costumes and the novels of R. F. Delderfield. The men tackle poet Keats and Duke Ellington.
- **8.35** EVER DECREASING CIRCLES: Martin organises a fund-raising function and is not pleased when Paul adds some innovations. Last in well-written series.
- **9.5** NEWS; WEATHER.
- **9.20** THAT'S LIFE: With Esther Rantzen.
- **10.5** EVERYMAN: Chilling insight into the mind of a torturer. Michalis Petrou, who worked for the Greek colonels, describes how he tortured opponents of the regime. With an account of how such men are trained to inflict pain on fellow humans.
- **10.45** THE WORLD OF COOKING: If you're not too confident about dishing up wakadori kuwayaki and oshi zushi, a Tokyo chef shows how it's done.
- **11.15** PHIL SILVERS* as Sergeant Bilko (rpt).
- **11.40** WEATHER; CLOSEDOWN.

## LWT

- **7.25** THOUGHT FOR A SUNDAY.
- **7.30** RUB-A-DUB-TUB: For children.
- **8.30** GOOD MORNING BRITAIN.
- **9.25** LWT INFORMATION.
- **9.30** ME AND MY CAMERA: Lord Lichfield shows how to take group photos (rpt).
- **10.0** MORNING WORSHIP from Victoria Methodist Church, Clifton, Bristol.
- **11.0** GETTING ON: Warmth, company, entertainment — Bingo's benefits to the elderly.
- **11.30** CRAFTS MADE SIMPLE: New series on how to draw and paint. With Ken Foord.
- **12.0** WEEKEND WORLD: Acid Rain — What is it doing to animal and plant life, and what can we do about it?
- **1.0** POLICE 5: Fight crime with Shaw Taylor.
- **1.15** THE BIG MATCH: Highlights of Liverpool v QPR, Southampton v Luton.
- **2.00** ENCOUNTER: How a young married couple are coping with the responsibilities they recently took on as wardens of a Church Army hostel in Central London.
- **2.30** LONDON NEWS then FILM: The Mouse That Roared.
- **4.30** JACK HOLBORN: Will the real Captain Sharingham step forward? Young Tom hasn't twigged that the man whose life he saved isn't the dashing buccaneer.
- **5.0** BULLSEYE: Norman Vaughan is guest on the darts-cum-quiz show.
- **5.30** SUNDAY SUNDAY: Gloria Hunniford's guests include Frankie Howerd.
- **6.30** NEWS
- **6.40** HIGHWAY: Harry Secombe visits Portsmouth Naval Base and meets Leading Wren Kim Toms who won the BEM for her work as a telephonist during the Falklands campaign.
- **7.15** FAMILY FORTUNES: Quiz show hosted by Max Bygraves.
- **7.45** FILM: Fear Is The Key.
- **9.45** NEWS.
- **10.0** SPITTING IMAGE: New comedy sketch series.
- **10.30** SOUTH BANK SHOW: Interview with hardhitting left-wing playwright Trevor Griffiths, whose notable credits include Comedians, Bill Brand, Through The Night and the film Reds. He talks about the problems involved in writing drama that deals with political and social issues.
- **11.30** LONDON NEWS then THE PROTECTORS: A hit man has Harry Rule cornered in a railway carriage (rpt).
- **12.0** NIGHT THOUGHTS; CLOSEDOWN.

## CHANNEL 4

- **1.5** MAKING OF BRITAIN: The Vikings and Alfred the Great's defence of Wessex.
- **1.30** IRISH ANGLE.
- **2.0** TENNIS: Davis Cup. Great Britain v Italy live from Telford, Shropshire.
- **4.15** JACK'S GAME: Rough Shoot. Jack Charlton and friends have a day out rough shooting in Durham.
- **4.45** THE MOTOR SHOW: Engine rebuilds; Nick Mason's fascinating garage; testing the XJS Convertible.
- **5.15** NEWS then 7 DAYS: Moral questions raised by the week's news.
- **5.45** FACE THE PRESS: Guest is Rt. Rev. Hugh Montefiore, Bishop of Birmingham.
- **6.15** TENNIS: Davis Cup from Telford. Highlights of Great Britain v Italy. Report on U.S. v Romania.
- **7.15** WORLD AT WAR: The Polish uprising; Arnhem; Hitler's Ardennes push.
- **8.15** THE JEWEL IN THE CROWN: Repeat of last Tuesday's Part 8.
- **9.15** THE FIRST CHRISTIAN: How Paul's letters to the Corinthians influenced Christian attitudes — particularly to women.
- **10.15** FILM*: The Mystery Of Mr X.
- **11.50** CLOSEDOWN.

## BBC2

- **6.25** OPEN UNIVERSITY.
- **1.55** CEEFAX PAGES.
- **3.0** RUGBY: John Player Cup. Bristol v London Welsh.
- **3.50** NEWSNIGHT'S FEBRUARY: Rerun of recent items: report on Argentina.
- **4.40** SWIMMING: Britain v West Germany at Crystal Palace.
- **5.10** WALES! WALES? Series on the recent history of Wales starts with the question of Welsh identity.
- **6.0** NEWS REVIEW.
- **6.30** MONEY PROGRAMME: Wine as an investment — an idea that could turn sour?
- **7.15** PRO-CELEBRITY GOLF: Kenny Lynch and Tom Watson v Alex Higgins and Greg Norman.
- **8.5** ONE PAIR OF EYES: Mentally handicapped Simon Trehearne hearteningly shows how people like himself can live independent lives.
- **8.35** ALL THE WORLD'S A STAGE arrives at the age of Marlowe and Shakespeare. Paul Rogers as Faustus, Jeremy Irons as Hamlet.
- **9.30** DID YOU SEE? Diverse Reports, Everyman, and All The World's A Stage.
- **10.15** NEWS; WEATHER.
- **10.20—12.0** FILM: My Brilliant Career.

# 1 The world of entertainment

## 1.1

1 Look at the headlines on page 95 and try to decide what the ambiguous meaning, or 'play on words', is in each case. Discuss your ideas with a partner, and consult your dictionary if necessary. Your teacher will tell you whether you were right.

2 Look at the theatre advertisements on page 96 and make a note of which theatre you would choose to go to if:
   a) you liked dance;
   b) you had children with you;
   c) you were fond of 18th century literature;
   d) you liked classical music.

3 Work in pairs. Ask each other which theatres you chose, and why. Then find out what your partner would most like to see, and the reasons why.

## 1.2

Work in pairs. One of you is A and the other one B. A should look closely at page 97 and then phone B to make plans for the weekend. B should not look at the page.

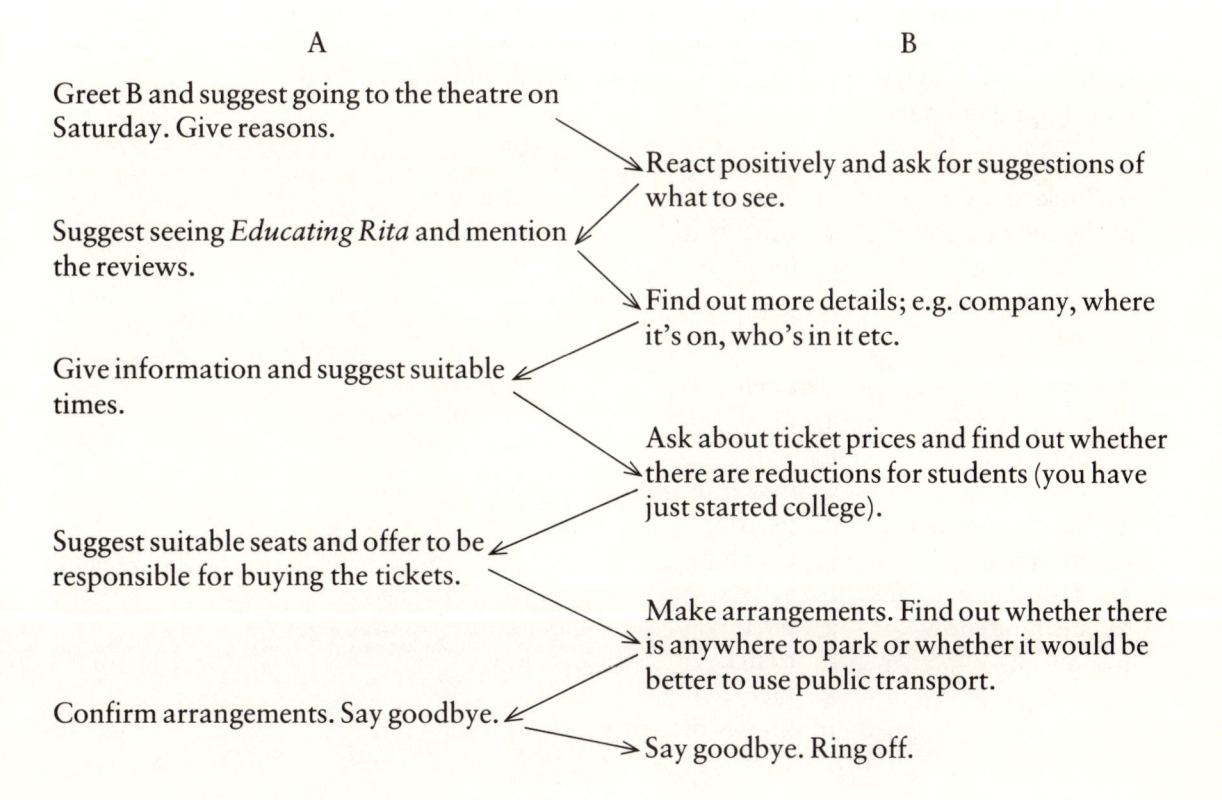

| A | B |
|---|---|
| Greet B and suggest going to the theatre on Saturday. Give reasons. | |
| | React positively and ask for suggestions of what to see. |
| Suggest seeing *Educating Rita* and mention the reviews. | |
| | Find out more details; e.g. company, where it's on, who's in it etc. |
| Give information and suggest suitable times. | |
| | Ask about ticket prices and find out whether there are reductions for students (you have just started college). |
| Suggest suitable seats and offer to be responsible for buying the tickets. | |
| | Make arrangements. Find out whether there is anywhere to park or whether it would be better to use public transport. |
| Confirm arrangements. Say goodbye. | |
| | Say goodbye. Ring off. |

*Leisure*

## 1.3

1 Read through the film reviews on pages 98–9 quickly, and make a note of which film:
   a) has been adapted from a play;
   b) is about a son who investigates the death of his parents;
   c) is about a famous model;
   d) has background music by a famous pop artist;
   e) is based on a meeting because of a funeral.

2 Look at the reviews again. Decide as quickly as you can which film you would *most* like to see and which film you would *least* like to see. Make a note of your reasons, under various headings such as: *director*, *actors*, *story*, *photography* etc. If you have already seen the film, decide whether you agree/disagree with the review. Discuss your ideas in groups and report back to the class.

3 Choose two of the films, read the reviews and note down all the words and expressions which indicate a *positive* or *negative* reaction to the film. Discuss your answers as a class.

4 Look at the same two reviews again and try to guess the meanings of these words and phrases in their context. Discuss your answers in pairs or groups, with students who have read the same reviews as you, and then check them by using a dictionary.

*Rumble Fish*
a) looks up to
b) homing pigeon
c) absorbing
d) billowing smoke
e) play up

*Daniel*
a) inspired
b) conspiring
c) unravels
d) 'red under the bed'
e) graphic

*The Big Chill*
reminisce

*Star 80*
a) estranged
b) fated
c) submitting
d) hung on in there
e) epitomises
f) flashy
g) steal the show
h) low key

*Betrayal*
a) illicit
b) slyly
c) makes us privy
d) prattle
e) chitchat
f) artless
g) portray
h) twitch
i) face saving
j) knows the score

5 Work on the following dialogue in pairs. One of you should take the part of 'you' and the other is your 'friend'. 'You' should consult the cinema guide on page 98. Your 'friend' should not look at this page.

You:     Why don't we go and see .................... tonight?

Friend:  Could do. What's it about?

You:     ........................................................................................

Friend:  Where's it on?

You:     ........................................................................................

Friend:  It'll have to be a late show. I'm working till 6.00.

You:     ........................................................................................

Friend:  ........................................................................................

6 Write a review of a film or play you have seen recently. Remember to mention the story, acting, costumes, photography etc. and to give some kind of conclusion in the form of a recommendation or otherwise.

## 1.4

1 Think of the television programmes which you like watching and note them down under headings, e.g. *comedy programmes*. You could look at page 106 for some suggestions of headings. Now read the interviews with four famous people on pages 100–1 and put a tick (✓) next to the programmes they mention which are on your list. Compare your notes with a partner.

2 Find words in the text which are similar in meaning to the following. Discuss your answers in pairs and check them with the dictionary.

*Neil Kinnock*
a) timetable
b) television
c) wonderful
d) quick look at
e) adore

*Barbara Cartland*
a) (I) like
b) acted/played
c) tired of / fed up with
d) boring
e) domestic
f) obvious

*Toyah Wilcox*
a) very interesting
b) agree with

105

*Leisure*

3 These are some of the types of programme which you find on television. Look at the TV guide on page 102 and note down one or two examples of programmes next to each of the headings below. Add any more programmes that you know of next to the appropriate headings, and compare your notes with a partner.

*Current affairs*: ....................................................................................

*Children's programmes*: ......................................................................

*Religion*: ...............................................................................................

*Educational programmes*: ...................................................................

*Documentaries*: ...................................................................................

*Sport*: ....................................................................................................

*Films*: ...................................................................................................

*Drama series*: ......................................................................................

*Quiz programmes*: ...............................................................................

*Chat shows*: .........................................................................................

*Hobbies*: ...............................................................................................

*Comedy*: ...............................................................................................

4 Imagine that you are choosing your evening's entertainment from the TV guide. Note down what you would *definitely* like to see, *quite* like to see and definitely do *not* want to see. Discuss your preferences with a partner and try to reach a compromise so that you agree on what to watch. Remember to give good reasons for your choice.

**Before reading the texts in section 2 more carefully, look at the exercises on pages 115–19.**

# 2 The sporting life

## It might be entertainment but...

### IS IT SPORT?

IF SNOOKER is a sport, surely chess is too? If angling is, why not deer-stalking? If bowls, why not marbles? What do you reckon is a sport, and what is not?

Probably no two people in any 10 would share an understanding of the word. When the Sports Council asked the question of the public, 7 per cent would not even agree that soccer was a sport, though 11 per cent thought cooking was; rugby, tennis, badminton and boxing were up to 96 per cent acceptance, but snooker was down as low as 46 per cent.

The fact that the Sports Council included flower arranging, knitting and watching TV on their questionnaire (they all got the thumbs down) might seem stupidly provocative; and the fact that there actually were positive votes for ornithology and Monopoly brings doubt on the validity of the whole operation.

The Sports Council obviously need to know what the public think are sports, since they distribute the Government's grant to the needy. Half a dozen stern requirements must be fulfilled before the Council will dispense the largesse, but the one most relevant to general understanding is that the activity should involve 'an acceptable balance of physical skill and effort'.

**Croydon Housewife:**
'WHAT is sport? I suppose it's anything they can make competitive or entertaining enough to be good television.'

**Collins Dictionary of the English Language, 1979:**
'SPORT – an individual or group activity pursued for exercise or pleasure, often involving the testing of physical capabilities . . .'

**Dick Palmer, General Secretary of the British Olympic Association:**
'WHEN I was on the Sports Council we had an application for a grant from the Association of Leisure Gardeners. They seemed to fulfil the conditions: they worked to rules, that was sure. They were intensely competitive. And if you don't think gardening is physical you've never dug a potato patch. But of course we knew it wasn't sport.

'The tighter you try to draw the rules around this thing, the more absurd it becomes. You say it must be physical, so you rule out chess. But you also rule out small-bore rifle shooting, and do you think that's right? As soon as you try to define it, you're on shaky ground. You come up immediately against the exceptions that you know belong to sport.

'You have to admit it's a slightly philosophical business. There was a Dutchman who tried to identify the features of sport, and he probably got it about right. As far as I remember, he said sport was a conflict of which you didn't know the outcome, played within defined areas and with defined rules. The greater the conflict, the greater the sport. If Sebastian Coe is running against High Wycombe's third string 800 metres man, that's not sport. But if Coe is running against Ovett, that's sport.'

**Bob Surtees, nineteenth century sportsman:**
'NO MAN is fit to be called a sportsman wot doesn't kick his wife out of bed on a haverage once in three weeks.'

**Christopher Brasher, Olympic gold medallist:**
'SPORT is any game or recreation played to a set of rules. A fisherman sitting on a bank is indulging in a recreation until he does it competitively; aeromodelling is a recreation, but put some rules on it and it becomes a sport.'

**Geoffrey Nicholson, sports writer:**
'SPORT is a contest of physical strength or manipulation or more probably both (if it involves mental agility, so much the better, but that's no criterion). So bar billiards and tabletop football are sports, however low on the scale. Bridge and chess are not; they are games.

'A sporting contest is artificially structured; it has an agreed set of often quite arbitrary laws, and a system of scoring or measurement which yields a self-evident winner (or produces an equally self-evident draw). That in itself rules out most blood sports, except perhaps match angling. So, too, climbing which, in strictly sporting terms, is simply vertical hiking. It also invalidates certain contests – ballroom dancing for example – where the result depends on a jury's subjective assessment of the competitors' style and technique.

'It follows that sport is a contest of human abilities: animals and machines can't understand the rules. So greyhound racing is obviously out; and motor racing and equestrian events can only be considered as marginal sports.

'Sport may involve direct physical combat and risk of injury, but ceases to be a sport when it turns to violence or when injury is deliberately inflicted within the rules. So wrestling is sport, boxing is not (a pity that it makes such good copy).'

---

*dispense the largesse*: give out money
*rule out*: eliminate
*on shaky ground*: having difficulties

Leisure

# Further shores of fitness

**Choosing the sport that you *stick* with could mean looking beyond the nearest aerobics class. The search starts here!**

*Martial arts* teach you self-discipline — and self-defence. "You learn to be in control of your body," explains Caesar Andrews, 2nd Black Belt in Shotokan Karate and chief instructor at the Budokwai Club, London. "You have to concentrate — which is relaxing. It makes you more aware; reflexes become automatic." The options? T'ai chi, karate, kung fu, judo for starters.

Take ball games beyond tennis and squash with *basketball, volleyball*. "The skill's the thing," says reader Karla Rayment, who plays for Herne Bay's Ladies Basketball Team. "You have to control how you throw the ball. Timing's vital, too. Basketball's competitive — and you're playing with a team. You need to build endurance, so l jog, too."

Try a high-flying sport for real thrills. "I wanted to prove to myself that I could really achieve something," says celebrity Paula Yates of her stab at *parachuting*. "The training is rigorous, but the actual jump is wonderful because it's absolutely quiet and you fall slower than you expect which gives you lots of time to admire the view . . ."

Skipping with a rope, of course, is terrific aerobic exercise. New York's Double Dutch team skip fast and furiously 'twixt several spinning ropes, without missing a beat.

Dance classes keep you moving; go to a specialised one and you learn a new skill. "I took up *tap* because it's fun and gives you a great sense of rhythm," enthuses star dancer Linda-Mae Brewer. "Your feet become musical instruments! Anyone can tap because you set your own pace." Exotic dancing — and wearing likewise costumes — loosens inhibitions. '*Belly dancing* is energetic, sensuous — and it tightens the pelvic area," says Eileen Fairbane, teacher of stretch/jazz and belly dancing at London's Dance Centre. "There are so many beautiful undulations and shimmies, sensuous hand movements, facial expressions — even the veil is mysterious. It's a culture of its own." Or why not try *folk* or *square dancing* for kicks — and a great aerobic workout.

*Hula hooping* is another fitness-for-kicks sport that's easy to pick up. "It's like riding a bike; once you get the feel for it, you never lose it," explains world champion Chico Johnson. "If you're right-handed, spin the hoop to the left, and vice versa." And when you've mastered the waist twist, you can move on to elbows, feet, and nose, Chico points out.

"It's chess on feet," says former modern Pentathlon world champion Kathy Taylor of *fencing*. "The aim is to outwit your opponent mentally as well as physically. You learn speed and stamina. And those fast lunges tone legs!"

Perhaps the ultimate challenge is *rock climbing*. "There's tremendous satisfaction when you've reached the top," says climbing and abseiling fan, journalist Kay Yarnall. "You have to strengthen arms and wrists — plus be pretty fit. And you need lots of stamina. *Abseiling*'s exhilarating; you can climb up a rock face or sea cliff. Secured by a rope to the top, you walk over the edge of the cliff backwards and whizz down to the bottom!" Of course, you might enjoy orienteering (army assault-type courses). Or how about *windsurfing*? Or *trampolining*? *Acrobatics*? The list is, literally, endless . . .

---

*Martial arts*: sports relating to war
*thrills*: excitement
*twixt*: between
*shimmies*: dance movements
*lunge*: sudden move forward
*tone*: improve the condition of

## 2 The sporting life

## FITNESS THROUGH SPORT

All exercise may be good for you but different types of exercise affect the body in different ways. The jogger who pounds round the local park, for instance, will have more stamina than the gymnast – who has flexibility and suppleness of body. One of the attractions of keep-fit exercises such as those mentioned above is that they are structured to improve all-round fitness. But toe-touching hardly has the intrinsic appeal of participating in a sport.

Some people will use exercises or jogging simply to achieve sufficient fitness to take part in their favourite sports; others will hope that sport itself will get and keep them fit. It all depends, of course, on the sport they wish to pursue, and on their own state of fitness. In the tables that follow, we have rated sixty-four sports and other activities for their differing physical effects on the human body.

The tables are adapted from the findings of an International Committee on the Standardization of Physical Fitness Tests. Medical experts from thirty-seven countries were represented on this committee, whose research provided the basis of a minutely-detailed textbook, *International Guide to Fitness and Health,* published by Crown Publishers Inc. of New York. Some British doctors believe their American counterparts underestimate the potential for fitness in activities such as gardening and DIY. We have therefore included a few of the domestic and non-sporting activities contained in the *International Guide's* tables in order to provide a comparison of their fitness potential with some of the most popular sports.

### The fitness ratings of sport
A. General Endurance
B. Muscular Strength
C. Mobility of Joints

The potential effect of each activity in each category is indicated by three ratings:
1. Great effect (***)
2. Moderate effect (**)
3. Little or no effect (*)

The table shows the differences between sports. The common denominator, though, is pleasure. And because sports are a social pleasure, and doing well at them is part of this pleasure, there is a greater chance that you will not only keep at them but also train for them. This makes it far more likely that you will reach and maintain a healthy level of fitness. You can get fit through sport, therefore, but do not expect to do so with one weekly game of squash or tennis. Nor should you expect much pleasure if you are too unfit to enjoy a sport. Some sports demand a reasonable level of fitness *before* you take them up – football, for instance.

|  | General Endurance | Muscular Strength | Mobility |
|---|---|---|---|
| 1. Archery | * | ** | * |
| 2. Badminton | ** | ** | ** |
| 3. Baseball | * | * | ** |
| 4. Basketball | *** | ** | ** |
| 5. Billiards | * | * | * |
| 6. Bowling (American) | * | * | * |
| 7. Boxing | *** | *** | * |
| 8. Canoeing | ** | *** | * |
| 9. Climbing stairs | ** | ** | *** |
| 10. Cricket | * | * | ** |
| 11. Croquet | * | * | * |
| 12. Curling | * | * | ** |
| 13. Cycling (Speed) | *** | ** | * |
| 14. Dancing | ** | * | * |
| 15. Darts | * | * | * |
| 16. Digging in Garden | ** | *** | ** |
| 17. Driving | * | * | * |
| 18. Fencing | * | ** | *** |
| 19. Fishing | * | * | * |
| 20. Football (American) | ** | ** | ** |
| 21. Football (Soccer) | ** | ** | ** |
| 22. Golf | * | * | ** |
| 23. Gymnastics | * | ** | ** |
| 24. Hiking | ** | ** | * |
| 25. Hockey | ** | ** | * |
| 26. Horse Riding | ** | * | * |
| 27. Housework | * | * | ** |
| 28. Hunting | ** | * | * |
| 29. Ice-hockey | ** | ** | * |
| 30. Jogging in place | ** | * | * |
| 31. Judo | * | ** | ** |
| 32. Jumping (Ski) | * | ** | ** |
| 33. Karate | * | ** | ** |
| 34. Kayaking | ** | *** | ** |
| 35. Lacrosse | ** | ** | ** |
| 36. Mountain climbing | *** | ** | ** |
| 37. Mowing lawn | * | ** | * |
| 38. Orienteering | ** | ** | * |
| 39. Rowing | *** | *** | * |
| 40. Rugby | ** | ** | ** |
| 41. Running (Sub-maximal) | *** | ** | * |
| 42. Sailing | * | ** | ** |
| 43. Sawing | ** | *** | * |
| 44. Scuba diving | ** | * | ** |
| 45. Sculling | *** | *** | ** |
| 46. Shooting | * | * | * |
| 47. Skating (Ice) | ** | ** | * |
| 48. Skating (Roller) | ** | ** | * |
| 49. Skin-diving | *** | * | ** |
| 50. Skiing (Cross-country) | *** | *** | ** |
| 51. Skiing (Downhill) | ** | ** | ** |
| 52. Snooker | * | * | * |
| 53. Squash | ** | ** | *** |
| 54. Surfing | * | ** | ** |
| 55. Swimming (Sub-maximal) | *** | *** | *** |
| 56. Table tennis | * | * | ** |
| 57. Tennis | ** | ** | ** |
| 58. Volleyball | * | * | ** |
| 59. Walking briskly (over 1 hr.) | ** | * | * |
| 60. Washing/polishing car | * | ** | ** |
| 61. Water polo | *** | ** | ** |
| 62. Water skiing | ** | ** | ** |
| 63. Weight lifting | * | *** | * |
| 64. Wrestling | ** | *** | ** |

Even hill-walking or orienteering at the non-competitive 'Wayfarer' level need a rudimentary fitness. If you are unfit, then choose a sport where you can select your own level of exertion – solo canoeing or swimming, for instance – and can thereby do more to improve your own fitness.

## Leisure

*Idle v. active: the Calorie balance*

The illustration compares the Calories used in the typical daily activities of an active man and one who eats the same food but chooses a lazier way of life. Both need Calories to keep the body ticking over, but at the end of the day the active man will have used nearly 1,000 more Calories than his sluggish counterpart – who will gain an average of ½ kg (1.1 lb) in weight about every five days.

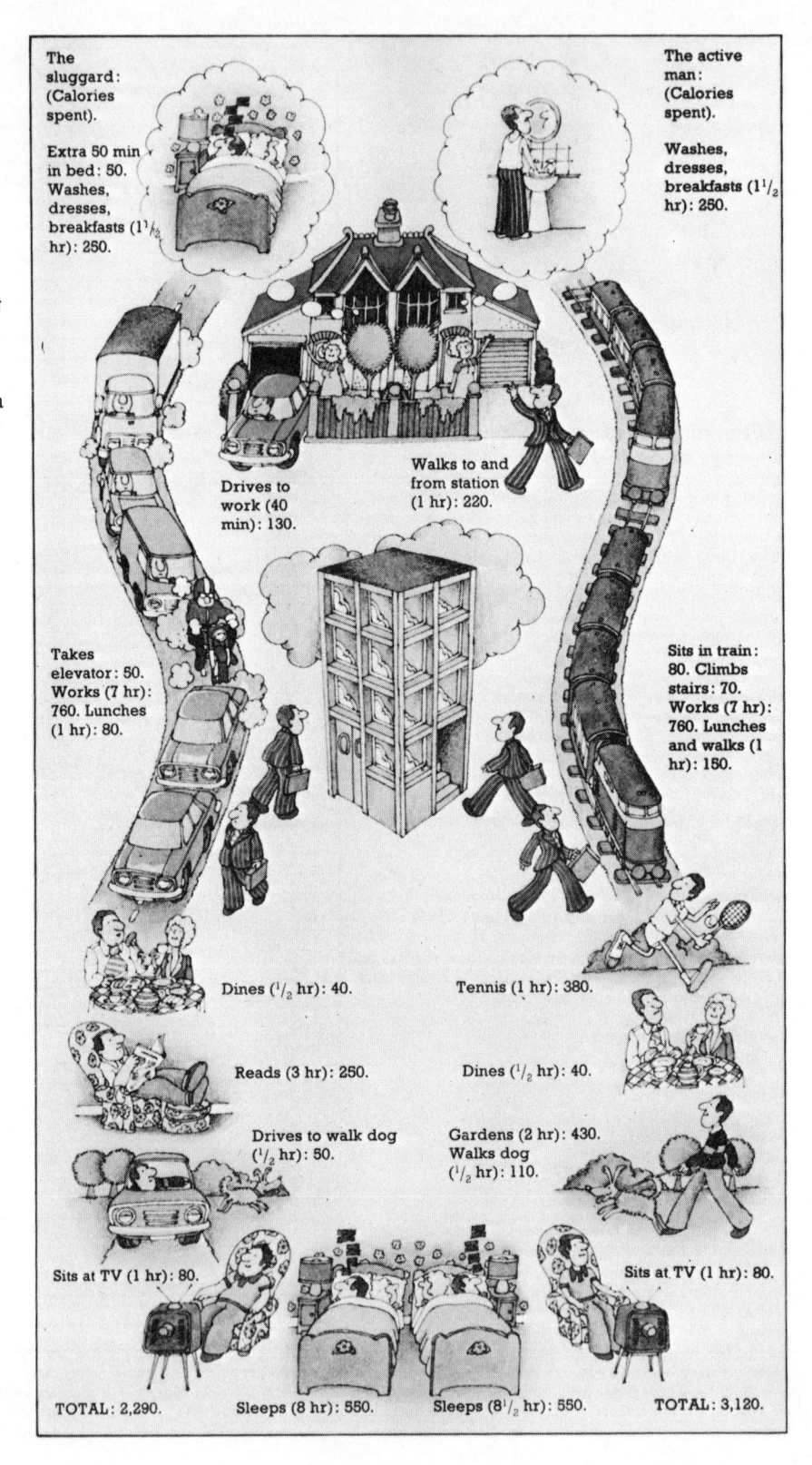

The sluggard: (Calories spent).

Extra 50 min in bed: 50. Washes, dresses, breakfasts (1½ hr): 250.

The active man: (Calories spent).

Washes, dresses, breakfasts (1½ hr): 250.

Drives to work (40 min): 130.

Walks to and from station (1 hr): 220.

Takes elevator: 50. Works (7 hr): 760. Lunches (1 hr): 80.

Sits in train: 80. Climbs stairs: 70. Works (7 hr): 760. Lunches and walks (1 hr): 150.

Dines (½ hr): 40.

Tennis (1 hr): 380.

Reads (3 hr): 250.

Dines (½ hr): 40.

Drives to walk dog (½ hr): 50.

Gardens (2 hr): 430. Walks dog (½ hr): 110.

Sits at TV (1 hr): 80.

Sits at TV (1 hr): 80.

TOTAL: 2,290. Sleeps (8 hr): 550. Sleeps (8½ hr): 550. TOTAL: 3,120.

## 2 The sporting life

**Which sport?**
**Swimming** is considered an ideal exercise for all ages. It uses most muscles and is smooth and rhythmic as well as offering many different strokes.
**Squash,** like swimming, is easy for city dwellers to take up because courts are readily available as are swimming pools. Very heavy activity so should not be played strenuously by the unfit.
**Ping-pong,** again, is easy for the city dweller and gives light to moderate exercise.
**Archery** is suitable for all ages and a sport you can play into old age. Quite a lot of standing about.
**Skiing** is a sport the middle aged and some elderly practised skiers can also enjoy. Moderate exercise when a combination of downhill skiing and being hauled back up a slope. (Cross-country skiing as native to Scandinavia is more arduous.)
**Golf** gives you exercise that is mostly walking, as long as you do walk and don't use a cart. It can vary depending on how fast you go round the course including waiting for your opponent to play his stroke and find lost balls. A good golfer will play less strokes than a novice.
**Gardening** is an ideal exercise for the not so young since a gardener can choose how energetic he wants to be and can do light, moderate or heavy work.
**Walking** is perhaps the basic 'sport' and a good first step to keeping fit as it uses most muscles. Again, the walker can choose his own pace.
**Jogging** is a good exercise, but it is important not to overdo it. The best pace is one that allows you to talk easily to anyone who happens to be beside you.
**Cycling,** like swimming, is smooth and rhythmical and the cyclist can choose his own pace.

**Important**
Although physical activity carries less risk to health than inactivity, anyone doubtful about his or her health should consult a doctor before embarking on any strenuous sport he or she is unused to.

**Calorie expenditure in some everyday sports**
The figures given indicate the Calorie expenditure per minute by men. Women expend approximately one Calorie less per minute. These figures are average since no two people are likely to expend the same amount of energy. One may run all over the court in a tennis match, while the other stands at the net and volleys every shot, moving much less.
 The figures are deceptive in another way. Squash, for example, demands more energy than tennis, but a tennis match is likely to last longer with the result that the total amount of energy used could be greater.

| Sport | Calories |
|---|---|
| Cricket | 2.5 to 3.7 to 6.6 |
| Sailing | 2.5 to 3.7 |
| Trampoline | 2.5 to 3.7 |
| Archery | 2.5 to 5.2 |
| Fishing | 2.5 to 5.2 |
| Croquet | 2.5 to 3.7 |
| Bowls | 2.5 to 3.7 |
| Golf | 2.5 to 7 |
| Tennis | 5.2 to 6.6 |
| Squash | 7.9 and over |
| Badminton | 3.7 to 5.2 |
| Surfing | 3.7 to 5.2 |
| Rowing | 5.2 to 7.9 and over |
| Underwater swimming | 5.2 to 6.6 |
| Swimming | 5.2 to 7.9 and over |
| Climbing | 5.2 to 7.9 and over |
| Skating | 5.2 to 6.6 |
| Skiing | 5.2 to 7.9 and over |
| Basketball | 5.2 to 6.6 |
| Football | 5.2 to 7.9 and over |
| Hockey | 5.2 to 6.6 |
| Rugby | 6.6 to 7.9 and over |
| Fencing | 5.2 to 6.6 |
| Karate | 5.2 to 6.6 |
| Wrestling | 7.9 and over |
| Boxing | 7.9 and over |

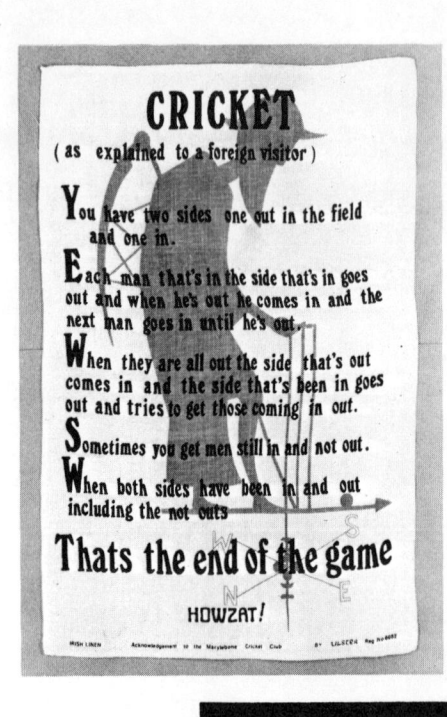

## Leisure

### CRICKET
*(as explained to a foreign visitor)*

**Y**ou have two sides, one out in the field and one in.

**E**ach man that's in the side that's in goes out and when he's out he comes in and the next man goes in until he's out.

**W**hen they are all out the side that's out comes in and the side that's been in goes out and tries to get those coming in out.

**S**ometimes you get men still in and not out.

**W**hen both sides have been in and out including the not outs

**Thats the end of the game**

**HOWZAT!**

---

### Linton Village College
Community Education Programme
### CRICKET COACHING 1984

Two new coaching courses — Get set for a really good season by undertaking pre-season training and coaching in our indoor nets.

**FOR ALL OVER 15 YEARS**

Sunday, 12th February to Sunday, 15th April

Course A: 9.30-11.25 am — Ten sessions
Course B: 11.35-1.30 pm — Ten sessions

Fee for each course £11.00 (full time students and unemployed £7.50) or per session £1.30 (full time students and unemployed £1.00)

KIT: Please bring your own white kit. Indoor gym shoes with light coloured soles. Your own bat, gloves and pads where possible.

Enrolment and further details from:

R. J. Webb, Linton Village College. Tel: Cambridge 891233 or David Bywater, Cambridge 892595.

---

### INTENSIVE SPORTS COACHING

Cricket ★ Tennis ★ Horse Riding ★ Squash ★ Badminton ★ Trampolining
Judo ★ Gymnastics ★ Basketball

With our extensive modern facilities we provide the chance for children aged 11-14 to undergo a week of intensive coaching in any two of the above sports. The emphasis is on developing individual skills under the supervision of highly qualified instructors.
Following the great success of our 1983 Sports Holidays, we are accepting bookings for the weeks commencing 22nd and 29th July, 1984.
The cost is £80 including tuition, meals and accommodation for the week with a £10 supplement for horse riding.
Further information from
Nick Mills Meldreth Manor School, Meldreth, Royston, Hertfordshire.
Telephone Royston 60771 (24 hours)

---

## England's fans leave trail of violence in France

Fifteen English football supporters were taken to hospital in Paris last night after clashes with French supporters and riot police.

Knives and bottles had earlier been used in skirmishes involving English supporters on a cross-Channel ferry on their way to the match between England and France.

Duty-free shops were looted, seats ripped and lifejackets thrown overboard. Four people were taken to hospital after arriving in Dunkirk.

Riot police at the Parc des Princes stadium used small amounts of tear gas at one stage. In one corner they moved in with batons to break up minor clashes between the French and English, several of whom appeared to be severely beaten before being taken away.

It was clear that some English supporters had managed to buy tickets for other areas of the stadium. They lobbed missiles down on French fans below while other French supporters behind one goal ripped up seats and hurled them at the English on a lower level.

After the ferry carrying 550 English supporters docked, several of them began an impromptu stock car race in the port parking area when they found a consignment of new British Leyland cars.

---

*fans*: enthusiastic supporters
*clashes*: } fights
*skirmishes*:
*looted*: robbed (with violence)
*batons*: sticks carried by the police
*lobbed*: threw
*docked*: arrived at the port

## 2 The sporting life

# NIGHT OF MADNESS
## Drunken English soccer hooligans run riot

**ENGLISH** soccer fans were involved in ugly clashes with French riot police during England's international here last night.

Fifteen supporters were in hospital—mostly with head injuries—after they had been baton-charged at the Parc des Princes Stadium.

And after a day of hooliganism by drunken supporters in the city, one was in intensive care with stab wounds.

Helmeted police charged the English fans after they started ripping up seats and hurling them at French fans.

The trouble had started on the journey from England, with rival gangs clashing on the late-night Victoria-Dover train.

They fought with bottles and knives, and stole steel bars, screwdrivers and axes from the train.

The fights continued on the ferry St Elois, which was packed with more than 500 England supporters. The duty-free shops were looted, seats ripped and life-jackets thrown overboard.

When the ferry docked at Dunkirk, the rampaging fans continued to cause havoc.

### Arrests

At the dockside they played their own version of dodgems with a dozen British Leyland cars parked at the port. Two vehicles were written off.

And on the train journey to Paris the hooligans smashed windows, ripped curtains and emptied fire extinguishers.

Once in Paris, the English supporters broke the plate glass windows of a bar near the stadium. Three people were arrested.

As the English fans left the stadium after seeing their side lose 2-0 Football Association chairman Bert Millichip said:

"I'm not totally satisfied that they were all English fans involved, but I do know that this sort of behaviour must stop.

"I hope the Government or somebody can tell us how to prevent it."

And Denis Howell, Labour spokesman on law and order, said: "This is another blow to the good name of British football.

"I am seeking an urgent statement from the Home Secretary to find out what advance action was taken by the police and other law authorities.

"We are all sick and tired of the continual besmirching of the country's name by these nauseating yobs."

**RIOT:** English fans go on the rampage. *Picture:* MONTE FRESCO

---

*fans*: enthusiastic supporters
*soccer*: football
*stab wounds*: injuries caused by a knife
*charged*: rushed forward
*rampaging*: behaving violently
*havoc*: destruction
*dodgems*: a game played at fun fairs, knocking cars into each other
*written off*: destroyed
*hooligans*: noisy, badly behaved young people
*besmirching*: giving a bad reputation
*nauseating*: disgusting
*yobs*: (colloquial) unpleasant people

*Leisure*

## 15 fans in hospital after England game

**From Paul Johnson in Paris**

Fifteen English soccer fans were in hospital last night after the France-England friendly international in Paris, which France won 2-0.

Most of those injured had been beaten up by baton-wielding police, and had head wounds. One man, in his twenties, was in intensive care after being stabbed three times in the back. A doctor said one of the wounds was close to a kidney.

There was trouble before and during the match. Riot police fought with English supporters before the kick-off, and there were clashes at both ends of the Parc des Princes stadium as flag-waving English fans climbed barriers to get at rival French supporters.

Scores of seats were broken and used as missiles.

Several French fans were kicked to the ground and led away bleeding before the CRS squads moved in. They chased groups of English fans away from the French, and used their batons when some visiting supporters, whose flags indicated that they came from London and Nottingham, tried to fight back.

Bottles and other missiles were hurled on to the pitch as police massed inside the stadium.

Just before half-time there was more fighting, and again the English fans appeared to start it. French supporters were punched and kicked to the ground while God Save The Queen was sung by many of the 2,000 English fans.

The CRS moved in again, hitting out wildly with their batons, and kicking out at random. Several fans were manhandled out of the stadium, and one of them was pitched over a concrete wall. The supporters were kicked and beaten by the police as they went.

Earlier, in the depressingly familiar style of English soccer fans abroad, supporters travelling to the match smashed up part of a train, wrecked cars, and fought among themselves with iron bars and knives. Police had to stop and board a Dunkirk-Paris train at Lens as groups of Chelsea and West Ham fans clashed.

In Paris windows were smashed, people were threatened, and taxis were damaged. Attempts to segregate the fans had clearly failed, and tickets were being bought openly.

Trouble began early yesterday on the ferry St Eloi, and four fans were injured. After fighting on the ferry, some supporters got into a British Leyland depot at Dunkirk and damaged several cars.

Nearly three dozen British Transport Police were sent to Dunkirk to meet the fans and escort them across the Channel early today.

## Men of the world

*Saturday? No, sorry, I'm always tied up on a Saturday. Didn't you realise? Okay, so your brother's getting married—is it my fault he chooses to get married when Liverpool's playing Arsenal? Mind you, I'm not saying it's going to be the match of the century—were you there for their last game, for instance? What a farce! As far as I'm concerned, Arsenal just doesn't count as a team, not compared with Liverpool, or even Sheffield, come to that. Interesting about Keegan, I know, but who can say where that's going to lead? World Cup? Don't talk to me about that! I mean, it just wasn't soccer, was it? No, I'm a football man, myself, and nothing can get in the way of that, a sportsman, a born sportsman, that's me...*

---

*soccer*: football
*fans*: enthusiastic supporters
*kick off*: beginning of the game
*missiles*: objects that are thrown

*segregate*: separate
*tied up*: (colloquial) busy
*farce*: ridiculous situation
*Keegan*: a famous footballer

*Liverpool*:
*Arsenal*: } the names of football teams
*Sheffield*:

## 2 The sporting life

# SHAME OF THE SOCCER THUGS

A SPECIAL squad of British Transport Police was sent to Dunkirk last night to escort home England's shameful army of soccer thugs.

And Sealink were planning to bring the mob across the Channel on a freight ferry little used by passengers.

The three dozen BT officers were called up after a day of wanton vandalism and drunken violence had further tarnished Britain's reputation on the Continent.

A British Rail spokesman said: 'These officers know exactly how to deal with this sort of crowd. They are not the type to take any nonsense – and that's a nice way of putting it.'

One 20-year-old English fan was in intensive care last night with stab wounds in the back. Fifteen others were being treated for injuries.

Hundreds of supporters staged a near-riot in the Parc des Princes stadium in Paris during the match with France, which England lost 2–0. Seats were ripped up and there were skirmishes between rival fans.

But France's crack anti-riot squad, the CRS quickly moved in to deal with the trouble. Tear gas was used, and several England fans were beaten to the ground with rubber truncheons.

The helmeted police, carrying riot shields, were uncompromising in their approach and at least 25 arrests were made.

The trouble had begun earlier in the day on the Sealink car ferry Saint Eloi. Fighting broke out among the 550 fans wielding knives and bottles. Duty free shops were looted, seats ripped and life-jackets thrown overboard.

When the ferry docked at Dunkirk, the fans played dodgems with a dozen new BL cars at the port.

---

*soccer*: football
*thugs*: violent criminals
*mob*: large crowd
*freight ferry*: a boat transporting goods
*wanton vandalism*: destruction for no reason
*tarnished*: made dirty

## 2.1

1 Think of the names of as many sports as you can in English, and write them down.

2 Work in groups. Compare what you have written with one another.

3 Look at the list below and put a tick next to the activities which you would regard as sports. Check in the dictionary if you are not sure what the words mean.

| | | |
|---|---|---|
| chess | bowls | wrestling |
| snooker | marbles | gardening |
| angling | cooking | shooting |
| rugby | model aeroplane building | running |
| tennis | greyhound racing | fishing |
| table football | horse racing | hiking |
| soccer | badminton | knitting |
| bridge | boxing | flower arranging |
| dancing | Monopoly | bar billiards |
| climbing | ornithology (bird watching) | |
| blood sports (hunting etc.) | motor racing | |

*Leisure*

4 Discuss the activities with a partner and justify why you do or don't think of them as sports. Try to define what you mean by a 'sport'.

5 Now read the article on page 107 and see whether the people quoted in the article agree with you. Decide which of the definitions of sport you would most agree with and discuss in pairs or groups.

## 2.2

1 Work in pairs. Interview each other and find out what sports you play and what other hobbies you have. Find out why, and make notes.

2 Write up a paragraph from your notes, describing your partner's leisure activities.

3 Look at the list of sports below, and the comments made about them. Try to match the sport with the appropriate comment, by putting the appropriate letter next to the sport.

Martial arts    belly dancing
basketball      fencing
parachuting     rock climbing
tap dancing

a) It's fun and develops a sense of rhythm.
b) It's satisfying, takes a lot of energy.
c) It's skilful and competitive.
d) It's fast, energetic, good for the legs and the brain.
e) Uninhibited, sensuous, energetic.
f) Thrilling, rigorous.
g) You need to be self-disciplined, to concentrate, control yourself and be quick in your reactions.

Now read the article on page 108 and see if you were right.

4 Try to guess what the following words or phrases might mean in the context of the text. First discuss your ideas with a partner, then check with a dictionary.
   a) *options* (column 1, line 12)
   b) *vital* (column 1, line 23)
   c) *stab at* (column 1, line 33)
   d) *rigorous* (column 1, line 34)
   e) *set your own pace* (column 2, lines 17–18)
   f) *for kicks* (column 2, line 34)
   g) *outwit* (column 3, line 14)

## 2.3

1 Work in groups. Look at the 64 different sports listed on page 109, and look up the words you don't know.

2 Tick (√) which one of the following criteria is the most important to you when you decide which sport to take up.
   a) It helps you to develop endurance.
   b) It helps you to develop muscular strength.
   c) It helps mobility.
   d) It helps you to lose weight.

3 Depending on the criterion you choose, try to decide which of the sports listed would be *most* and *least* suitable for you and make a note below.

|    | Most suitable | Least suitable |
|----|---------------|----------------|
| a) |               |                |
| b) |               |                |
| c) |               |                |

Now check with the charts on page 109 (for the first three criteria) and page 111 to see if your predictions were correct.

## 2.4

After looking at the diagram and article on page 110 you decide to write a letter home. Your father (remember that you wrote a letter to him about his eating habits in *Living to eat*) is very lazy and rather overweight. Your brother is not much better, although quite young and much fitter. They both live in the city and tend to drive everywhere. Write a letter to them both suggesting how they could change their lifestyle and what sports they could take up.

## 2.5

1 Read the instructions for playing cricket on page 112. Think of a game you know well and write instructions for how to play it (you needn't write it in the same amusing style!).

2 Work in groups. Don't mention what game you have described, but circulate your instructions within the group and get the other students to try and guess what they refer to.

*Leisure*

## 2.6

1 Look at the four newspaper articles on pages 112–15. Before reading:
   a) try to predict what the articles might be about;
   b) try to predict what *fans* and *thugs* mean;
   c) try to predict which paper(s) is/are likely to be more objective in their way of reporting.

2 Your teacher will divide you into four groups and tell you which article to look at. *Each group will only look at one article*. Read your article as quickly as you can for the general meaning and make notes of the following information. (Don't worry if the information is not in your article.)
   a) Briefly, what happened?
   b) Where was the match held?
   c) How many English supporters were there?
   d) Who won the match?
   e) How many people were injured?
   f) How were they injured?
   g) How many are in hospital?

   The groups will now be reorganised so that each new group contains at least one member from each of the old groups. Exchange your information and try to put together all the relevant facts. Decide, too, if your predictions were correct. Don't worry for the moment about any other information.

3 In your original groups, read the *same article* once more, this time more intensively and make notes under the following headings.

   *Events before the match*
   a) on the train to Dover
   b) on the ferry to Dunkirk
   c) at Dunkirk
   d) on the train to Paris
   e) in Paris

   *At the match*
   a) the role of the French police
   b) the injuries
   c) damage and events during the match

   *After the match*
   a) action from Britain
   b) reaction of British people

   Again, the groups will be rearranged so that an exchange of information can take place and any contradictions can be discovered. This can be followed by a class discussion.

2 The sporting life

4 In your original groups, look through the article a third time, this time focusing on vocabulary.

   a) Find as many examples (nouns, verbs etc.) as you can of the language of violence (e.g. *beat up*).

   b) Make a note of any language which you regard as being particularly subjective or emotional, or typical of newspaper style. Discuss with a partner, and then as a group.

   c) Using only your notes and without referring back to the original articles, each write your own report of the event, and invent a title. Remember to make use of linking words. Decide whose report is the most effective.

   d) Discuss the problem of football violence and what should be done about it. Present your proposals to the rest of the class and then write up your conclusions in the form of a letter of recommendation to your Member of Parliament.

# Roleplay

For groups of three to five people.

## Roles (pages 160–4)

Alison O'Hanlon (role 3)
Jeremy O'Hanlon (role 6)
Tania Ealing (role 15)
Fred Hunter (role 12)
John Funston (role 9)

*Note:* roles 12 and/or 15 could be omitted if necessary.

## Situation

You are a group of friends who are discussing how to spend the evening, where to go, how to get there and so on. You all have different preferences and are not always willing to change your mind.

## Preliminary tasks

You will have some time to read through your role (at the back of the book) and decide where you want to go, how you are going to persuade the others etc. You can look through the texts in this unit if it is relevant, and consult the teacher. But you should only look at *your own* role (and no-one else's).

*Leisure*

## Procedure

Each person will have time to state their preference, as convincingly as possible. Try to persuade the rest of the group to do what you want, but the teacher will give you only a limited amount of time to reach a decision, so you may have to come to a compromise.

## Follow up

Write an entry for the day in your diary, describing how you eventually spent the evening.

# The environment

Look through the texts in both sections of this unit and try to answer the following questions *as quickly as possible*. Remember that you are not looking for any other information, so it is not necessary to study the texts in detail.

1. What could be in your cavity walls, according to an advertisement?
2. Which town may soon have its duck pond destroyed?
3. Who wrote *The Little Pot Boiler*?
4. Which organisation is advertising about ways to save energy?
5. What is the address of the World Wildlife Fund?
6. What kind of energy system is virtually inflation proof?
7. How many ideas are given for saving energy without spending any money?
8. What is the name of an organisation which aims to preserve the environment?
9. Why may it soon be impossible to see a tree?
10. Why does Schweitzer think that men will destroy the earth?

Check your answers with a partner before looking at the key on page 157.

Now look at the exercises on pages 129–33 before reading the texts in section 1 more carefully.

*The environment*

# 1 Preserving the countryside

'Man has lost the capacity to foresee and to forestall. He will end by destroying the earth.'

*Albert Schweitzer*

*Photograph donated by R. Ian Lloyd, Apa Photo Agency, Singapore.*

## A green earth or a dry desert?

*There may still be time to choose*

The World is destroying its tropical rainforests. Half the forests have gone, and the speed of destruction is accelerating. If this continues we will lose for ever the earth's greatest treasure house of plants and animals, perhaps our most valuable natural resource for the future. In the next 25 years the vast forests of Malaysia and Indonesia could be gone forever, leaving erosion to turn a green paradise into a barren wasteland.

It's happening partly because the local people depend upon the forests for their immediate needs for survival, partly because of demand in the developed world for tropical timbers.

In 1980 the WWF and other authorities published a plan for developing resources without destroying them. We need your help to ensure that it is put into action.

Write to WWF for more information. It could be the most important letter you ever write.

**World Wildlife Fund – UK, Panda House, 11-13 Ockford Rd., Godalming, Surrey GU7 1QU.**

**WWF FOR WORLD CONSERVATION**

*forestall*: prevent something happening
*accelerating*: getting faster
*resource*: supply of materials
*erosion*: process of eating away
*barren*: empty/unprofitable
*wasteland*: uncultivated land

*1 Preserving the countryside*

# FOLLOW THE COUNTRY CODE

## ENJOY THE COUNTRYSIDE AND RESPECT ITS LIFE AND WORK

More people than ever before enjoy exploring the countryside. Within a few miles there can be so many changes of scenery that there is always something new to see and do. Something more to enjoy.

Some people will want to discover little known paths and tracks. Others will become interested in architecture or farming, identify plants or observe birds and other wildlife. Many will be content to just sit and absorb the landscape, its features, colour, space and history.

Whatever the interest there is a lot to learn about the countryside – and that learning can be fun. This Code has been written to help you get all the pleasure you can from the countryside while contributing to its care.

It is a living countryside; part of our heritage which gives life to both resident and visitor, protecting it for their mutual interest.

### 1 PROTECT WILDLIFE, PLANTS AND TREES

The countryside today is threatened by many things.

The changing pattern of agriculture, through necessity, often means that in some places, traditional features such as hedgerows and woodlands and even whole species can disappear.

Building takes up more acres every year and there are now more visitors to the countryside than ever before.

It is up to all of us to look after our countryside and its wild things. To protect plants rather than pick them, to observe wildlife rather than destroy it.

The countryside has so much to offer and there's so much we can do to protect it. Isn't it worthwhile trying to do what we can?

### 2 USE GATES AND STILES TO CROSS FENCES, HEDGES AND WALLS

Did you know that you can tell the age of a hedge by the number of different trees growing in it? That drystone walls have such individual characters that, just by looking at them, an expert could instantly tell whereabouts he was?

Gates and stiles, too, change from county to county and you will find many to compare on your country walks.

Always use them to cross hedges, fences or walls where there is a right of way. It should never be necessary to break through a hedge or climb over a wall – this could cause damage and create a gap through which livestock could stray.

If you can't find a gate or stile, check your map, you may have wandered away from the path.

### 3 MAKE NO UNNECESSARY NOISE

Most animals are very timid. Sudden or loud noises can disturb them unnecessarily. Wild animals are so shy that at the slightest noise they will disappear altogether.

If you want to get the best out of the country go quietly. Stop frequently and listen to the life around you. Learn to pause at gateways and see what lies beyond before walking on. You'll be surprised at the activity you can detect even on a winter's day.

To see the countryside at its best you have to try to be part of it, to disturb it as little as possible and take nothing from it except happy memories.

### 4 TAKE SPECIAL CARE ON COUNTRY ROADS

Roads in the country serve many users. Round a tree-lined corner you could find a slow-moving tractor, a flock of sheep, children on their bicycles or a party of ramblers keeping into the side as best they may.

If you are in a car, take extra care, be patient and drive slowly. If you wish to park, make sure that you do not block a farm gateway.

Horse riders and cyclists need special consideration, a slow speed and a wide berth. They in turn should allow motor vehicles every opportunity to pass.

All roadusers need to show extra care on country roads.

*heritage*: what is passed down from the past     *livestock*: animals kept on a farm for breeding, sale, etc.

123

*The environment*

## 5 KEEP TO PUBLIC PATHS ACROSS FARMLAND

There are more than 100,000 miles of public paths providing rights of way throughout Britain. Most of them were there for a purpose – a short cut from one village to another. Often they date back for centuries and represent a real part of local history.

Today, with our road system, they are less often used for work, more for leisure.

They will be clearly marked on your Ordnance Survey map as footpaths and bridleways and many of them are waymarked and signposted. They will take you into the heart of the country, away from roads, away from other people.

Make sure you keep to the path and you can be sure you are not trespassing. You will be treading in the footsteps of generations of countrymen.

## 6 HELP TO KEEP ALL WATER CLEAN

Clear, bright water, either sparkling and tumbling as a mountain or moorland stream, silent and reflective in a lake or pond or flowing softly to the sea is one of the glories of our countryside.

All wildlife depends upon it. Even we depend on it, for much of it finds its way into our reservoirs. But it must be clean water. There is no sadder sight than a stream or pond fouled by debris or polluted by oil or chemicals. Broken glass can harm both livestock and children paddling, scraps of nylon fishing line can get entangled in water birds.

Help to keep all water clean for the sake of all living things.

## 7 KEEP YOUR DOGS UNDER CLOSE CONTROL

Dogs are friendly animals. At home they are loving and obedient but sometimes, in strange countryside, new sights and interesting smells can get the better of them.

Even if he's just playing, a dog which chases cows or sheep can do a great deal of harm and if there are young animals, calves or lambs about, they can easily be killed. The fact that the dog didn't mean any harm is no excuse.

Both you and your dog will enjoy your walk more if he's under control. If there is livestock about there's only one sure place for him. On the lead.

## 8 FASTEN ALL GATES

A gate is a great thing for leaning on and admiring the view. In itself it's a little piece of rural history – you will find different types of gate wherever you go in the country.

They all have one thing in common. They are there to prevent farm animals from straying either out of or into an enclosure. It is often just as important to keep them out of one field as it is to keep them in another.

So to be safe, always close and fasten a gate behind you, even if it was open when you found it – it may have been left open by accident.

It shouldn't be necessary to climb over a gate, but if you must, to follow a path, always do so at the end nearest the hinges. That's where it's strongest.

## 9 GUARD AGAINST ALL RISK OF FIRE

In summertime when it is most pleasant to be outdoors there is always a risk of fire. Hay, heathland and bracken can catch light so easily and once ablaze are very hard to put out.

A little care is all that's needed. Care with lighted cigarettes, pipes or matches. Care in preparing that campsite or barbecue. Don't run the risk of starting something you can't stop, and remember – fire spreads so quickly.

Know what to do if you see a fire break out. Tell the landowner or fire brigade as soon as you can. But, best of all, try not to let it happen in the first place.

*Ordnance Survey*: a government survey department which makes maps

# 10 TAKE YOUR LITTER HOME

Everyone likes a picnic. It's one of the best things about a day in the country. Children, especially, revel in eating outdoors.

Half the pleasure can be finding a quiet, secluded spot where you can be undisturbed, and when you have found one it is a place to remember for future visits.

Make sure you don't spoil it for yourself and others by leaving unsightly litter. Modern packaging materials like plastics don't rot or decay. They stay around and look unpleasant and can often harm wildlife and farm animals.

It's easy to take an empty bag with you and take your litter home.

---

I think that I shall never see
A poem lovely as a tree;
A tree that in the summer wears
A nest of robins in its hair.
*Alice Meynell*

I think that I shall never see
A billboard lovely as a tree.
Perhaps unless the billboards fall
I'll never see a tree at all.
*Ogden Nash*

'The earth has enough for every man's
need but not for every man's greed.'
*Gandhi*

## 'Once Upon'

Once upon an unfortunate time, there was a hairy thing called man. Along with him was a hairier thing called animal. Man had a larger brain which made him think he was superior to animals.

Some men thought they were superior to men. They became leader men. Leader men said 'We have no need to work, we will kill animals to eat.' So they did.

Man increased animals decreased. Eventually leader men said 'There are not enough animals left to eat. We must grow our own food.' So man grew food.

Now, the only animals man had not destroyed were tiny ones, like rabbits and mices, and these little animals were caught eating some of man's crops. 'These animals are a menace. They must die.'

In China they killed all the sparrows. In Australia they killed all the rabbits. Everywhere man killed all wild life. Soon there was none, and all the birds were poisoned. Leader man said 'At last! We are free of pests.'

Man's numbers increased. The world became crowded with men. They all had to sleep standing up. One day a leader man saw a new creature eating his crops. This creature's name was starving people.

'This creature is a menace!' said leader man . . .

(from *The Little Pot Boiler* by Spike Milligan)

"To begin with, my idea was to come to the country in order to raise rabbits"

*billboard*: a board to display advertisements
*nest*: a place where birds lay eggs
*robin*: a bird with a red breast
*crops*: plants grown as food
*a menace*: a danger
*pests*: destructive creatures (in this context: especially to crops)

# The environment

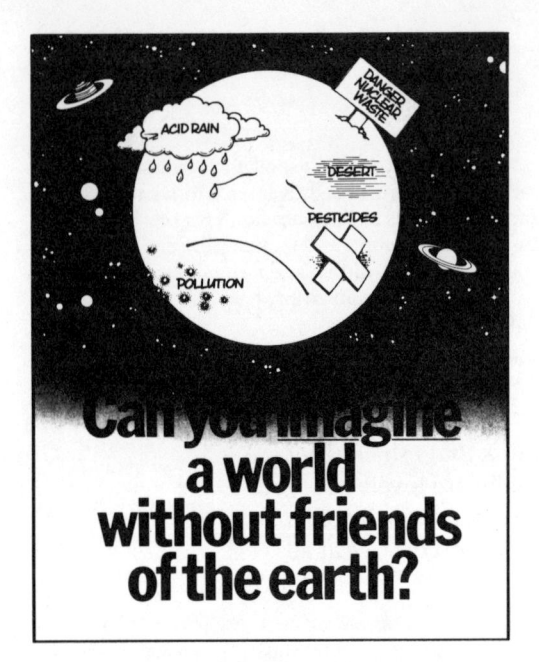

**Can you imagine a world without friends of the earth?**

... Nuclear and toxic wastes, pesticides, acid rain, asbestos; destruction of wildlife, countryside and tropical rain forests; depletion and mis-use of natural resources; the waste of unemployment — they all threaten our world now ...

### ... if we don't fight them, who will?

## The human hazards of a modern world.

We pay a price for the benefits of our industrial society. The risk of a nuclear accident, a waste train derailed, a chemical works explosion, a poisoned water supply, lead dust in the playground or asbestos in the home, are hazards we face daily. Cancer deaths increase our concern. Official secrecy makes matters worse. Poor control of pesticides on the farm, the sites of dangerous factories, land disposal plans for nuclear waste — facts hidden from near-by communities. We suffer the accidents, noise and stress of cities choked by traffic.

We waste energy and live in a throw-away dreamland. Conservation is a vital lifeline for the future.

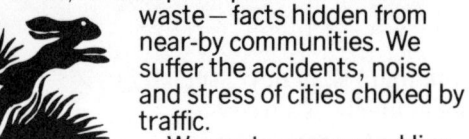

*The Hare — symbol of our campaign to protect wildlife habitats.*

## Nature under threat.

Large areas of Britain have lost many birds, plants and animals. Otters, kingfishers, many orchids, cowslips and other once-common species are threatened. Since 1949 we have destroyed 95% of our wildflower-rich meadows. Heaths, fens, mires and ancient woods have largely disappeared. Agribusiness, forestry and motorways are to blame. Across the globe life support grows more fragile. Poisons banned in the West are sold to the Third World. The rain forests are sacrificed because food and fuel are scarce. Wild species and vital seeds are lost. The climate is altered. Nations foolishly pollute the air and sea — upon which we all rely. Creatures and natural resources are exploited for short-term greed and gain.

Friends of the Earth, 377 City Road, London EC1V 1NA, Tel: 01-837 0731

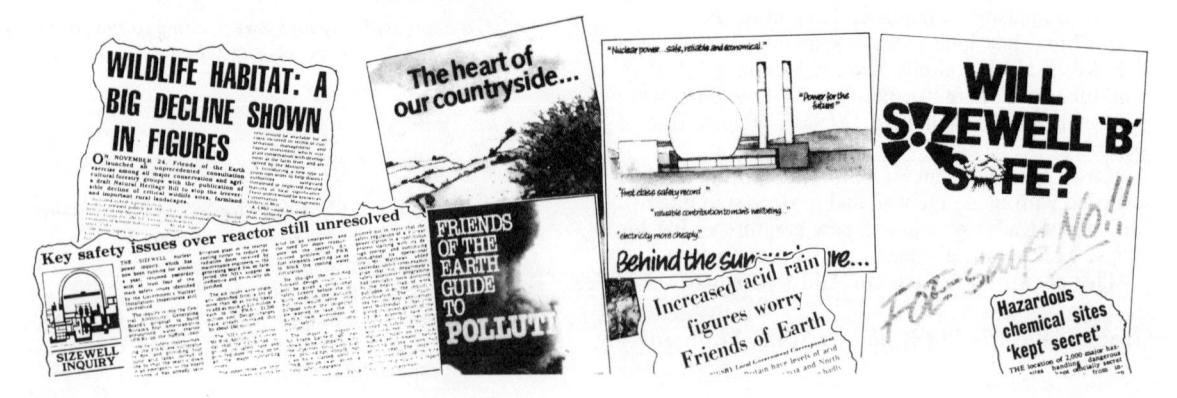

# 1 Preserving the countryside

## What is Friends of the Earth?

A well-organised non party-political, national pressure group. Part of an international network covering 28 different countries. Our campaigners seek to make people aware of the key issues and publicise the environmental case on T.V., Radio and in the press. We lobby politicians and government bodies. We press for changes in the law and in policies decided by the Town Hall or Whitehall.

*Radioactive nuclear waste — should they bury it at Bedford, Billingham and other secret sites in Britain?*

For example, our Natural Heritage Bill aims to protect special nature sites. We fought plans to build a nuclear reprocessing plant at Windscale. We attend public inquiries and provide evidence for Parliamentary Committees. We publish books and a wide variety of information materials. We have 20,000 supporters and 250 action groups who campaign at a local level.

*Nuclear Power is unreliable, expensive and unsafe. We are fighting the PWR at the Sizewell Inquiry.*

Together we are a highly effective force for conservation, public safety and a clean, lasting environment.

## What does FoE campaign on?

ENERGY:
**For:** Conservation, Home insulation and Renewable energy.
**Against:** Sizewell PWR and any further nuclear expansion.

NUCLEAR WASTE
**For:** Dry storage at the power stations. Open debate and research for future safe disposal.
**Against:** Reprocessing at Windscale, Transport across country, Dumping at sea or on land.

POLLUTION:
**For:** Controls on use of pesticides, More information on hazards at work and in the home, Ban on strawburning.
**Against:** Acid rain, Industrial secrecy, Over-use of nitrate fertilisers.

WILDLIFE & COUNTRYSIDE:
**For:** New Natural Heritage Bill, More money for conservation.
**Against:** Over-intensive, big-business farming, Destruction of habitats and Tropical Forests, Whaling and Seal culling.

TRANSPORT:
**For:** Your public bus service and rail network. Safe cycling facilities.
**Against:** Heavy lorries, Car-dominated cities, Closure of Settle-Carlisle line.

## A FoE Local Group in Action.

Wheatley FoE, Oxfordshire

Otmoor and Bernwood Forest (Britain's best butterfly wood) are threatened by the M.40 extension route. Wheatley FoE have campaigned since 1978 to save this unspoilt area of semi-wetland. The Group recently bought 2.3 acres of ancient meadow and sold plots to 3000 people, many overseas.

*Over half Britain's ancient woodlands have been felled since 1945. 140,000 miles of hedgerows have disappeared.*

The Government are faced with a unique legal quandary — the wild flowers of Otmoor may yet survive!

## How you can help our work.

- All the campaigns are run on a shoestring budget. We urgently need your donation and/or membership to carry on the fight.
- Persuade your friends to join FoE — the more supporters we have, the more work we can do.
- Join a local FoE Group — there will be one not far from you — or form a new one. We have staff and materials to help you.
- Many FoE Groups and supporters devise and run job creation schemes such as home insulation, bottle recovery, wastepaper collections and cycle route building.

*FoE wants to save Public Transport in the town and country; and promote safe, cheap travel*

---

*toxic waste*: poisonous remains
*pesticides*: chemicals used to destroy pests
*depletion*: use of, until there is little or nothing left
*hazards*: dangers
*otters*: mammals which live in and near water
*kingfisher*: a kind of bird
*orchids*: } wild flowers
*cowslips*:
*heaths*: areas of uncultivated land
*fens*: low wet land

*mires*: areas of muddy land
*globe*: the world
*scarce*: very little
*network*: organised system
*lobby*: try to influence
*Whitehall*: government building
*whaling*: } killing of animals for profit
*seal culling*:
*M40*: a motorway
*shoestring budget*: very little money

*The environment*

## CHILDREN'S PLEA TO COUNCIL

# 'Don't wreck our pond'

**CHILDREN** from St Mary's Junior School, Saffron Walden, have launched a campaign to save the duck pond in Freshwell Street from being destroyed by a new car park.

Seventy children signed a petition last week which they have sent to MP Mr Alan Haselhurst following news that Uttlesford District Council may decide to build a car park on Swan Meadows where the pond is situated.

The petition, composed by Elizabeth Rybicki and Joanne Gough, both aged ten, says: "I have heard that the pretty meadow behind the duck pond is to be changed into a car park. It would really spoil our enjoyment and nearly all the children's in our town.

"I go there often and find it a lovely place. Sometimes there are horses there as well. I often see mothers and their children down there feeding ducks and even in winter I still enjoy it.

"If we do need a car park so badly please will you try and put it in a different place."

Mr Mark Ferland, headmaster of St Mary's said: "I am very pleased to see the children use their initiative like this. They have a very conservation-minded teacher and I think she has probably inspired them."

Mr Haselhurst said this week that he would pass the views of the children to Uttlesford District Council.

He felt there was a definite need for more car parking in the town. "It's a question of striking a balance between maintaining the economic life of the town and insuring that one doesn't spoil its heritage."

The Council's policy and resources committee recently agreed to proceed with plans to acquire land and develop a car park there.

It would cost around £100,000 to provide access and parking for about 100 cars adjacent to the pond and a further 250 spaces could be created at an extra cost of £75,000. At a later date a further 250 spaces could be added if required.

*launched a campaign*: began an organised attempt to get public support
*MP*: Member of Parliament

# 1 Preserving the countryside

## 1.1

1 Look at the advertisement on page 122 and answer the following questions.

    a) What is likely to happen to the tropical forests in the next 25 years?
    b) Why is this happening? (*two reasons*)
    c) What do the initials WWF stand for?
    d) What is the WWF trying to do?
    e) What does the WWF want you to do?

2 Look at the article again and decide what the following words refer to.

    a) *its* (line 1)        f) *your* (line 20)
    b) *this* (line 4)       g) *it* (line 20)
    c) *It* (line 12)        h) *It* (line 23)
    d) *their* (line 14)    i) *you* (line 23)
    e) *them* (line 19)

## 1.2

1 The Country Code is a set of rules which aims to protect the countryside. Work in pairs. Before looking at pages 123–5, try to predict why the Country Code states that you *should* or *should not* do the following, when you are in the country. After discussing possible reasons with each other, look through the texts and see if you were correct.

    a) You should use gates or stiles rather than climb over walls, hedges etc.
    b) You shouldn't pick flowers, or destroy trees or wildlife.
    c) You shouldn't be noisy.
    d) You should stay on the paths which are shown on the maps.
    e) You should take care if driving on country roads.
    f) You should keep (even well-behaved) dogs under control.
    g) You should close gates carefully.
    h) You should be careful with matches, cigarettes and even barbecues.
    i) You should take your rubbish home with you.
    j) You should help to keep the water clean.

2 Look through the texts again quickly and, in groups, find the answers to the *Countryside Quiz*.

    a) What kinds of things do people like doing when they are in the country?
    b) How can you tell how old a hedge is?
    c) What should you do if you have a dog with you in the country?
    d) Why were public paths originally there?
    e) Find four different names for areas of water.
    f) Why are some traditional features of the countryside disappearing?

*The environment*

    g) What should you do if a fire starts in the country?
    h) What kind of people may you meet on country roads?
    i) If you have to climb over a gate, which side should you climb over?
    j) What are public paths marked as on the map?

3 Look at the relevant text number and find words in the text that are similar in meaning to the following.

*1*
a) a group of the same kind (animals, birds, plants etc.)
b) a measurement of land

*2*
a) steps which enable people to get over hedges, walls etc.
b) immediately
c) animals such as cows, pigs etc. (kept for profit)
d) walk away and get lost

*4*
a) a group of walkers
b) plenty of room

*5*
a) a quicker way of getting somewhere
b) a path for people on horses
c) to go on someone's land, illegally

*6*
a) a place where water is kept
b) made dirty
c) walking in the water

*7*
a) tempt them to do something (out of character)
b) a leather strap, used for taking dogs for walks

*8*
joint on which a gate swings

*9*
a) on fire
b) start

*10*
a) enjoy
b) isolated
c) bits of paper etc.
d) go bad

## 1.3

1 Look at page 125, 'Once Upon'. Read the text through once, quickly, and decide if the following statements are true or false according to the passage. Write T or F next to each statement.

   a) Animals are inferior to men.
   b) Men killed animals instead of working.
   c) Some men who were better than others were chosen as leaders.
   d) The reason that men started growing food was that they hadn't many animals left to eat.
   e) Small animals were allowed to live at first.
   f) Birds were regarded as harmless.
   g) After all the animals had been killed, there were enough crops for all men.

2 Look at the passage a second time and decide what the following words and phrases refer to. Make a note of your answers.

   a) *him* (line 2)
   b) *him* (line 4)
   c) *they* (line 5)
   d) 'So they *did*' (lines 7–8). Did what?
   e) '*These* animals' (line 15)
   f) 'Soon there was *none*' (line 18). No what?
   g) '*This* creature' (line 24)

3 In pairs, discuss what you think the writer's purpose was in this text (e.g. to inform, complain, amuse etc.). Refer closely to the text.

## 1.4

1 Look at the picture on page 126 and, in pairs, discuss which of these problems you have in your own country and what, if anything, is being done to help.

2 Look at the headline 'The human hazards of a modern world' and, individually or in pairs, make a note of as many environmental problems as you can think of that are caused by the growing industrial society. Then read the paragraph and add any other problems which are mentioned there.

3 Tell your partner of any events which have occurred recently in your own country (or another) which illustrate the growing danger to the environment.

*The environment*

4 Read the paragraph 'Nature under threat' and find out:
   a) why so many wild animals, birds, plants and parts of the countryside are disappearing;
   b) why species of animals and natural resources are being used and exploited.

5 In groups, select one or more of the problems which are mentioned in these two paragraphs, and discuss what could be done about it/them.

6 Write a letter to a newspaper drawing attention to the problem(s) and suggesting what might be done.

7 Look through the text on pages 126–7 again, and then try to complete the following summary, using the words from the list which follows (they are in mixed-up order).

Friends of the Earth is a (1) .................... which aims to (2) .................... the environment. It has 250 (3) .................... action groups, but also works at a national and (4) .................... level, trying to get maximum (5) .................... for environmental problems and trying to (6) .................... the law.

One of its aims is to (7) .................... energy and (8) .................... nuclear expansion, as well as investigating ways of (9) .................... of nuclear waste safely. It is opposed to (10) .................... at sea or on land.

The group is very concerned about the problem of (11) ....................; among other things, it is looking for greater (12) .................... of pesticides on (13) .....................

One of its other interests is the protection of (14) .................... and the (15) ..................... One of the things it is trying to do is prevent the killing of (16) .................... and (17) .....................

In its efforts to cut down on heavy traffic it is in favour of (18) .................... transport and of encouraging (19) .....................

In order to carry on its work, Friends of the Earth needs (20) .................... and wants to encourage you to (21) .................... a local group or start a new one. Many groups are working to reduce (22) .................... by creating jobs such as (23) .....................

a) pollution         c) prevent
b) countryside       d) group

132

1 *Preserving the countryside*

e) publicity
f) money
g) seals
h) farms
i) dumping
j) local
k) change
l) unemployment
m) public
n) control
o) disposing
p) international
q) conserve
r) whales
s) wildlife
t) join
u) wastepaper collection
v) protect
w) cycling

## 1.5

1 Look at the newspaper article on page 128 and decide whether the following statements are true or false according to the text. Write T or F next to each statement.
   a) Children at a junior school are complaining that Saffron Walden doesn't need another car park.
   b) The children are worried about losing the duck pond.
   c) Alan Haselhurst has decided to build a car park near the duck pond.
   d) The headmaster of their school told the children to complain.
   e) Mr Haselhurst has ignored the children's request.
   f) More than 150 spaces could be provided immediately in a new car park.

2 Find another word in the text that means approximately the same as each of the following.
   a) to destroy
   b) a written request
   c) to act on their own / think for themselves
   d) gave them the idea
   e) what has been given by the past
   f) to go on with
   g) next to

**Before reading the texts in section 2 more carefully, look at the exercises on pages 141–4.**

133

*The environment*

## 2 Conserving energy

# CUT YOUR HEATING BILLS

**WHERE THE HEAT GOES AND HOW TO STOP IT**

## 2 Conserving energy

# Energy, Money and You

More and more people are becoming worried about the dangers of nuclear power. We are told that we need it to meet our future energy requirements, but is it really the answer?

After 30 years of development nuclear power supplies less than 2% of the energy we use. It is too complicated and expensive to substitute for fossil fuels (coal, gas and oil) as they become scarce. We need to find quicker, safer and cheaper ways of meeting our energy requirements.

Most of the energy we use is for heating buildings and water. By doing this more efficiently we can immediately reduce the demand for fossil fuels so that they will last longer.

We can all heat our own homes and water tanks more efficiently by installing insulation, choosing the right heating system and using energy economically.

There is a further good reason for taking these measures: fuel prices are going to rise considerably faster than wages and may double by the year 2000. For an increasing number of people the only way to keep warm and be able to pay fuel bills is to save energy wherever possible.

Below are some suggestions for saving energy.

### INSULATION

On average 65% of the energy we use in our homes is for space (room) heating. The heat escapes from a typical, uninsulated, semi-detached house through the walls (35%), roof (25%), floor (15%), draughts (15%) and windows (10%).

These figures are a useful guide but can vary considerably, depending on the age, type and size of home. By insulating our homes we can slow down the rate at which heat escapes.

### Draught-Proofing

This is easy and cheap and can save a lot of money, particularly in older houses. Using a variety of strips and fillers (available from hardware and D.I.Y. shops) windows, doors, letter boxes, skirting and floor boards and unused fireplaces can be sealed against draughts. Remember though that some ventilation is necessary to prevent condensation and to ensure safe-burning of fuel appliances. Usually draught-proofing costs only a few pounds and pays for itself in less than a year.

### Loft Insulation

Glass fibre matting is the material most commonly used. The thicker the layer of matting, the more effective it will be. 200mm (8 in) of glass fibre can cut the rate of heat loss through the roof by 90%. It costs about £150 (all prices for 1980) to buy the matting for an average sized semi from a builder's merchant.

### Wall Insulation

Brick walls come in two types, each requiring a different form of insulation. **Cavity walls** have two layers of brick with a gap in between. Heat losses can be reduced by injecting insulating material into the cavity. This has to be done by a contractor and will cost about £200 for an average semi. It will cut the rate of heat loss through the walls by 60% or more and can save up to 20% on heating bills.

Older houses usually have **solid walls.** External wall insulation can improve the appearance of the house and will, in time, pay back its cost in energy savings. Insulation should be at least 100mm thick and will cost around £15 per square metre if the work is done by a contractor. Insulation can be applied internally, though it is difficult to install.

### Floor Insulation

Heat losses are greatest through **suspended timber floors.** The simplest way of keeping heat in is to put a layer of insulating material under the floor covering. Aluminium foil, hardboard or softboard are suitable. The most effective method is to fix glass fibre matting (at least 100mm) under the floor.

**Solid concrete floors** keep heat in better but are cold to stand on. An insulating floor covering, such as cork or a thick carpet and underlay will create a warmer surface.

### Window Insulation

The rate of heat loss through windows can be halved by double-glazing. Adding secondary panes clipped to existing window frames costs about £10 per square metre. A very cheap and almost equally effective alternative is the fixing of cling-film (transparent food-wrapping material) across the inside of the frame. Perspex or polythene can also be used. Replacing single-paned windows with wooden frames with aluminium-sealed double-glazing units does not result in a significant saving of energy because the heat escapes more quickly through the metal frames. Heavy lined curtains can reduce heat loss as effectively as double-glazing. Shutters constructed from insulating material are more effective still.

### Insulating the Water Tank

21% of the energy consumed in our homes is for water heating. If you have an immersion heater make sure it has a thick, tight-fitting jacket of insulating material. A 75mm thick jacket will cost under £10 and pay for itself in a few weeks. A thicker jacket will save even more in the long run. Hot water pipes should be lagged at the same time.

### CHOOSING THE RIGHT FUEL

Using electricity is the most inefficient way of heating our homes. 85-90% is produced by burning coal or oil in expensive power stations. Only 30% of the energy is turned into electricity; the rest is lost at the power station as waste heat. Nuclear power stations are even more expensive to build and many have been unreliable in operation.

In Denmark, West Germany and Holland many homes are now heated by Combined Heat and Power (C.H.P.) schemes. Instead of being wasted the heat produced by power stations is utilised by piping it directly to people's homes. C.H.P. schemes should be built in Britain's major towns and cities.

Meanwhile North Sea gas is the best fuel to use for domestic heating. Oil or coal fired central heating is the best option for homes which cannot be connected to the gas mains.

---

*insulation*: method of preventing heat loss by covering things
*draught proofing*: method of preventing loss of heat because of currents of air
*hardware shop*: shop which sells electrical goods etc.
*DIY*: Do It Yourself
*loft*: room in the roof

*The environment*

# FREE SAVINGS

Insulating and draughtproofing your house means spending money – even though you're going to get it back later.

But there are steps you can take which cost nothing. Here are 10 tips.

**1** **Check what you're spending:** read your meters at least once a month, and keep a record of the readings. Try to explain any increases which aren't due to colder weather.

**2** **Draw the curtains:** thick curtains, when closed, can be almost as effective as double-glazing. Close them at dusk, but make sure they don't hang in front of your central heating radiators or the hot air will travel up behind the curtains and through the windows. Do this in rooms you're not using, too.

**3** **Turn down thermostats** a few degrees, as long as you're still comfortable. Reducing the air temperature by 1°C throughout the house could save around five per cent on your fuel bill. But remember older people and young children generally need higher temperatures.

**4** **Experiment with timers:** set your heating to come on later and go off sooner – especially as it gets warmer in spring – and see whether you notice. And, of course, make sure it's set to go off at night and while you're out at work. Turn off the heating in summer and set the boiler to come on for just long enough to heat sufficient hot water.

**5** **Turn the heat down in rooms you're not using,** and keep the doors shut. You can probably keep all the upstairs rooms at a lower temperature most of the time – but keep downstairs doors shut or warm air will rise upstairs.

**6** **Keep windows shut:** if you feel too hot, turn the heating down instead.

**7** **Turn off extractor fans** when not needed. A fan working unnecessarily is drawing cold air in from outside.

**8** **Use cheaper electricity:** if you're already on Economy 7 tariff, your immersion heater and *any* other electrical appliance you use at night or early in the morning will be on the off-peak rate. Off-peak electricity is available for a period of seven hours between midnight and 8am GMT. The exact times may vary in different areas – check with your Electricity Board.

**9** **Wear warmer clothes:** obvious perhaps, but a thick pullover could be equivalent to 1°C or more on your thermostat.

**10** **Shop around for solid fuel:** take advantage of any summer discounts, and buy in bulk – perhaps with a neighbour.

*double glazing*: an extra layer of glass for the window (to keep in heat)
*in bulk*: a lot at one time

## 2 Conserving energy

## Why Solar Energy?

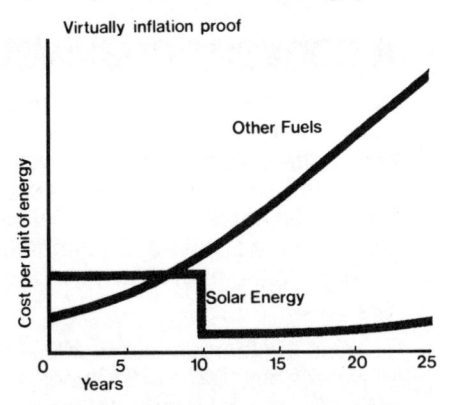

The sun is a vast inexhaustible furnace. It is our greatest energy resource. So great is its power, that in only three days it provides our planet with as much heat and light as would be produced by burning all the earth's remaining reserves of oil, coal and timber. It is an economically, ecologically and politically desirable source of renewable energy. It is pollution free, requires no distribution network, and is not subject to political embargo.

Most important of all, economically speaking, the cost of energy delivered by a solar heating system is virtually inflation proof. This is because one can purchase energy at today's prices for use in future years, while operation/maintenance costs remain almost negligible.

## 1

## A Solar System

A special fluid that will not boil, freeze or corrode is circulated around a closed circuit (B). As the fluid passes through the collectors (A) it absorbs heat. The hot liquid then passes through the solar coil, the coil gets hot and heats the water in the solar tank (C). The fluid, now cooled, is pumped back to the collectors and the cycle is repeated continuously as long as there is sufficient solar radiation. The hot water in the storage tank is either stored for later use, or transferred to where it is needed. The control system (D) ensures that the whole system functions quite automatically as conditions dictate.

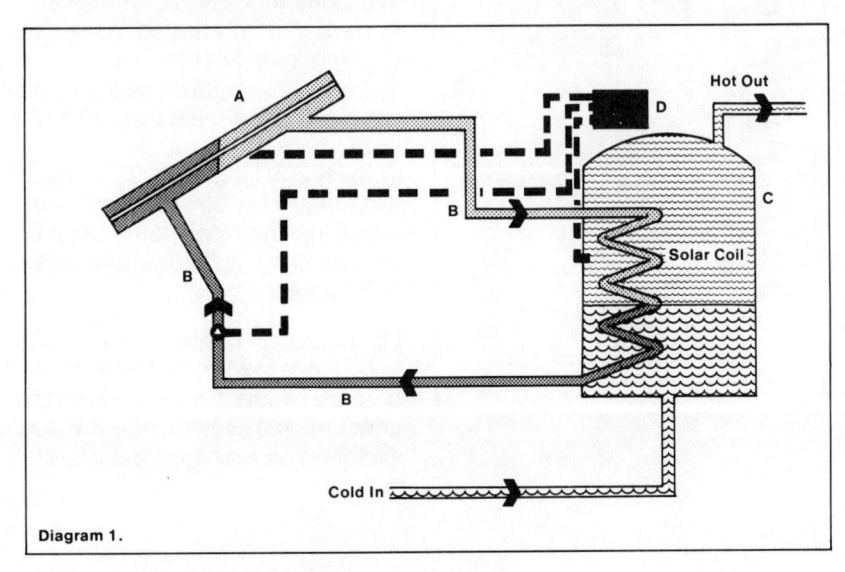

Diagram 1.

*a furnace*: a place for heating something   *timber*: wood   *an embargo*: a prohibition

*The environment*

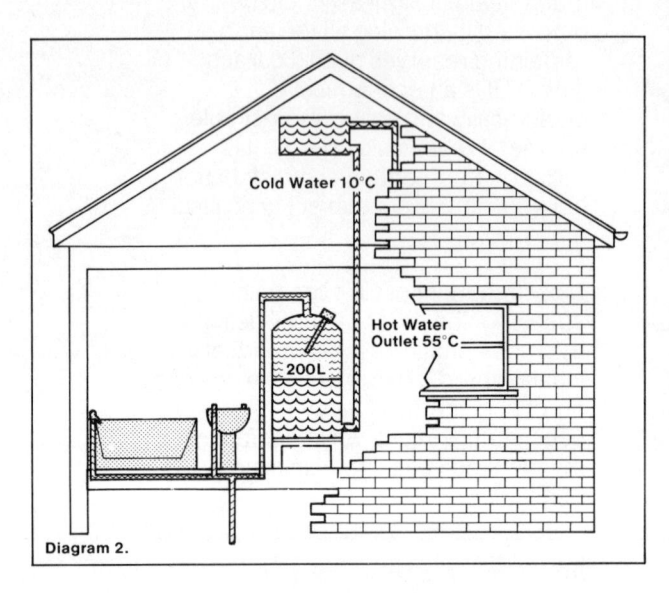

## 2
## A conventional System

In a Conventional System cold water from the mains supply at say 10°C enters the tank and is heated by an oil or gas fired burner, or an electrical immersion heater. Conventional fuel is burned up until the water temperature is raised to the required temperature of say 55°C.

To raise the temperature of 200 litres* of water from 10°C to 55°C uses 10.5 kWh of electrical energy. At today's prices this could cost £174 per year. If fuel prices increase at the rate of 20% per year, the annual cost would be £898 by 1990.

* Typical daily consumption for a 4 person family.

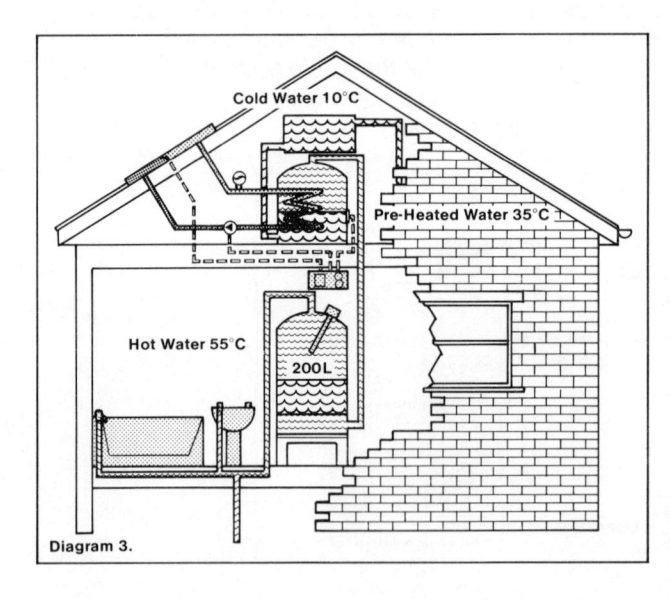

Diagram 2.

## 3
## A Solar plus conventional System

In a Combined System the solar system is simply added to the existing Conventional System. The solar system either partially or totally heats the water depending upon conditions.

To heat 200 litres from 35°C to 55°C uses only 4.65 kWh of electrical energy — less than half the energy required by a conventional system receiving cold 10°C water.

Of course, on bright sunny days the solar system will heat the water to 55° or more, without any help from the conventional system, which will stay switched off — saving costly fuel.

Diagram 3.

2 Conserving energy

# Want to know the difference home insulation makes? Stuff this paper up your jumper.

Almost immediately you'll feel the extra warmth. Of course, there's a simple reason why.

The more layers there are between you and the cold outside, the less body heat you lose.

Exactly the same principle applies to your home. These days, most people have some insulation. What they generally don't have is enough.

Did you know, for example, that the most efficient depth of loft insulation is at least 4 inches?

Or that with cavity insulation you can significantly cut the heat loss through your walls?

A modern jacket around your hot water tank can cut heat loss by 75%.

And with the proper use of your time switches and thermostats, you could reduce your annual central heating bill by up to 20%.

All over your home there are areas where you can save energy and money, no matter what fuel you're using.

The Energy Efficiency Office exists to help you do just that.

Complete the coupon and we'll send you our free booklet, 'Make the most of your heating'. It's packed with facts and easy ways to save precious energy.

Look out for our 'Energy Saver Show', too. It will be in your area soon.

Meanwhile, post the coupon.

For the price of a stamp, you could knock pounds off your fuel bills.

To: The Energy Efficiency Office, P.O. Box 702, London SW20 8SZ. Please send me a free copy of 'Make the most of your heating'.

Name_____

Address_____

_____

**ENERGY EFFICIENCY OFFICE**

*stuff*: push

*The environment*

# If this is all that's filling your cavity walls, it's costing you £50 a year.

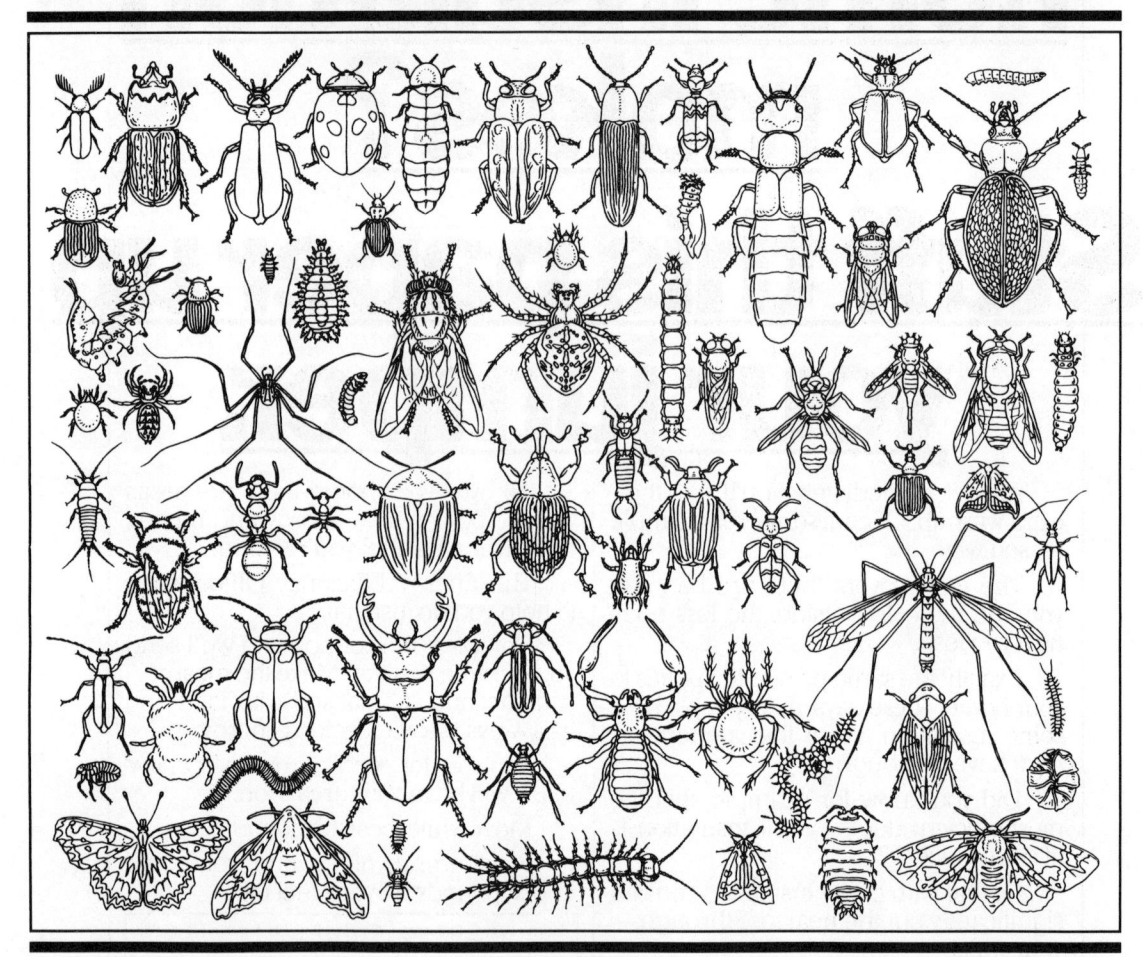

If you have uninsulated cavity walls, they're costing you at least £50 a year in wasted heat.

All that wasted heat doesn't disappear. Some of it ends up trapped between the two brick walls. And turns the cavity between into a five star hotel for all the characters on this page.

Because it's sheltered. It's dry.

And thanks to you, it's also lovely and warm. What cockroach could ask for more?

Cavity wall insulation saves you so much money it could literally pay for itself in just 3 years.

And you'll have a warm insulating blanket around your home instead of a breeding ground for lots of creepy-crawlies.

The Energy Efficiency Office has a free booklet which shows you how to save hundreds of pounds by insulating your home completely.

For instance, under £10 spent on a thick tank jacket could easily save you £40 a year. For a building society to offer that kind of return, they'd have to pay over 400% interest!

If you're bugged by the size of your fuel bills, write for your free copy of 'Make the most of your heating' to the Energy Efficiency Office, FREEPOST, P.O. Box 100, West Sussex RH16 1TY. It won't even cost you the price of a stamp.

**ENERGY EFFICIENCY OFFICE**

*cockroach*: an insect (a household pest)
*breeding ground*: an area where more insects are produced
*bugged by*: (play on words) annoyed by

## 2 Conserving energy

# If these bugs ARE filling your cavity walls your house may well interest David Bellamy

**By GILL SWAIN**

CREEPY-CRAWLIES make many people cringe. And the sight of 70 of them drawn in meticulous detail is designed to send a shudder down the average spine.

So the Central Office of Information was well pleased with its energy conservation advertisements featuring a dramatic collection of insects and headlined: 'If this is all that's filling your cavity walls, it's costing you £50 a year.'

It is spending around £300,000 on the advert to persuade people to invest in insulation, and millions of people have turned the pages of their favourite newspaper to be startled and appalled by the sight of the bugs, making a five-star hotel of their walls.

But it was the COI's turn to shudder yesterday when it learnt that most of the featured insects would rarely be found in a cavity wall, that none makes it its natural habitat, and that two are completely foreign to these shores.

Botanist David Bellamy first spotted the mistake and was worried in case the collection included any endangered species.

His query ended up on the desk of eminent entomologist Dr Paul Whalley, of the Natural History Museum, who said yesterday that none was endangered, but added: 'I would be very surprised to find 80 per cent. of these insects in a cavity wall. And I would be quite excited if I found the caterpillar of the lobster moth in my wall.'

He said there was a Japanese insect and a Buprestid beetle which were never found in Britain. The wood tiger moth and one of the stag beetles were rare. All the insects, except the silverfish, would avoid cavity walls.

COI and the Energy Efficiency Office scrambled to pass on the blame to the advertising agency, Young and Rubicam, which drew up the advert.

Garfield Meredith, marketing director of the Energy Efficiency Office, said: 'We asked for all these points to be checked.'

Rupert Howell, account director at Young and Rubicam, said he had been assured by the National Cavity Insulation Association that all these insects could be found in cavity walls. 'It may be they have strayed in there, but insulators are constantly surprised by what they find in walls. Some things are found which were not shown . . . like wasps nests.'

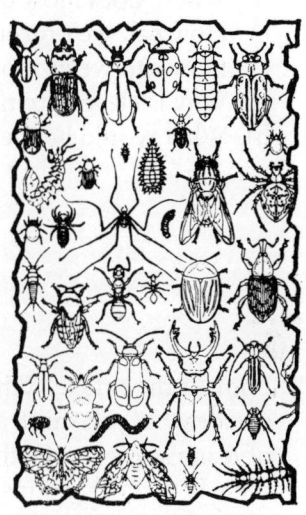

*Advert of errors?*

*entomologist*: an expert on insects

## 2.1

1 Work with a partner. Look at the picture on page 134 and try to decide where most of the heat escapes from in a normal house, and how you could stop it escaping. Make notes.

2 Report back on your ideas in a class discussion about how you can conserve energy.

3 Read the text on page 136 and check whether it contains any ideas on saving energy that you did not think of.

*The environment*

4 Look at the article on page 135 and see how quickly you can find the answers to the following questions. Discuss your answers in pairs, and then as a class. Remember to make close reference to the text.

   a) Why is it so important to find ways of conserving energy?
   b) What are 'fossil fuels'?
   c) Where does most of the energy we use go?
   d) Where does most of the heat escape from in our houses?
   e) How can we prevent this happening?
   f) How can we economise on hot water?
   g) Why is electricity not a good way of heating the home?
   h) What would be the best fuel to use for heating our homes?

## 2.2

1 Look at the article 'Why Solar Energy?' on page 137. Before you read it, decide what you think are the economic, ecological and political advantages of using solar energy for heating and lighting. Make notes, and discuss them in pairs or groups. Then read the article and see if it puts forward the same advantages as you did.

2 Read the article again and decide if the following statements are true (T) or false (F), according to the article.

   a) The sun can never run out of energy.
   b) We could survive for a long time if we used the earth's resources for energy, instead of the sun.
   c) With a solar heating system, the price of energy will almost never go up.
   d) It costs a lot to operate a solar heating system.

3 a) Divide into groups of three (A, B and C). Each person should look at *one* of the texts on pages 137–8 and *one* diagram.

   A: Read text 1 and be prepared to give B and C the following information:
      – what the letters A, B, C and D refer to in diagram 1.
      – how a solar system works.

   B: Read text 2 and be prepared to give A and C the following information:
      – how a conventional system works;
      – how much it costs to heat water for the average family of four (per year);
      – how much it may cost by 1990.

C: Read text 3 and be prepared to give A and B the following information:
– how much less energy is required to heat 200 litres of water in a combined system than in a conventional system, and why;
– why you can't use just solar energy on its own.

b) In your groups, make notes under the following headings. You will need to talk to the other members of your group and refer to the diagrams on pages 137–8 to find all the information.
*How a solar system works*
*The disadvantages of a conventional system*
*The advantages of combining a solar system with a conventional one*

c) Using your notes, design a group poster which summarises the advantages of a solar heating system. Remember to make it attractive and eye-catching! Compare your poster with those of other groups.

d) In groups, discuss to what extent solar energy is used in your country/countries for light and heat. Discuss also why you think it is not used more often, if the advantages are so obvious.

## 2.3

1 Work in pairs. Look at one of the advertisements on pages 139–40. Your partner will look at the other one. Look through it quickly and try to decide what the aim of the advertisement is and how effective it is as a way of persuading you to do something. Try to convince your partner to do what is shown in the advertisement and answer any questions he or she has to ask.

2 Work in groups. Bring an example to class of an advertisement (in English or your own language) which you find particularly effective. Do the same for an advertisement which you do not find convincing, and discuss your reactions with members of your group. Remember to give your reasons.

3 As a class, decide on a product which is known to all of you. Then, in pairs, work out an advertisement for it, including a picture if possible. Show your advertisement to the rest of class. Decide which is the best, and why.

## 2.4

1 Look at the article on page 141. Read through it quickly and find out who the following people are.
   a) David Bellamy    c) Garfield Meredith
   b) Paul Whalley     d) Rupert Howell

*The environment*

2 Read the article again and answer the following questions.
   a) What do the initials COI stand for, and what is one of the activities of this organisation?
   b) Why is the advertisement on page 140 so controversial?
   c) Find two other words in the article which mean the same as *insects*.
   d) Find as many names of insects as you can from the article, and add any others you know in English.

3 Find a word or phrase in the text which is similar in meaning to each of the following:
   a) (to make) a movement of fear (*two different words*)
   b) showing
   c) very surprised
   d) to be filled with fear, shocked
   e) home
   f) this country
   g) noticed
   h) inquiry
   i) important
   j) were in a hurry / hurried
   k) created
   l) lost their way

# Simulation

## Situation

There is shortly to be a conference where representatives of several countries are to meet in order to discuss their environmental problems. The aim of the conference is to draw up a list of the most important problems, which will then be published in the form of a report designed to draw public attention to the seriousness of these issues.

The conference will be held in Brussels, and will focus on two main areas of interest:
a) rural problems (the erosion of the countryside, the extinction of some species of plant and animal life etc.)
b) urban problems (pollution, the energy crisis, traffic problems etc.)

## Preliminary tasks

*Mixed nationality groups*

1 Working on your own, make notes on what you consider to be the most serious rural and urban problems in your country, what (if anything) is being done about them and what you would suggest should be done.

2 You will be given time to discuss your notes with other people from your country (if there are any) so that you can come to some agreement on the main problem areas. One of the group should make notes on what you decide, to report back to the rest of the class at the 'meeting'.

## 2 Conserving energy

*Groups of the same nationality*
You will be divided into two groups; Group A will consider the *rural* problems in your country, and Group B the *urban* problems.

1 Working on your own, make notes on what you consider the main problems to be, what (if anything) is being done about them, and what you suggest should be done.

2 You will be given time to discuss your views with the rest of your group (i.e. A or B) and you should try to come to some agreement on what the main problems are. One of the group should take notes on what you decide, to report back to the rest of the class at the 'meeting'.

## Procedure – the meeting

One person will be appointed as the chairperson, to lead the meeting and to make sure that a representative from each group is given the opportunity to report back on the feeling of his/her group.

A secretary should take notes of the main points of the meeting.

1 Within the time given, each group of different nationality, or both groups (in the case of mono-national groups) should report back, via a spokesperson, on:
   a) environmental problems in their country
   b) what is being done
   c) suggestions of the group as to what might be done.

2 The chairperson should allow time then for a general discussion and questions before agreement is reached on the main problems which are common to all countries, and possible ways of solving them. This information is to be published in the report.

## Follow up

Write up the report, based on decisions and opinions voiced at the meeting. Organise it into four main paragraphs:
a) Rural problems
b) Urban problems
c) How the country/countries is/are trying to solve them
d) Suggestions of the meeting as to what could be done

# Key

## Food and drink

1. menu: pages 4, 5, 6, 7, 12
   review: page 8
   article: pages 5, 6, 9, 13, 19, 21, 22
   chart: pages 21, 22
   coupon: page 23
   cartoon: pages 7, 8, 20
   advertisement: pages 4, 5, 10, 11, 12, 20, 23
   form: page 23
2. You lose coordination, and you can't handle a car or even a pen. (page 20)
3. £17.80 (or £19.95 on St Valentine's Day) (page 5)
4. 11 stone 8 lbs (or 162 lbs) (page 22)
5. He said he'd come to do the washing up. (page 9)
6. BBC2 (page 19)
7. prawn cocktail, steak and gateau (page 5)
8. The Daily Mail (page 9)
9. by using Weight Watchers new food plans (page 23)
10. home cooking – good and wholesome (page 12)

## 1 Living to eat...

### 1.1

1. a) mussels, (lemon) sole, prawn, crab, haddock, cod, scampi, plaice
   b) (roast) beef, pheasant, steak, game, duck(ling), spare ribs, chicken, pork, veal

4. fry, grill, bake, roast, poach, sauté ('seethe' and 'salamander' are not very common)

### 1.3

2. a) F   f) T
   b) F   g) F
   c) T   h) F
   d) F   i) T
   e) F   j) F

3. a) arrive
   b) arrive
   c) use legal means to make you pay
   d) insist
   e) show an example of a typical menu
   f) look carefully at the small writing
   g) the usual cost
   h) Be careful
   i) include in the price
   j) as well as

### 1.4

1. a) Pasticceria Amalfi
   b) Geales
   c) Tzabar Falafel House
   d) Porters
   e) Chez Louisette

# Key

3  *Chez Louisette*
   a) the people who work there
   b) to say very quickly (and mechanically)
   c) large
   d) looks good
   e) very busy

*Tzabar Falafel House*
   a) a taste you get used to
   b) wonderful

*Pasticceria Amalfi*
there in the restaurant

*The Crown Tavern*
clocks

*Geales*
   a) a small complaint
   b) to cost you

## 1.5

2  a) T    f) F
   b) F    g) F
   c) F    h) T
   d) F    i) F
   e) F    j) T

3  a) the British diner
   b) Christopher Driver, the editor of the guide
   c) the overgrown tasteless tomato
   d) that kind of attitude (something being indiscriminately marketed and pushed in front of the customer)
   e) in France
   f) the restaurateur
   g) the fishermen
   h) say they are inspectors
   i) as saying thank you
   j) the *Good Food Guide*

## 1.6

1  a) Grove Tavern
   b) George Inn
   c) Sherlock Holmes
   d) Nags Head
   e) Old Star

2  a) a leaflet
   b) tavern/inn
   c) grub
   d) ale
   e) handy, close to/by, within easy reach, nearby, just around the corner from

## 1.7

1  a) – they could take the children with them.
   b) – the occasional pub has facilities for children.
   c) – children under 14 can't go into a room in a pub where alcohol is being served.
   d) – age limits should apply to drinking alcohol in pubs but not to entering them.
   e) – a lot of teenage drunkenness would be avoided.

2  a) a pint            g) sidestep
   b) chores            h) convivial
   c) sampling          i) shuffled off
   d) admit             j) haven
   e) barring           k) kids
   f) broadminded       l) misfits

3  a) – to pretend not to notice
   b) – to enjoy yourself without inhibition
   c) – to race around noisily

# 2 Or eating to live

## 2.1

2  a) 700,000
   b) 10,000
   c) Yes, in moderation
   d) 6 units (e.g. 3 pints of beer) for men per day; 4 units for women.
   e) By checking your health, providing a social base, and helping you to cut down on your drinking.

147

Key

3  a) tuning in        f) hugely
   b) dire             g) a screening
   c) prematurely      h) tips
   d) scrap            i) soft
   e) paunches         j) a sip

## 2.2

2  a) The National Advisory Committee on Nutrition Education
   b) to cut down the high rate of heart disease, strokes and cancer
   c) It says that processed food can often be better for you than red meat.
   d) Because the Department of Health and the British Nutrition Foundation felt that the report didn't have enough evidence. *Or* because the Foundation is funded by the food manufacturers.
   e) There is too much fat.
   f) High fibre foods, fish, poultry, fruit and vegetables.
   g) Fat, sugar and salt.

## 2.3

1

|            | always | a little | never |
|------------|:------:|:--------:|:-----:|
| meat       | ✓      |          |       |
| fish       | ✓      |          |       |
| eggs       | ✓      |          |       |
| cheese     | ✓      |          |       |
| vegetables | ✓      |          |       |
| fruit      | ✓      |          |       |
| milk       |        | ✓        |       |
| bread      |        | ✓        |       |
| cereal     | ✓      |          |       |
| sugar      |        |          | ✓     |
| cake       |        |          | ✓     |
| sweets     |        |          | ✓     |
| rice       |        |          | ✓     |
| alcohol    |        | ✓        |       |

   h) Have smaller helpings.
   i) No.
   j) Exercise, less alcohol and no smoking.

# Christmas

1  3½ hours (page 33)
2  happy/drunk (page 32)
3  a soldier action man, a train set or a bicycle (page 38)
4  Prince Albert (page 30)
5  a reindeer (pages 38, 39)
6  A Christmas Carol (page 29)
7  Christmas is giving and kindness (page 36)
8  Santa Claus (pages 37, 39)
9  foil (Alcan) (page 33)
10 Peanuts (page 39)

## 1 The spirit of Christmas

### 1.1

1  a) Scrooge: (examples) miserable, unpleasant, pessimistic etc.
   b) the nephew: (examples) cheerful, happy, optimistic etc.

2  a) glow, ruddy, sparkled, smoked
   b) cheerful, merry, gaily
   c) cross, sternly, indignantly
   d) dismal, morose

3  a) approached him
   b) idea/suggestion
   c) rubbish/hypocrisy
   d) enough of
   e) working out bills/money
   f) do what I want

148

## 1.2

a) turkey
b) roast goose
c) potatoes and (Brussels) sprouts
d) Christmas pudding and mince pies
e) Christmas falls earlier now than it used to.

## 1.3

1 *For*
It is fun for children.
It gets you out of the usual routine.
People are friendlier.
Giving presents is satisfying.
One can concentrate on non-commercial values.

*Against*
It is an un-Christian time.
It is purely an alcoholic occasion.
It is a waste of money.
It is hypocritical.
It is thoughtless.
People eat food they don't want.

# 2 Christmas is children

## 2.1

2  a) F    e) T
   b) F    f) T
   c) F    g) T
   d) T

## 2.2

1  *espoused*: married
   *unto*: to
   *Hail*: Hallo
   *thou that art*: you who are
   *highly favoured*: very privileged
   *salutation*: greeting
   *fear not*: don't be afraid
   *thou hast*: you have
   *behold*: look
   *thou shalt*: you will
   *thy*: your
   *bring forth*: give birth to

2
| | | |
|---|---|---|
| b) | pitcher | a well, water |
| c) | peasant | village |
| d) | shield | brightness |
| e) | carpenter | block of wood, hit my thumb |
| f) | drop in | just... to say hello |
| g) | startled | |

# Work

1  since 1975 (page 52)
2  two (page 53)
3  £204 (page 55)
4  He may have an early divorce, a poor sex life and an early death. (page 56)
5  Chivers (page 47)
6  £110 (page 48)
7  a gardener (page 47)
8  He need only work half time; he gets an allowance to cover some of what he would have been paid for the rest of the time. (page 46)
9  Michael Edwards (page 45)
10 L. Harper (page 54)

Key

# 1 In and out of work

## 1.1

2  a) F    d) F
    b) T    e) T
    c) F

3  a) – an unemployment allowance
    b) – to register as unemployed
    c) – one of the Houses of Parliament

## 1.2

a) half your normal hours
b) an unemployed person
c) £12.90 less
d) Because he can spend more time with his wife.
e) By sending off the coupon for some booklets, or picking them up from the Jobcentre.

## 1.3

a) the gardener
b) the junior assistant in Sweetens bookshop
c) the secretary/receptionist
d) the part time nursery assistant and non-teaching assistant
e) the customer service representative for Kelly Girl

# 2 A woman's place

## 2.1

2  *Personal qualities and skills*: You must be: intelligent, cheerful, outgoing, healthy, flexible, patient, discreet, kind, have a sense of humour.
You must be able to: budget and be competent in domestic skills, accept responsibility, act on your own initiative, negotiate house agreements, settle disputes.

*Knowledge*: You must know about: nursing and psychology.
You should know about: world affairs, the environment, sport, handicrafts, music, art, literature, drama.

*Qualifications*: no 'A' levels needed, no university degree, shorthand, typing or previous experience of any kind.

## 2.2

1  a) 11   g) 2    m) 3
    b) 8    h) 14  n) 7
    c) 13   i) 9    o) 12
    d) 5    j) 10  p) 6
    e) 1    k) 15
    f) 16  l) 4

2  a) yell/scream/bawl
    b) loathe/abhor
    c) washing and ironing
    d) children

3  a) dirty      f) look angry
    b) toilet     g) witch
    c) emptied  h) rush
    d) quite good i) fight
    e) fashionable j) soaking wet

## 2.3

1  a) an Army sergeant major, a bishop and a fire chief
    b) Legal & General Insurers
    c) because of inflation
    d) There is no evidence that it did.
    e) Thursday
    f) To employers, since husbands rarely think of insuring their wife's life.
    g) one in four
    h) no
    i) yes
    j) It ceases when you leave your job.

Key

## 2.4

3  a) T   c) F   e) T
   b) T   d) F

4  a) idle        f) carving
   b) washouts    g) coaxing
   c) pick        h) chore
   d) loo         i) appliances
   e) in the mood j) make up for

## 2.5

1  a) teenage schoolgirls
   b) 19-year-old students
   c) married women in their mid-twenties
   d) a doctor's wife of 65
   e) a prostitute in her mid-twenties

# Education

1  Bill Craddock (page 72)
2  four (page 69)
3  Alternative Prospectus (page 85)
4  Milton Keynes (page 81)
5  Mrs Griffiths, Mrs Davies, Miss Miller (page 64)
6  The Union Building (page 85)
7  Linguaphone (page 83)
8  weak (page 71)
9  6 million (page 84)
10 Carol Baker (page 78)

## 1 The happiest days of your life?

### 1.2

1  a) F   b) T   c) F   d) T   e) F

### 1.3

2

|  | Lucy Jackman | Jillian Hall | Stephen Parker |
| --- | --- | --- | --- |
| Age | 25 | 23 | 23 |
| Feelings about school | hated it | was happy | rather negative |
| Reasons | all the work, the petty discipline, one of the teachers hated her, convent made her 'hung up' | it was like a family to her, she was babied and cocooned; she got on well with everyone, decisions made for her | too sheltered, too oriented to university/profession, made him naïve |
| Present job | journalist | bank clerk | student of accountancy |
| Feelings about job | loves it | doesn't like it, but too nervous to move | quite likes it but would be equally happy elsewhere |

151

*Key*

3 a) *loathed*: hated
*boarder*: someone who lives at school
*dormitory*: a bedroom for a lot of children
*bunch of kids*: a group of children
*petty*: unimportant
*a soft spot*: a liking
*dragon*: (here) a severe woman
*load of lines*: a written punishment
*drive*: determination

b) comfortable/peaceful: *settled down*
emotionally disturbed: *hung up*
tying: *doing up*
acted very emotionally: *freaked out*
speak severely to someone about their faults: *tell off*
giving out: *handing out*
make (someone) exasperated: *drive round the bend*
hated: *couldn't stand*
became clear: *dawned on*

c) *that*: the convent school which she went to for a couple of years
*it*: being a boarder at the convent school
*it*: life at the school
*It*: life at the school
*that*: pretending
*all that*: feeling hung up and guilty
*them*: the teachers
*people like that*: petty people
*therefore*: because she liked her
*that . . . it*: (into) the choir . . . (with) music
*that woman*: the Deputy Head
*it*: about Lucy refusing to do her lines
*that*: that once you stop being afraid teachers can't hurt you
*it*: leaving school

d) loathed / detested / couldn't stand — *strong hate*

fond of / enjoyed / had a soft spot for

love — *strong liking*

*indifference*

4 a) *babied*: looked after / treated like a baby
*form teacher's pet*: the class teacher's favourite student
*cocoon*: protective environment

b) had a good relationship with: *got on with*
told to leave: *thrown out*
reached the end, despite inefficiency: *muddled through*
only just succeeded: *scraped through*
work very hard: *slog (my) guts out*
ignored: *left out*
to make (yourself) popular with: *get on the right side of*
be independent: *stand on my own two feet*

5 a) *the be all and end all*: the only important thing
*wholeheartedly*: absolutely
*suspended*: told to leave school for a while (as a punishment)
*conflict*: argument
*in the long run*: eventually
*guaranteed*: sure to get

b) agreed with / supported: *backed up*
in favour of: *right behind*
earning lots of money: *raking the money in*
arranged/planned: *mapped out*
not having a regular job: *bumming around*

# 1.4

1 a) since September 1967
b) in Saffron Walden, or within eight miles (possibly less now)
c) exam results above the national average
d) two gymnasia, with changing rooms and showers, an open air heated swimming pool, playing fields, tennis courts etc.
e) clubs, societies and extra-curricular activities, and educational visits
f) sixth form private study, common and dining rooms, seminar rooms
g) everyone except the sixth form
h) phone or write

Key

# 2 Beyond the classroom

## 2.1

2  a) Education is compulsory, but school is not.
   b) Unless one of the parents gives up work, there are great problems in organisation.
   c) Local Education Authority
   d) Usually it is cooperative.
   e) – looking at the timetable/curriculum
      – having an informal chat
      – visiting the home
   f) Reasons of principle, or practical reasons.
   g) You have to de-register the child, by writing to the headmaster and the LEA.

4

|   | The Fullwoods | The Wilkins | Nicholas Everdell |
|---|---|---|---|
| a) | eldest child's work got worse when a new head teacher came with different methods; dismissed as 'slow child' though IQ above average | reasons of principle | problems at school, e.g. bullying, feeling of isolation – affected his health |
| b) | 2 years | 9 months | since he was 13 |
| c) | a.m. – 3 hours' work, including maths and spelling<br>p.m. – playing | a.m. – domestic chores, then a couple of hours' work, then refreshments and story<br>p.m. – out of doors | studying for exams, following interests, e.g. electronics/radio |
| d) | practical problems, e.g. dirty house | some doubts about whether Sally could handle it; a break from routine, no time for parents to follow own interests | feeling of loneliness and isolation |
| e) | developing responsibility and self discipline | developing at own pace, independent, happier and more creative – more harmonious atmosphere at home | more confident, had time to read more and be more inventive |

5  The Fullwoods
   a) trendy
   b) plummeted
   c) IQ
   d) catch up on lost ground
   e) well ahead
   f) on the right track
   g) joins in
   h) a soft option
   i) shirk

   The Wilkins
   a) withdrew
   b) prompted
   c) chores
   d) uneasy
   e) clinched
   f) flourished

   Nicholas Everdell
   a) runt
   b) thinking it over
   c) cut off
   d) respite
   e) bullying
   f) hanging around
   g) hindsight

153

*Key*

## 2.2

2  a) Yes
   b) You study at home.
   c) None.
   d) Those under 21, and those living abroad.
   e) Teaching material, the television and radio, home experiment kits (for some subjects).
   f) No, you have a personal tutor, there are local study centres and you can go to a summer school.
   g) There are 138 courses.
   h) You have to get six credits.
   i) Yes, although there are grants if necessary.
   j) By sending off the coupon.

## 2.3

|    | *Mrs O'Shea* | *Mrs Homer* | *Rev. Davis* |
|----|-------------|-------------|--------------|
| a) | She had time to spare after her husband died, and she wanted a challenge. | She wanted a diversion from her personal problems. | He wanted to do something more demanding, keep his mind occupied, have more discipline. |
| b) | 77 | 35 | 66 |
| c) | None – a grandmother. | A former model. | A vicar. |
| d) | She found it fruitful and enjoyable, although rather 'a bind' at times. | She liked it a lot; it opened new doors. | He enjoyed it and found it valuable. |
| e) | An Arts Course (specific subjects not mentioned). | A Humanities degree in history of art (including Greek and Roman art up to the Renaissance). | Sociology. |
| f) | Possibly to do an honours degree. | She would like to do research. | ? |

## 2.4

1  a) by going to the Cambridge College of Further Education
   b) similar to 'O' levels (grade 1 is equal)
   c) Return to Study
   d) at the Cambridge Computer College
   e) the Linguaphone method
   f) St Marks Community Centre
   g) the RSA Preparatory Certificate in TEFL
   h) the RSA and City and Guilds
   i) at the Job Centre Education desk or at the Careers Library

## 2.5

1  a) the Travel Office
   b) phone Niteline
   c) the Cellar bar
   d) the Founders bar
   e) the Welfare Office
   f) the Games room

## 2.6

1

|   | Advantages | Disadvantages |
|---|---|---|
| a) | there is a friendly atmosphere, social functions, television, laundry etc. | restrictive meal times, only tolerable food |
| b) | more freedom, cheaper, not so many rules and regulations, don't have to clear out your room in the holidays | you have to look after yourself, no choice of flatmate when you first arrive, no organised social life |
| c) | you can live with who you want | often overpriced and substandard |

# Leisure

1  Because he has to go to a football match (page 114)
2  Willy Russell; the Royal Shakespeare Company (page 97)
3  *Lianna* (page 98)
4  four (page 102)
5  over 15; £1.30 per session (page 112)
6  the Barber of Seville (page 96)
7  Paris (pages 112–15)
8  What television programmes she liked/ disliked (page 101)
9  the International Guide to Fitness and Health (page 109)
10  18 (page 98)

## 1 The world of entertainment

### 1.1

1  'Magistrates act . . .':
   a) act in the theatre
   b) do something
   'Queen sees Fonteyn take 10 curtains':
   a) appear to the audience after a performance
   b) steal
   'Star's broken leg hits office':
   a) affects
   b) hits (physically)

2  a) the Royal Festival Hall
   b) the Westminster Theatre / Aldwych
   c) the Lyric
   d) Wigmore Hall

155

*Key*

## 1.3

1. a) *Betrayal*
   b) *Daniel*
   c) *Star 80*
   d) *Rumble Fish*
   e) *The Big Chill*

4. *Rumble Fish*
   a) respects/admires
   b) a bird which returns home
   c) interesting
   d) waves of smoke
   e) exaggerate

   *Daniel*
   a) gave the idea
   b) working together secretly
   c) finds out bit by bit
   d) anti-Communist
   e) explicit

   *Star 80*
   a) separated from
   b) a person to whom something bad was sure to happen
   c) offering
   d) persisted
   e) is an example of
   f) a person who likes showing off
   g) make the strongest impression
   h) not exaggerated

   *Betrayal*
   a) secret and forbidden
   b) cleverly/secretly
   c) shows us
   d) superficial talk
   e) superficial talk
   f) innocent
   g) play
   h) a sudden quick movement
   i) defensive
   j) knows what is happening

   *The Big Chill*
   talk about the past

## 1.4

2. *Neil Kinnock*
   a) schedule
   b) box
   c) miraculous
   d) glimpse
   e) (am) besotted about

   *Barbara Cartland*
   a) appeals to (me)
   b) portrayed
   c) sick to death of
   d) dreary
   e) kitchen sink
   f) overt

   *Toyah Wilcox*
   a) intriguing
   b) (be) all in favour of

3. *Current affairs*: Newsnight's February, News Review, 7 Days, Weekend World
   *Children's programmes*: Rub-a-dub-tub, Postman Pat
   *Religion*: Worship, Songs of Praise, The First Christian, Thought for a Sunday, Morning Worship
   *Educational programmes*: Open University, Maths Help, Greek, Making of Britain, Making the Most of the Micro
   *Documentaries*: Everyman, Weekend World, One Pair of Eyes, World at War, Encounter, Wales, Wales
   *Sport*: Rugby, Swimming, Golf, Tennis, The Big Match
   *Films*: The Bells of St Mary's, My Brilliant Career, Fear is the Key, The Mystery of Mr X, The Mouse that Roared
   *Drama series*: Goodbye Mr Chips, The Jewel in the Crown, Ever Decreasing Circles
   *Quiz programmes*: Mastermind, Bullseye, Family Fortunes
   *Chat shows*: Face the Press, Sunday Sunday, Did you see?, South Bank Show
   *Hobbies*: Me and my Camera, Indian Cookery Course, The Motor Show, The World of Cooking, Crafts Made Simple, Jack's Game
   *Comedy*: Spitting Image

Key

## 2 The sporting life

### 2.2

3. a) tap dancing
   b) rock climbing
   c) basketball
   d) fencing
   e) belly dancing
   f) parachuting
   g) Martial arts

4. a) alternatives
   b) essential
   c) an attempt
   d) very difficult/tiring
   e) do it in your own time
   f) for fun
   g) to be better (cleverer) than the other person

# The environment

1. insects (page 140)
2. Saffron Walden (page 128)
3. Spike Milligan (page 125)
4. the Energy Efficiency Office (pages 139–40)
5. 11–13 Ockford Rd Godalming Surrey GU7 1QU (page 122)
6. Solar energy (page 137)
7. ten (page 136)
8. Friends of the Earth (page 126)
9. because of all the billboards (page 125)
10. They have lost the capacity to foresee and forestall. (page 122)

## 1 Preserving the countryside

### 1.1

1. a) They may be eroded away into a barren wasteland.
   b) – the local people need the forests to survive.
      – there is a demand for tropical timber in the developed world.
   c) World Wildlife Fund
   d) develop resources without destroying them
   e) to write for more information

2. a) the world's
   b) the destruction of tropical rain forests
   c) the destruction
   d) local people
   e) the resources
   f) the readers
   g) the plan
   h) the letter
   i) the reader

### 1.2

1. a) Because you could cause damage, and livestock could get out.
   b) Because a lot of traditional features of the countryside are disappearing.
   c) You may disturb wild animals.
   d) They will take you into the heart of the countryside, and it will prevent you trespassing.
   e) Because you may meet horses, cyclists, sheep, tractors etc.
   f) Because they can do harm to livestock even if they are only playing.
   g) To prevent farm animals getting out/in.
   h) Because there is a danger of starting a fire.
   i) It looks awful, and can harm animals.
   j) Humans and wildlife depend on clean water.

157

*Key*

2 a) exploring the paths, looking at the architecture, farming, etc., plants, birds, wildlife – or just sitting and looking at the scenery
b) by the number of different trees in it
c) keep it on a lead
d) as a short cut from one village to another
e) stream, lake, pond, sea
f) because agriculture is changing, there is more building and more visitors
g) tell the landowner or call the fire brigade
h) ramblers, children on bikes, cyclists
i) the side nearest the hinges
j) footpaths and bridleways

3   1  a) species
       b) acre

    2  a) stiles
       b) instantly
       c) livestock
       d) stray/wander

    4  a) a party of ramblers
       b) a wide berth

    5  a) short cut
       b) bridleways
       c) trespass

    6  a) reservoir
       b) fouled
       c) paddling

    7  a) get the better of
       b) a lead

    8  hinges

    9  a) ablaze
       b) break out

    10 a) revel in
       b) secluded
       c) litter
       d) rot/decay

## 1.3

1 a) F  e) T
  b) T  f) F
  c) F  g) F
  d) T

2 a) a hairy thing called man
  b) man
  c) some men
  d) killed the animals
  e) the small animals
  f) wildlife
  g) starving people

## 1.4

4 a) because of modern farming techniques (agribusiness), forestry, motorways, etc.
  b) they are used for food and fuel

7 (1) d   (9) o    (17) g
  (2) v   (10) i   (18) m
  (3) j   (11) a   (19) w
  (4) p   (12) n   (20) f
  (5) e   (13) h   (21) t
  (6) k   (14) s   (22) l
  (7) q   (15) b   (23) u
  (8) c   (16) r

## 1.5

1 a) F  d) F
  b) T  e) F
  c) F  f) T

2 a) wreck
  b) a petition
  c) use their initiative
  d) inspired them
  e) heritage
  f) proceed
  g) adjacent to

## 2 Conserving energy

### 2.1

4  a) People are worried about the dangers of nuclear power, which we will have to use if we exhaust our present supply of energy.
   b) coal, gas and oil
   c) on heating (buildings and water)
   d) through the walls, the roof, the floor, draughts, the windows
   e) by insulating our houses
   f) by insulating the immersion heater
   g) it is inefficient
   h) North sea gas

### 2.2

2  a) T     c) T
   b) F     d) F

### 2.4

1  a) a botanist
   b) an entomologist
   c) the marketing director of the Energy Efficiency Office
   d) the accounts director of an advertising agency (Young and Rubicam)

2  a) The Central Office of Information – one of its activities is energy conservation
   b) because it is suggested that some of these insects are never found in Britain
   c) bugs / creepy crawlies
   d) caterpillar, lobster moth, beetle, tiger moth, stag beetle, silverfish, wasp

3  a) cringe/shudder
   b) featuring
   c) startled
   d) appalled
   e) habitat
   f) these shores
   g) spotted
   h) query
   i) eminent
   j) scrambled
   k) drew up
   l) strayed

# Roles

### 1    *Guest 1*

You are on a diet but, since the meal is paid for, you would like to have all three courses if they are not too fattening.

You will be disappointed if you can't have what you want, but can be persuaded to change your mind as long as it is slimming food.

### 2    *Jack Frost*

You work hard all year, and really look forward to relaxing at home at Christmas with lots of food and drink and the old films on the television. The only thing wrong with Christmas at home is that your wife's mother always comes, and you don't get on with her.

You are not going to be persuaded to go abroad because it would be too expensive, and you hate foreign food. Anyway, you like being at home. You think Cherry should go on her own and take Grand Ma with her.

### 3    *Alison O'Hanlon*

You get on very well with John and you are looking forward to a long chat with him. You would like to go to a nice restaurant where you can catch up on the news at the same time as having a lovely meal. You think it would be a nice idea to take John and pay for him since you are both staying with him. Since there are five of you, you think it would be a sensible idea to take a taxi to wherever you are going.

## Guest 2

You are an American, visiting Britain on business, and so you want to eat something typically English. You have heard that English food is simple and plain, so you want to avoid anything cooked in rich sauces. You want to drink English beer with the meal.

You have very definite ideas about what you want, and would rather have nothing at all than second best.

## Holly Frost

You find Christmas, with all the shopping, cooking etc. very tiring and you always seem to do all the work. You would like a change of scenery, but there are two problems. You know your mother (Grand Ma) won't go on a plane and you won't go without her, and you will be upset to miss the traditional side of Christmas (the carols, mince pies etc.).

## Jeremy O'Hanlon

You and your wife, Alison, live in Bristol, where you teach English. You are spending the weekend with your friend John who you haven't seen for a few months and who lives in London.

You have been looking forward to going to the theatre this weekend. You don't mind what you see, as long as it is not opera or ballet, which you find boring. Something light such as a musical would be ideal. Look through *Entertainment*, and choose a show. You will be disappointed not to go to the theatre, but would even prefer the cinema to a restaurant or a pub.

## Guest 3

You are a vegetarian and don't eat any meat or fish except the occasional bit of chicken. You don't like eggs either, but you love pasta and rice, and all kinds of vegetables.

## Roles

### 8 Cherry Frost

Your best friend's family want your family to go abroad with them, and you think it's a fantastic idea. You find Christmas boring, and you hate all the relations coming. You are very excited at the idea of going abroad and the idea of flying. You would much prefer to go without the rest of the family but you are sure they won't let you, so persuade them to go. Persuade them that it will not be much more expensive than buying all those presents, food etc.

### 9 John Funston

You are pleased to have Jeremy and Alison staying with you and look forward to seeing Fred and Tania for the evening, but are not to keen on going out as it is very cold and you haven't got much money at the moment. You would really prefer to stay in, listen to music and chat. There is a good film on the television, and an excellent place where you can get takeaway food at the end of the road.

If you are forced to go out, you would prefer something relaxing such as a concert as long as it is not too expensive. Suggest getting a bus, as there is not much traffic at this time.

### 10 Guest 4

You live near the sea and are an expert on fish, which must be very fresh to please you. You are allergic to shellfish. You hate alcohol and anything cooked in it.

### 11 Nicky Frost

You don't really care what you do as long as you get your presents as usual. Your sister annoys you because she only thinks of herself. Going away may be fun but you are worried about missing your sports training and being away from your friends. The other problem is who would look after your dog and rabbit if you went away. You will not leave them with Aunt Joan as she over-fed your goldfish last time, and it died.

You like Grand Ma as she always buys you presents. You are bored with the discussion and try to end it quickly so that you can go out.

## Fred Hunter   12

You are a student at art college in London. You are going to visit your friend John tonight with your girlfriend Tania. You would like to spend the evening at the pub, playing darts or snooker and then take fish and chips back to his flat later on. You hate spending money on food and you never go to the theatre. You also hate walking, so suggest either going to the local pub or getting a bus.

## Inspector   13

You love exotic foreign food, imaginatively cooked, in sauces etc. Decide what you would like to eat and then make a note of questions to ask your friends (e.g. you will want to know if they were satisfied with the choice and why / why not) and the manager (e.g. why he chose those particular dishes for the menu).

## Aunt Joan   14

You know a beautiful hotel in Scotland which has wonderful food, as well as good nightlife, sports facilities etc. You think this would be a good solution, as your sister needs a rest and Nicky can carry on with his sport.

You don't like Cherry, so ignore her. Offer to have Nicky's pets, as you know the hotel won't, and encourage them to take Grand Ma with them (as otherwise she will have to stay with you).

You have a special interest in persuading them to go to this hotel as one of your friends owns it and the agreement is that if you send enough people there in the winter you will have a free summer holiday! (Don't tell your relations this, of course.) Do your best to convince them that this is the perfect solution.

## Tania Ealing   15

You and your boyfriend, Fred, are meeting up with your friend John this evening. You get bored sitting in a pub all evening so you want to persuade John to go to a film with you. However, you don't mind too much what you do, as long as it doesn't cost more than £6, which is all you have. You love Italian food, and you are also a health fanatic, so would prefer to walk to wherever you are going.

*Roles*

## 16 Restaurant manager

Prepare a menu that will cater for all tastes, including people on a diet, vegetarians and people who don't like foreign food.

Look through the texts in *Food and drink* and choose a maximum of six first courses, six second courses and six desserts. Be prepared to defend your choice, though very politely of course!

The only problems this evening are:
a) you have no green vegetables, as they are very expensive;
b) you are not sure how fresh the fish is, so try to encourage them to have something else (you have a little shellfish);
c) you have no fresh fruit.

The restaurant does not serve beer as it likes to create a more sophisticated image!

# To the teacher

## Components of *Variety*

### The texts

The wide variety of texts focus on the kind of material that students are likely to want to read, and include, among others, letters, newspaper and magazine articles, advertisements, menus, cartoons and extracts from novels. They are unsimplified and reproduced in their authentic state, and cover a range of different styles and registers, from the very colloquial to the more formal.

The texts are organised around such everyday topics as work, education and leisure and their content is likely to interest those who want to know more about life in Britain today.

### The exercises

*Variety* is a workbook, which means that although the texts provide valuable exposure to the language, and are interesting in their own right, the exercises and activities, which are closely linked to the texts, are an integral part of the book.

One of the aims of the exercises is to provide a genuine purpose and motivation for reading a particular text or group of texts and to develop systematically skills and strategies for dealing with ungraded material. The activities are skills-based rather than a test of linguistic comprehension and the emphasis is on helping students learn how to transfer the reading techniques which they have in their own language to a foreign or second language.

Another very important aim of the texts in *Variety* is that they should be a stimulus to speaking and writing activities. There is plenty of scope throughout the book for different types of oral fluency work in pairs or groups, and the reading and speaking activities provide the motivation for creative writing tasks.

(For further detailed discussion on skills activities in *Variety* see below.)

## Who is *Variety* for?

*Variety* is intended for intermediate level students who may have a passive knowledge of grammar but who feel the need to enlarge their range of vocabulary and idiomatic expressions, develop a feel for style and register and become aware of aspects of discourse and textual convention in different varieties of written language. It can be used by students working alone, who are able to assess their own progress by means of the key; or it may be read by people who merely want to increase their exposure to the language and read for pleasure.

*To the teacher*

However, *Variety* can be used to its best advantage in class, or at least with other students, since one of the aims is to activate a passive knowledge of English by giving foreign learners something interesting to speak and write about, so that they will develop their confidence and fluency in using the language for a communicative purpose.

## *How is Variety organised?*

There are six units, each covering a specific theme – Food and drink, Christmas, Work, Education, Leisure and the Environment. The themes are independent of each other and can be worked through in any order.

To make the units manageable they are divided into two sections, each section dealing with a specific aspect of the main theme. At the beginning of each unit is a series of questions which require students to scan quickly all the texts in that unit to look for specific information. The idea behind this is for students to get a 'feel' for the kinds of texts which are in the unit and to encourage quick and efficient reading, making use of linguistic and textual clues. You are recommended to set a time limit for this, and treat it as a kind of competitive exercise to be done individually or in groups. The exercises which follow the texts in each section should be looked at *before* reading, since they will help to determine suitable reading strategies. At the end of each unit there is a full-scale fluency activity such as a roleplay or class discussion, which includes a written follow up; the input comes from the reading and discussion throughout the unit, and the activity should lead on naturally from this.

## Skills activities

### *Reading*

Reading texts are often the most accessible form of exposure to language outside the classroom and yet students will sometimes hesitate to approach authentic reading material as they have developed the habit of reading in a linear fashion, pausing to look up every new word, and can therefore be dispirited by the lack of progress, and the time it takes.

We have deliberately included in *Variety* material which is rather above the level of average intermediate students so that they will gradually learn to overcome the feeling of panic when they do not understand every word.

The motivation to read the text may come from some form of pre-reading activity where, for example, learners relate the text to their own ideas or experiences, or predict from linguistic or textual clues what the text will be about.

The purpose for reading will often be provided by a 'while reading' exercise, which will also determine the strategy for reading (which in the first language is usually unconscious). So the reason for looking at a page of job advertisements may be to find a suitable job for a particular person, and students will need to scan the page to find one. A poem, on the other hand, may require careful reading to appreciate exactly what shades of meaning the author is trying to convey.

The 'while reading' exercises may also focus on such sub-skills as guessing the meaning of unknown words in context, working out the function of the text and purpose of the writer, inferring meaning and analysing cohesive devices such as pronoun reference or discourse markers.

# To the teacher

Although reading is essentially an individual activity, discussion of answers in pairs or groups helps students to think about their reading strategies and how to improve them. Many of the exercises encourage students to think for themselves and become more autonomous, using the teacher and the dictionary as resources rather than automatically depending on them to provide the answer.

## Speaking

The idea of providing students with the opportunity to use language in a relaxed environment, not only practising what they have learnt consciously, but also experimenting with and forming hypotheses about language they have acquired subconsciously, is now becoming recognised as a very important principle in communicative language teaching. Tasks which enable learners to focus on *what* they are saying rather than *how* they are saying it can also provide you with useful feedback on the stage their 'interlanguage' has reached; subtle monitoring of such activities might enable you to identify persistent errors, omissions or impediments to communication, providing useful input for future remedial work.

In order to be motivated to speak, the learner must have a genuine communicative purpose. This may arise naturally; for example, in *Variety*, the activities which involve students exchanging information about how the life and customs in their own country differ from life in Britain are genuinely communicative if they take place in a mixed-nationality class. Indeed, in any class there may be a genuine 'opinion gap' which will provoke a lot of spontaneous discussion.

*Variety* uses communicative techniques such as jigsaw reading, and other information gap activities such as roleplay, to encourage communicative interaction. Roleplay also encourages experimentation with different levels of appropriacy and use of language functions.

How much emphasis is put on communicative oral activities will, of course, depend on the particular teaching situation and the needs of the students. In addition, the themes of *Variety* lend themselves very well to project work, which could lead on to further activities such as interviews, informal talks etc. as well as spontaneous discussion which may well arise out of reading specific texts.

## Writing

The function of the writing tasks in *Variety* is not to give controlled practice of language items but to provide an opportunity to experiment with writing different types of texts in different registers and an incentive to write creatively.

The writing tasks lead on naturally from specific reading and/or speaking activities, which means that the student has a genuine communicative purpose for writing but the output will be experimental, rather than modelled on a specific text. You may want to pick out certain aspects of language structure, register, discourse features, written conventions or particular types of text etc. if you feel that it is necessary to make the learners conscious of them in order to improve a particular kind of writing.

Unless the students are preparing for examinations such as the Cambridge First Certificate, when they will need to be able to write most of these kinds of texts, you may well choose not to ask your students to do all the writing tasks set in *Variety*. Alternatively you may treat them as a springboard for free writing, with feedback

*To the teacher*

focusing only on linguistic aspects – students may, for example, be encouraged to monitor, and correct one another's work.

## How can *Variety* fit into a language programme?

*Variety* provides a coherent and integrated way of teaching language skills, particularly if it is combined with relevant listening material at this level. Each unit could provide the basis of several skills-focused lessons over a period of several weeks, and its thematic organisation means that it is always possible to add other material where appropriate.

Constraints of time might mean that some or all of the wider reading and perhaps many of the writing tasks will need to be done out of class, with class time spent on discussion of reading exercises, pair and groupwork activities and possible remedial input based on the oral and written activities.

The skills approach in *Variety* could be complementary to, and run parallel with, a more formal 'accuracy based' programme, or alternatively it could be approached in a cyclical way with a period of emphasis on language work being followed by a period of focus on skills.

*Variety* would be suitable for short courses or, in courses where a predetermined syllabus is not possible, it may help to identify common gaps or problems for future teaching.

## Conclusion

The approach we have used in *Variety* is based on the belief that it is necessary to give students not only a wide exposure to many different kinds of authentic language, but also the motivation to interact in some way with the texts. At the same time, it is equally important to provide opportunities to use language creatively and in an uncontrolled situation if students are to form hypotheses as to how language works and therefore acquire it subconsciously.

At the same time, awareness, discussion and monitoring of the skills involved, not only in reading authentic texts but also in speaking and writing the target language are very important to students if they are to become truly efficient and effective communicators both inside and outside the classroom.

# Acknowledgements

The authors and publishers are grateful to the authors, publishers and others who have given permission for the use of copyright material identified in the text. It has not been possible to identify the sources of all the material used and in such cases the publishers would welcome information from copyright owners.

The George Hotel, Bishops Stortford, and The Eight Bells, Saffron Walden, for the menus on pp. 4–5; *Caterer & Hotelkeeper* for the article on p. 5; Syndication International Ltd for the articles on pp. 6 (from *Woman*) and 13 (from *Honey*), the 'Andy Capp' cartoon on p. 20, the extract on p. 52 ('Great Opportunities for Women', from *Woman's Own*), the articles on pp. 56 ('Man about the house, you're lazy') and 113 (both from the *Daily Mirror*), 64 (from *Woman's Own*), 66–7 (from *19*), the reviews of *Rumble Fish* and *Star 80* on pp. 98–9 (from *Woman's Journal*); London Express News and Feature Services for the 'Gambols' cartoon on p. 7; Singer Communications Inc. for the cartoon by Joseph Farris on p. 7; The National Magazine Company Limited for the reviews on p. 8 (from *Company*), the review of *The Big Chill* on p. 99 and the article on p. 108 (from *Cosmopolitan*); Joe Dwan for the cartoon on p. 8; Associated Newspapers Group plc for the articles on pp. 9, 45, 56 ('Will your success make your marriage a failure?'), 115, 141 (all from the *Daily Mail*) and on p. 21 (from the *Mail on Sunday*); *Private Eye* for the picture on p. 9 (from the *Bumper Book of Boobs*); Whitbread & Co. Ltd for the leaflet on pp. 10–11; Matthew Brown P.L.C., Brewers at Blackburn & Workington, for the menu on p. 12; the Radio Times for the article by Hilary Macaskill on p. 19; Seagram Overseas Sales Company for the advertisement (prepared by Warwick, Welsh & Miller Inc.) on p. 20; WeightWatchers for the advertisement on p. 23; Patrick Hardy Books for the cartoons by Fritz Wegner on pp. 29 and 39 (from *Don't Look Now but it's Christmas Again*, © Patrick Hardy Books 1983); The Lygon Arms, Broadway, Worcs., for the programme and menu on pp. 30–1; the British Turkey Federation and Ogilvy & Mather for the advertisement on p. 33; Val Antopolski and the children of Bourn Parochial School, Bourn, Cambridge, and Emily and Sarah Ducker for the sayings and illustrations on p. 36; Fay Maschler for the poem on p. 37; United Feature Syndicate Inc. for the 'Peanuts' cartoon on p. 38; *Family Circle* for the play extract on p. 40; Mel Calman for the cartoons on pp. 45 and 55; COI for the advertisement on p. 46, reproduced with permission of the Controller of Her Majesty's Stationery Office; Chivers Hartley for the advertisement on p. 47; Kevill Brown & Co., Lancashire County Council, the King's School, Macclesfield, Lancashire Constabulary, Office Equipment World Wholesale Ltd, Preferred Assurance Company Ltd, Safeway Food Stores Ltd, Kelly Girl Service Ltd, Sweetens Bookshop Ltd and International University Europe for advertisements on p. 48; *Woman's*

## Acknowledgements

*World* for the cartoons on pp. 52 and 65, the review of *Daniel* on p. 98 and the extract ('Men of the World') on p. 114; Times Newspapers Ltd for the Sex Discrimination Act notice on p. 52 (from the *Times Educational Supplement*), the article on pp. 53–4 (from the *Sunday Times Magazine* 7 May 1978), the article by Lorna Bourke on p. 55 (from the *Times* 11 November 1981), the article by Hunter Davies on p. 57 (from the *Times* 2 May 1982) and the article on p. 112 (from the *Times* 1 March 1984); DCT Syndication for the letter on p. 54 (from *Jackie*); *Living* magazine for the articles by Brian Jackson on p. 65 and Carol Baker on pp. 78–80; the County High School, Saffron Walden, for the prospectus on p. 68; Penguin Books Ltd for the extracts on p. 69 from *The School that I'd Like* ed. Edward Blishen (Penguin Education 1969), selection copyright © Penguin Books and contributors 1969, reprinted by permission of Penguin Books Ltd; *Options* magazine for the extract on p. 69; Hutton Grammar School for the 'Code of Conduct' on p. 70; ALI Press Agency Ltd for the cartoons on pp. 70 and 125; Mrs A. M. Walsh for 'The Bully Asleep' from *The Roundabout by the Sea* by John Walsh (OUP); the Open University for the advertisement on p. 81; the *Cambridge Evening News* for the articles on pp. 82–3; the Linguaphone Institute for the advertisement on p. 83; The Association of Certified Accountants, the Bell School of Languages, the Cambridge Computer College, St Mark's Community Centre and the Education Alliance (TUC) for the advertisements on p. 84; the University of Birmingham Guild of Students for extracts from the *Alternative Prospectus* (prepared by the Education Committee of Birmingham University Guild of Students) on pp. 85–7; *Punch* for the cartoon by Ed Fisher on p. 95; the English National Opera, the Lyric Theatre, Michael WhiteLtd (Cambridge Theatre Co.), Hetherington Seelig, London, Ray Cooney productions and the Westminster Theatre for advertisements on p. 96; the Royal Shakespeare Company for the advertisement on p. 97 (design Bob Paton-Walker); Prue Lightfoot for the article on pp. 100–1; E. Lange for the cartoon on p. 101; the *Observer* for the article on p. 109; Michael Joseph Ltd for the extract from *The Sunday Times Book of Body Maintenance* (ed. Gillie and Mercer) on p. 109; Mitchell Beazley Ltd for the extract from *Living Well* on p. 110; Marshall Cavendish Books Ltd for the extract from *The Body Book* on p. 111; Linton Village College Community Council and Meldreth Manor School for the advertisements on p. 117; the MCC for 'Cricket, as explained to a foreign visitor' on p. 112; the *Guardian* for the article on p. 114; the WWF/Ogilvy & Mather for the advertisement on p. 122; the Countryside Commission for extracts from *The Country Code* on pp. 123–5; Norma Farnes for 'Once Upon' from *The Little Pot Boiler* by Spike Milligan on p. 125; Friends of the Earth for the leaflet on pp. 126–7 and the extract on p. 135; the *Saffron Walden Reporter* for the article on p. 128; the Consumers' Association for the extracts on pp. 134 and 136 (from *Which?* September 1983, published by Consumers' Association); ESTEC for the extracts on pp. 137–8; the Energy Efficiency Office for the advertisements on pp. 139–40, Crown ©, reproduced with permission of the Controller of Her Majesty's Stationery Office.

The drawing on p. 37 is by Hugh Marshall. Artwork by Gecko Ltd, Wagstaffs Design Associates and Wenham Arts.
Book design by Peter Ducker MSTD